A DREAMER FOR THE PEOPLE

T0369725

Paseo de Andalucía by Francisco de Goya with kind permission from the Prado Museum, Madrid

HISPANIC CLASSICS – Modern Drama

Antonio Buero Vallejo
A DREAMER FOR THE PEOPLE
(Un soñador para un pueblo - 1958)

translated with an introduction and notes by

Michael Thompson

ARIS & PHILLIPS — WARMINSTER — ENGLAND

ISBNs   cloth   0 85668 553 4
        limp   0 85668 554 2
ISSN HISPANIC CLASSICS 0953 797 X

British Library Cataloguing-in-Publication Data
A catalogue record for this book is available from the
British Library.

The publishers gratefully acknowledge the financial assistance of the Dirección General del Libro y Bibliotecas of the Ministerio de Cultura de España with this translation.

Printed and bound by CPI Group (UK) Ltd, Croydon, CR0 4YY

Contents

Illustrations

Stills from *Esquilache* reproduced with kind permission from **Sabre Films**, Madrid.

Preface

The translation

This is the first translation into English of *Un soñador para un pueblo*. The original Spanish text is taken from the Espasa Calpe edition (Colección Austral), first published in 1972, and re-issued in 1989 with minor corrections and an excellent introduction and footnotes by Luis Iglesias Feijoo. I have used the 1989 text with virtually no alterations: one or two misprints have been corrected, and some of the stage directions have been attached to the end of the preceding line of dialogue, rather than set out separately.

The translation aims at a satisfactory balance between fidelity to the original and readability — ideally, actability — in English. A bilingual edition imposes its own discipline. The presence of the original Spanish on the facing page discourages extreme inventiveness, but at the same time keeps in sight the linguistic context that may allow the need for a risky departure from the obvious to be appreciated. The language of Buero's dramatic texts tends towards literariness, in that it is carefully controlled, it expresses ideas concisely and powerfully, and it builds up a core of significance based upon extended metaphors. Nevertheless, it lends itself well to a conventional, broadly naturalistic style of acting in which one can feel that the characters are being made to express themselves convincingly. My version aims to achieve a similar effect in English, without losing the general awareness that the cultural context is Spanish.

In this play, Buero does not attempt to recreate an eighteenth-century idiom: only forms of address and certain words referring to things specific to the period stand out as obviously archaic. Period pastiche is certainly not the objective. On the other hand, anything with a specifically twentieth-century flavour is avoided. There are a few terms whose cultural and period specificity is of crucial significance, and have therefore not been translated (which is another way of saying that they are impossible to translate satisfactorily): *majo, maja, embozado* and *cesante*. These words appear mostly in stage directions (and as character labels) rather than in the dialogue itself, and are explained in footnotes.

The upper-class characters are not restricted to formal language: they frequently speak in a relaxed, mildly colloquial style, but this should not begin to sound racy. The speech of the lower-class characters is clearly colloquial, but is not dominated by slang or regional forms. There is a well-loved Spanish tradition of popular theatre based on an exaggeratedly colourful Madrid dialect (an effect similar to using Cockney rhyming slang in English), with its origins in the period covered by this play. Buero resists this temptation in favour of an all-purpose idiom that manages to be lively without blatantly calling attention to itself.

Spanish theatre employs a convention for the designation of left and right in stage directions which is the opposite of the normal practice in English-language theatre. The Spanish convention assumes the point of view of the spectator looking at the stage, whereas in the English tradition the point of view is that of the actor looking out from the stage towards the auditorium. I consider it preferable to retain the Spanish

convention in the translation, rather than violate normal linguistic logic by having — on facing pages — *izquierda* matched with "right" and *derecha* with "left". For the designation of areas of the stage from the front (nearest to the audience) to the back (furthest from the audience), Buero uses the expressions *primer término, segundo término* and *fondo*. These have usually been translated as "downstage" and "upstage" (and in some cases, "the back of the stage").

There is also the question of the title. It may seem perverse to turn "*un* pueblo" into "*the* people". The implication of the indefinite article in the Spanish is that the existence of a unified entity that can be defined as "the people" is in doubt. Near the end of the play, the king puts a rhetorical question to Esquilache: "¿Hay un pueblo ahí abajo?" ("Is there a people down there?", which I have rendered as "Is there a real people down there?") (p.167). The dreamer seeks to find or define an authentic *pueblo*, or perhaps the *pueblo* can only define itself as such by finding its own dreamers: what is needed is "un soñador para un pueblo", or more precisely, "para que haya un pueblo" ("in order that there should be a people"). The "para" of the title recalls the phrase mentioned in the text as the motto of enlightened absolutism: "todo para el pueblo, pero sin el pueblo" ("everything for the people, but without the people") (p.55). However, "a people" seems less meaningful in English than "un pueblo" in Spanish. The two words have different semantic ranges: apart from the shared idea of national or ethnic group, *pueblo* often refers to a village or a rural environment, whereas *people* (without an article) is a very loose, neutral way of referring to any number of human beings (equivalent to *gente* in Spanish). The Spanish word feels rooted in a down-to-earth peasant way of life, and this association colours it even when it is used to encompass the entire national population. In English, only with the definite article does the phrase carry the implication that the essence of *people* is defined by the notion of commonalty; "a people" seems politically more neutral, to do with nationhood or race rather than class. My version has therefore sacrificed some of the precision of the original, with the intention of making the title more obviously meaningful in English.

My notes serve three purposes. Firstly, they identify people and places when they first appear or are mentioned. Secondly, there are some that clarify or elaborate upon linguistic matters. And thirdly, they draw attention to certain significant discrepancies between the dramatic action and the historical record. A full discussion of Buero's treatment of his source material forms the main part of the introduction. The aim is only partly to supply interesting contextual information to enrich the reading experience (or the viewing experience — some of this material could be turned into programme notes for a performance). The idea is also to look at *Un soñador para un pueblo* as a case study of historical theatre: to observe the process of turning history into drama and analyse the relationships between various readings of the history and of the text itself.

Acknowledgements

My thanks go to Antonio Buero Vallejo for his help and encouragement in the preparation of this edition. His unfailing courtesy and goodwill in response to all enquiries about his work have become legendary, and I hereby add one more tribute. I also wish to express my gratitude to those who made invaluable contributions to the polishing of the translation: David Johnston, and Ian and Sheila Macpherson.

Further Reading

This is a brief selection of the most useful reading relevant to *Un soñador para un pueblo*. A very full bibliography on Buero Vallejo is given in: Marsha Forys, *Antonio Buero Vallejo and Alfonso Sastre* (Metuchen: Scarecrow, 1988). References to other sources are given in the notes to the introduction and the translation.

On drama and historical drama in general

Jean-Paul Borel, *El teatro de lo imposible*, translated by G. Torrente Ballester (Madrid: Guadarrama, 1966)

A. Buero Vallejo, 'Acerca del drama histórico', *Primer Acto*, 187 (1981), pp.18-21

Martha Halsey & Phyllis Zatlin (eds.), *The Contemporary Spanish Theater* (Lanham: University Press of America, 1988)

Herbert Lindenberger, *Historical Drama: The Relation of Literature and Reality* (Chicago: University, 1975)

Francisco Ruiz Ramón, *Historia del teatro español: Siglo XX*, 8th ed. (Madrid: Cátedra, 1989) (1st ed. 1970)

Francisco Ruiz Ramón, 'Pasado/presente en el drama histórico', *Estreno*, 14 (1988), pp.22-4

On Buero Vallejo and *Un soñador para un pueblo*

Ricardo Doménech, *El teatro de Buero Vallejo* (Madrid: Gredos, 1973)

J.M. García Escudero, 'Un soñador para un pueblo', *Ya* (27 December 1958), p.5

J.M. García Escudero, 'Un pueblo para un soñador', *Ya* (1 January 1959), p.5

Luciano García Lorenzo, Mariano de Paco & Ricard Salvat, *Antonio Buero Vallejo: Premio "Miguel de Cervantes", 1986* (Barcelona: Anthropos, 1987)

Martha Halsey, 'The rebel protagonist: Ibsen's *An Enemy of the People* and Buero's *Un soñador para un pueblo*', *Comparative Literature Studies*, 6 (1969), pp.462-71

Martha Halsey, 'More on "Light" in the tragedies of Buero Vallejo', *Romance Notes*, 11 (1969), pp.17-20

Martha Halsey, *Antonio Buero Vallejo* (New York: Twayne, 1973)

Martha Halsey, 'El intelectual y el pueblo: tres dramas históricos de Buero', *Anthropos*, 79 (1987), pp.46-9 (special issue entitled 'A. Buero Vallejo: la tragedia, transparencia y cristal de la palabra')

Luis Iglesias Feijoo, *La trayectoria dramática de Antonio Buero Vallejo* (Santiago de Compostela: Universidad, 1982)

Robert Nicholas, *The Tragic Stages of Buero Vallejo* (Chapel Hill: University of North Carolina, 1972)

Mariano de Paco (ed.), *Estudios sobre Buero Vallejo* (Murcia: Universidad de Murcia, 1984)

Pilar de la Puente Samaniego, *A. Buero Vallejo: Proceso a la historia de España*
(Salamanca: Universidad, 1988)

Historical sources

Manuel Danvila y Collado, *Reinado de Carlos III*, vol.10 of A. Cánovas del Castillo
(ed.), *Historia general de España* (Madrid: El Progreso, 1891)
Conde de Fernán Núñez, *La vida de Carlos III*, 2 vols. (Madrid: Fernando Fé, 1898)
(new edition Madrid: Fundación Universitaria Española, 1988)
Antonio Ferrer del Río, *Historia del reinado de Carlos III en España*, vol. 2 (Madrid,
1856)
John Lynch, *Bourbon Spain, 1700-1808* (Oxford: Basil Blackwell, 1989)
José Navarro Latorre, *Hace doscientos años: Estado actual de los problemas históricos
del "Motín de Esquilache"* (Madrid: Instituto de Estudios Madrileños, 1966)

Antonio Buero Vallejo. Photographed by Gyenes.

Introduction

Antonio Buero Vallejo: a sense of balance

Buero's career as a playwright represents a remarkable synthesis of potentially contradictory elements.[1] In circumstances that have frequently been hostile to him personally and to his profession, he has consistently displayed intelligence, integrity, humanity, and an admirable sense of balance — political, ethical and artistic.

Buero was born in Guadalajara in 1916, and was studying in Madrid at the outbreak of the Civil War in 1936. As a consequence of serving on the side of the Republic during the war, he was condemned to death in 1939, although this sentence was then commuted to imprisonment. He was given conditional release in 1946, but not considered sufficiently free of suspicion to be allowed to travel abroad until 1963. He was therefore one of the *vencidos*, the defeated, an adherent of a cause and a whole way of thinking that Franquism claimed to have eradicated. And yet he has become the most distinguished living playwright in Spain, a member of the Royal Academy, and holder of numerous theatrical and literary prizes, including the prestigious Premio Cervantes (1986): from a virtual non-person to an almost universally respected member of the Establishment.

Although he displayed an early enthusiasm for the theatre, his first vocation was as a painter. His training at the San Fernando School of Fine Art was cut short by the war; by the time of his release in 1946, the skills seemed to have stagnated, and he turned his energies to writing. Despite this late start as a playwright, he achieved success relatively quickly with *Historia de una escalera* (*Story of a Staircase*, 1949), and has become a recognized master of dramatic craftsmanship, an influential theorist (particularly of tragedy), and a true man of the theatre. Moreover, the interest in painting has been brilliantly integrated into some of his most impressive plays: in *Las Meninas* (*The Maids of Honour*, 1960) and *El sueño de la razón* (*The Sleep of Reason*, 1970), powerful images by Velázquez and Goya become essential parts of the performance.

At first, Buero's reputation rested primarily on the success of plays such as *Historia de una escalera* and *Hoy es fiesta* (*Today's a Holiday*, 1956): a deliberately straight-forward, everyday, subdued kind of naturalistic realism. The impact of these works came from the unflinching honesty with which they observed contemporary Spanish life, rather than from any stylistic innovations. However, there was greater diversity in Buero's writing from the beginning, and he has subsequently proved himself to be a highly inventive explorer of dramatic form. At the same time, he has continued to be respected as a purveyor of big ideas. He has repeatedly carried off the extraordinary balancing act of satisfying conservative Madrid audiences and reviewers while

---

1   Useful biographical, autobiographical and bibliographical information, together with studies of Buero's plays, appears in *Antonio Buero Vallejo, Premio "Miguel de Cervantes" 1986* (Barcelona: Anthropos/Ministerio de Cultura, 1987) and in *Anthropos*, 79 (1987), a special issue entitled 'A. Buero Vallejo: La tragedia, transparencia y cristal de la palabra'.

maintaining a reputation as a playwright who tackles serious social and moral issues; upholding progressive, humanitarian values throughout the Franquist period without renouncing commercial success and without being completely neutralized by censorship.

The plays themselves suggest a similar quality of judicious balance and synthesis of potential opposites. Tough social problems and concrete historical circumstances tend to be given a metaphysical or mythical dimension, and the most everyday reality is imbued with a sense of mystery. The individual dilemma, the personal experience, the subjective point of view are always productively set off against collective, public and political perspectives. The necessary recognition of the prevalence of human weakness, selfishness, solitude and cynicism is illuminated by examples of strength of character, altruism, solidarity and idealism.

Buero's theatrical technique has remained essentially realist: in general, dialogue is rational and conversational, characterization is consistent and psychologically complex, stage space represents real locations, time flows in a logical and straightforward manner. Nevertheless, his work has been constantly enriched by the carefully controlled use of symbolism, fantasy and illusion; of temporal displacement, multiple or schematic staging techniques, and Brechtian devices of narration and distancing. Each new text generates a uniquely coherent theatrical structure in which such innovations are made to give the impression that they are essential, organic parts of a unified concept. Each project poses an intriguing technical problem: for example, the closed communal space of the staircase in *Historia de una escalera*; the strict regulation of stage time in *Madrugada* (*Before Dawn*, 1953); the translation into theatrical terms of the special ways of seeing the world embodied in well-known images by Velázquez and Goya in *Las Meninas* and *El sueño de la razón;* the recovery of fragments of real and fictional history in *El tragaluz* (*The Basement Window*, 1967); the violently lucid perceptions of a writer on the point of committing suicide in *La detonación* (*The Shot*, 1977); the guilt-induced delusions and obsessions of successful men in *Jueces en la noche* (*Judges in the Night*, 1979) and *Música cercana* (*Close Harmony*, 1989).

The constant focus of exploration is the relationship between the performance and the audience. Familiarity is destabilized by surprise, cathartic emotional involvement is complicated by techniques provoking self-consciousness and detached analysis. In *El tragaluz*, for example, the central dramatic action is set within a frame consisting of two 'researchers' several centuries later, who address the audience as if it were their (fictional) audience, in their time, viewing the fragmented results of their experiment in the reconstruction of past lives. It turns out that the play's structure is built upon a double bluff, since the time presented as past is in fact the present of the real (twentieth-century) audience, who are invited to participate in the emotional and imaginative reconstruction of a 'lost' world that is in fact their own world: the spectators are asked to pretend to be someone else pretending to be someone who turns out to be very similar to themselves. The 'someone else' is always oneself: "Ése eres tú, y tú, y tú..." ("That person is you, and you, and you...").[2]

This continuing exploration is closely related to an ambitious artistic objective, repeatedly declared by the author, which also acts as a powerful unifying factor: to

---

2   Antonio Buero Vallejo, *El tragaluz* (Madrid: Espasa Calpe, 1970), p.88.

create modern tragedy, that is, dramatic texts with the moral seriousness and emotional power of classical tragedy, yet able to do justice to the ideological complexity of the twentieth-century world. In a period in which the major theatrical innovations have been explicitly anti-tragic (expressionist, epic, absurdist, postmodernist), Buero has continued to write texts that imply a search for transcendent values. Particular historical circumstances tend to be presented as destructive and dispiriting, but there is a constant reaffirmation of the meaningfulness of human existence. Buero sees tragedy as an impassioned exploration of the necessary (and necessarily unresolvable) contradictions of human existence. At its core is hope, balanced between the two poles of absolute optimism and total pessimism. Works of tragedy are expressions of "la fe que duda" ("the faith that doubts").[3] Ultimately, the claim to tragic status rests not only upon the profundity of the moral and philosophical debate, but also upon the achievement of an aesthetic and emotional impact beyond rationality. The audience is challenged to re-examine their ideas, but is also faced with suggestions of ultimate mystery.

Historical theatre and *Un soñador para un pueblo*

Un soñador para un pueblo (written and premiered in 1958) is the first of an influential series of history plays by Buero. It was followed by *Las Meninas* in 1960, *El concierto de San Ovidio* (*The Concert at Saint Ovide*) in 1962, *El sueño de la razón* (The Sleep of Reason) in 1970, and *La detonación* (The Shot) in 1977. Except for *El concierto de San Ovidio*, which is set in eighteenth-century France, all of these plays reassess important moments in Spanish history: the clash between forces of conservatism and reform in the 1760s in *Un soñador para un pueblo*; signs of decay in the Hapsburg empire during the reign of Felipe IV (the 1650s) in *Las Meninas*; the crushing of the spirit of the Enlightenment by Fernando VII in the 1820s in *El sueño de la razón*; the frustration of liberal and Romantic protest in the 1820s and 1830s in *La detonación*. *Un soñador para un pueblo* also marks the beginning of a significant trend among Spanish playwrights: since the early 1960s, Alfonso Sastre, José María Rodríguez Méndez, José Martín Recuerda, Carlos Muñiz, Antonio Gala, Manuel Martínez Mediero, Jerónimo López Mozo, Ana Diosdado, José Sanchis Sinisterra and others have produced searching critical reappraisals of periods of Spanish history ranging from the Middle Ages to the recent past of the Civil War (1936-39) and the Franquist dictatorship (1939-75).[4]

---

3   Antonio Buero Vallejo, 'La tragedia' in Guillermo Díaz Plaja (ed.), *El teatro: Enciclopedia del arte escénico* (Barcelona: Noguer, 1958), p.77.

4   Recent studies emphasising the importance of this preoccupation with Spanish history include: various articles in *Estreno*, 14 (1988); Martha Halsey, 'The politics of history: Images of Spain on the stage of the 1970s' in Halsey and Zatlin (eds.), *The Contemporary Spanish Theater* (Lanham: University Press of America, 1988), pp.93-108; Martha Halsey, 'Dramatic patterns in three history plays of contemporary Spain', *Hispania*, 71 (1988), pp.20-30; Francisco Ruiz Ramón, 'Apuntes para una dramaturgia del drama histórico español del siglo XX' in S. Neumeister (ed.), *Actas del IX Congreso de la Asociación Internacional de Hispanistas*, vol.2 (Frankfurt: Vervuert, 1989). An important earlier

4   INTRODUCTION

The history plays produced by these writers performed a particularly important function during the 1960s and 1970s by challenging the Franquist hijacking of ideas and ideals of national identity. The regime imposed a monolithic, unashamedly partisan view of history, which developed a myth of divinely-ordained destiny based on the central role of the Catholic Church and the necessity of national unity. The official version went roughly as follows: Spain's identity had been forged in the crusading fervour of the medieval reconquest, and the nation united in the faith by Fernando and Isabel at the end of the 15th century; the national destiny had become a universal destiny with the carrying of Catholic civilization into the Americas; the decay of a vast and glorious empire had been brought about largely by foreign treachery and pernicious liberal ideas, culminating in the humiliating loss of the last colonies in 1898; the Republic established in 1931 had threatened the very foundations of Church, State, family and traditional values; the military rebellion of 1936 had set in motion a new Crusade that had saved Spain from anarchy and heresy; and now the nation, reunited and fervently Catholic, had rediscovered its historic destiny and its true identity. History had been brought full circle, the apotheosis had been reached, no other way was conceivable.[5] Even when the fascist and imperialist fervour of the 1940s had given way to the more moderate tone of the 1950s, official propaganda still celebrated the idea of Spain as the last bastion of Christian civilization in a world corrupted by communism on the one hand and liberal democracy on the other.

The work of some playwrights, such as José María Pemán, reflected or even celebrated this distortion. The task facing those who opposed it was nothing less than the reclaiming of their history. In place of the closed, smug, backward-looking official mythology, their texts attempt a redefinition of historical perspective, presenting history as a dynamic, open, ambiguous process. Historical events and personalities are reinterpreted, national identities are re-examined. Previously idealized elements are questioned, while neglected or despised elements are brought into clearer focus. Links with the present are sometimes explicitly signalled by means of anachronisms or framing devices, or suggested by the construction of analogies with particular features of conditions in Franco's Spain. One advantage of using a historical setting in a time of strict political control is that it may afford a disguise under which specific criticisms can be smuggled past the censors. However, none of these new history plays has such limited aims. Most of them are sophisticated examinations of the ways in which multiple pasts give rise to multiple present possibilities, or in which attitudes and ideologies in the present rewrite the past. Historical drama is recognized as offering a special opportunity for the creative exploration of audiences' responses through the tensions between temporal distance and aesthetic distancing, between historical time and stage time, between recorded fact and dramatic fiction. Dramatization personalizes history, making it accessible, comprehensible, palpable; at the same time, a historical setting underlines the general, collective significance of individual dramatic conflicts.

---

discussion appears in Francisco Ruiz Ramón, *Estudios de teatro español clásico y contemporáneo* (Madrid: Fundación Juan March/Cátedra, 1978), pp.215-42.

5   Some stunning examples of this kind of rhetoric can be found in Julio Rodríguez Puértolas (ed.), *Literatura fascista española*, vol.2 (Madrid: Akal, 1987).

Three principal approaches to the dramatization of history can be identified in the work of these playwrights:

(a) the serious re-evaluation of well-known historical figures or episodes (motives are explored, ambiguities are exposed, human depths are revealed, events are seen in a new, more complex light);

(b) the satirical or grotesque debunking of officially sanctioned myths (often described as *desmitificación*, and often influenced by the aggressively expressionist *esperpentos* written by Valle-Inclán in the 1920s);

(c) the rediscovery of marginalized or suppressed interests, voices and communities (historical events are seen from the point of view of the victims, folk culture is rescued from paternalism and sentimentality).

Buero is the supreme exponent of the first of these strategies (usually combined with some element of the third). Each play is built around an exceptional individual: an artist or intellectual whose importance lies not so much in being the prime mover of events as in being an unusually perceptive observer of them. Esquilache (*Un soñador para un pueblo*), Velázquez (*Las Meninas*), Goya (*El sueño de la razón*) and Larra (*La detonación*) develop a special understanding of the impact of historical processes on the lives of the people around them. The personal crisis of each protagonist is intricately linked, through a structure of powerful theatrical images, with the public crisis of the historical moment. The privileged perspective of each of them is complemented by a relationship with a representative of the powerless masses: Esquilache learns from Fernandita, Velázquez from the beggar Pedro Briones, Larra from his servant, also called Pedro, and Goya from Leocadia (although in this play, the emphasis is more on the painter's lack of contact with ordinary people). In each case, the tragedy is both individual and collective. Both the hero and the nation fail to achieve progress or self-fulfilment, and yet some kind of inner victory is won. Hope is invested in the potential of the *pueblo*, in the continuing influence of the ideas or creations of the protagonist, and in the future. History is shown to be driven largely by crude forces of self-interest and abuse of power, but certain individuals afford glimpses of a special moral awareness. They learn, and then offer to the audience, the difficult lesson that real human progress can only be made through individual and collective empowerment — the enabling of people's (and the people's) latent capacity for understanding mutual needs and taking their own decisions. These history plays, in common with all of Buero's other works, end on a positive note, affirming human potential and the possibility of true understanding on a personal as well as a public level.

Within this context of revisionist history plays by Buero and other writers, *Un soñador para un pueblo* is something of an exception, in that it sets out to defend a monarch and a government denigrated by Franquism, rather than the more usual pattern of attacking or discrediting the ruling classes of every period. According to the mythology of imperial destiny, the eighteenth century was a time of betrayal of the true faith and the true character of the Spanish people. The Bourbon dynasty established by Felipe V in 1700 brought with it considerable French (and later Italian) influence, which was despised by the nationalists of the 1940s. Reforms that had been designed to limit the secular power and wealth of the Church were seen as attacks on religion itself. As one survey of historical research on the eighteenth century observes, "the postwar period was not a favourable one for research on the Age of Enlightenment. [...]

Historians of the time preferred to devote their efforts to the study of periods with a greater affinity to the 'national spirit' proclaimed by the new authoritarian regime".[6]

Some new, more objective studies of the period by foreign historians were beginning to emerge by the late 1940s, but it was not until the end of the 1950s that work by Spanish historians on the eighteenth century was given official encouragement by

> the group of technocrats who were brought into government after the abandonment of the policy of economic self-sufficiency and the end of international isolation. The rise of these new administrators generated a need to find in the Spanish past some kind of precedent that could help to legitimize their political programme, and nothing served this purpose better than the study of the achievements of the enlightened ministers of Carlos III. The eighteenth century in Spain had the advantage in their eyes of being a period of reforms designed to promote "economic progress" without the need to change the fundamental structures of a system which, although destined to collapse, could be presented as having been destroyed by purely external forces.
>
> (Fernández, pp.22-3)

In order to assess what contribution *Un soñador para un pueblo* makes to this debate, we now turn to a detailed analysis of the play's treatment of historical material.

The *motín de Esquilache*: re-ordering the evidence

Un soñador para un pueblo is set in March 1766, at the time of the popular uprising in Madrid known as the *motín de Esquilache*. As Buero's representation of the period and the particular episode generated some controversy when the play was first staged, it is important to establish exactly what the dramatist does with the historical material at his disposal. The main events on which the action of the play is based are as follows:

1759	August: Carlos succeeds his brother as king of Spain. December: he arrives in Madrid, bringing Esquilache with him as secretary. The only change he makes to the Government is to appoint Esquilache as Finance Minister.
1760	Reforms and building programmes are set in motion by the king, Esquilache and other ministers. A plan to introduce a measure banning long capes and wide-brimmed hats is abandoned. Ensenada is brought out of exile, but not into government.
1761	Work begins on the paving of the streets of Madrid and the installation of sewers.
1762-63	War against Britain (opposed by Esquilache) proves unpopular and expensive, and leads to the replacement of Ricardo Wall as Minister of War by Esquilache (who also retains the post of Finance Minister). The huge cost of the war results in the introduction by Esquilache of a new tax.
1763-65	Droughts and crop failures cause food shortages, price rises and widespread hardship.
1763-66	The Government is increasingly dominated by Esquilache and Grimaldi. Administrative, economic, military and educational reforms continue.
1764	More than twenty people are killed by Walloon guards controlling the crowds at the wedding of the Infanta María Luisa.

---

6 Roberto Fernández, 'Introducción' in Roberto Fernández (ed.), *España en el siglo XVIII: Homenaje a Pierre Vilar* (Barcelona: Crítica, 1985), p.18. The English versions of quotations from this and other sources in Spanish are mine.

1765	Esquilache introduces free trade measures to ensure the continuity of grain supplies. Work begins on the installation of street lights in Madrid. The winter of 1765-66 is harsh.
1766 January	The king and Esquilache decide to reintroduce the ban on long capes and wide-brimmed hats: it is successfully imposed on civil servants and members of guilds. The price of bread rises again.
9 March	Despite the reservations of its fiscal, Campomanes, the Council of Castile approves the general application of the capes and hats measure.
10 March	The order is made public: notices are posted in the streets of Madrid. During the night, all the notices are torn down and replaced by posters threatening revolt.
11-12 March	Notices are posted again, but are again torn down and replaced by lampoons attacking Esquilache and declarations calling for rebellion. Conspirators issue the *Constituciones y Ordenanzas*, an anonymous manifesto setting out objectives and rules of conduct for an uprising against Esquilache.
12-22 March	Measures are implemented to ensure that the order is obeyed, but some citizens openly defy the order and provoke armed skirmishes with the authorities.
23 March	(Palm Sunday) Soldiers who attempt to arrest two men provocatively strutting in long capes and wide hats in the Plaza de Antón Martín are ambushed and disarmed by thirty other rebels. A crowd forms and copies of the *Constituciones y Ordenanzas* are distributed. Gangs march through the streets shouting "God save the King! Death to Esquilache!", unstitching three-cornered hats, and smashing street lamps. Esquilache's house is ransacked; at Grimaldi's, the rioters do no more than break windows. On hearing that Esquilache is with the king, the crowd heads for the Royal Palace, somehow picking up the Duke of Medinaceli on the way. He is carried to the Palace to bear the rebels' message to the king: they remain loyal to the king himself, but demand Esquilache's head. During the night, the Palace guard is reinforced while the mob releases prisoners.
24 March	A very large crowd (20-30,000) has formed outside the Palace, calling for the king to come out and hear their demands. Walloon guards fire on the crowd, provoking ferocious retaliation. Formal demands are drawn up and taken into the Palace by a priest: Esquilache and his family to be exiled, other foreign ministers to be replaced by Spaniards, free trade measures to be abolished, the Walloon guard to be withdrawn from Madrid, restrictions on dress to be repealed, and food prices to be reduced. The king receives the priest and sends him back with an assurance that the demands will be met, then consults his advisers. Three of them advocate crushing the uprising by force; the other three favour concessions. Some of the protesters are allowed into the palace courtyard, and the king comes out onto a balcony to negotiate directly with them. The crowd surges into the courtyard, refusing to disperse until the king's acceptance of all the demands is written down point by point. In the early evening, official notices confirm the concessions and grant an amnesty to all involved in the rising; the insurrection breaks up in festive mood.
25 March	The royal family, with Esquilache and his family, leave for Aranjuez at two o'clock in the morning. News of this arouses popular suspicion in Madrid: the crowds cut communications with Aranjuez, seize weapons from barracks, release women from prison, and force the governor of the Council of Castile to draw up a document denouncing Esquilache. This document is taken to the king in Aranjuez. That evening, Esquilache and his family set off for Cartagena, from where they will sail to Naples.

26 March	The king's reply is brought back: he gives his word that the concessions promised on the 24th will be respected, which satisfies the protesters. They hand over their arms and disperse rapidly: the uprising is over. Twenty-one rebels and nineteen soldiers have been killed. Esquilache is replaced by Múzquiz (finance) and Muniáin (war), but Grimaldi stays in office.
April	The Count of Aranda is appointed President of the Council of Castile, with the job of restoring order and finding out who was responsible for stirring up the revolt. His enquiry, conducted by Pedro Rodríguez de Campomanes, puts the blame on the Jesuits, which leads to the expulsion of their order from Spain in 1767. Ensenada is exiled to Medina del Campo, and loses all influence in government. Military garrisons in Madrid are heavily reinforced, and the king remains in Aranjuez (until December). Riots and protests over food prices break out in cities and villages in various parts of Spain.
June	Most of the concessions made by the king in March are annulled. The enforcement of the order imposing short capes and three-cornered hats is aided by a new clause decreeing that the only man permitted to wear the traditional wide-brimmed hat is the public executioner.

Buero's principal sources of historical information were classic accounts published in the nineteenth century. Antonio Ferrer del Río[7] and Manuel Danvila y Collado[8] present a generally favourable picture of the reign of Carlos III, reflecting some of the same liberal, reformist values that came to be despised by the crusading hardliners of Franco's regime in the 1940s. The Count of Fernán-Núñez was a member of Carlos III's court, and an eye-witness to some of the events portrayed; an edition of his biography of Carlos published in 1898[9] also presents the king and his project of reform in a reasonably favourable light. Buero keeps a careful record of all the material he uses, of all the interesting snippets collected from his enthusiastic and wide-ranging reading from and about the eighteenth century: Torres Villarroel's *Piscator* almanacs, the texts of government decrees and of popular lampoons against Esquilache, Sainz de Robles's *Historia y estampas de la Villa de Madrid* (Barcelona: Iberia, 1933), José María Cossío's *Los toros* (Madrid: Espasa Calpe, 1943), plays by Ramón de la Cruz, a French history of the Walloon guards, a natural history of Asturias in which Fernandita's remedy using cream of tartar is mentioned.

Buero remains very faithful to these sources. Woven into the dialogue and the action of *Un soñador para un pueblo* are many of the themes and incidents emphasised (with minor discrepancies over points of detail) by Fernán-Núñez, Ferrer and Danvila. In Part 1: the scurrilous *letrilla* peddled by the blind man; the possibility that the capes and hats decree has been suggested to Esquilache by Ensenada; the shameless avarice of doña Pastora, and the favouritism enjoyed by their children; the unhealthy state of Madrid before the introduction of sewers and paving; staff cuts in the civil service; the

---

7   Antonio Ferrer del Río, *Historia del reinado de Carlos III en España*, 2 vols. (Madrid, 1856).

8   Manuel Danvila y Collado, *Reinado de Carlos III*, vol. 10 of A. Cánovas del Castillo (ed.), *Historia general de España* (Madrid: El Progreso, 1891).

9   Conde de Fernán-Núñez, *La vida de Carlos III*, 2 vols. (Madrid: Fernando Fé, 1898). A new edition was published in 1988 (Madrid: Fundación Universitaria Española) to mark the bicentenary of the death of Carlos III.

decree itself, its initial application to civil servants, and the tearing down of the notices; the paving of the Plaza Mayor; the poster threatening to raise 3,000 rebels against Esquilache; the installation of tailors in doorways to trim capes and stitch up hats; the defiant phrase "porque no me da la gana" ("because I don't feel like it"); the king's insistence on punctuality, devotion to hunting, and patronizing comparison of the Spanish people with children who must be forced to have their faces washed; reports of meetings of conspirators in Madrid and El Pardo; the *Constituciones y Ordenanzas*; popular discontent over the rising price of bread; the installation of street lighting; the deliberate provocation of troops at the Plaza de Antón Martín; and the smashing of streetlamps.

Significant details in Part 2 taken from the source texts include: the mob's occupation of Esquilache's house; the presence of ringleaders reported to be wearing expensive shirts and stockings; the killing of a stable boy who resists the attack on the house; the seizing of firearms; the gangs roaming the streets unstitching hats and forcing people to join in the shouts of "¡Viva el rey! ¡Muera Esquilache!"; the freeing of prisoners; the king's protection of Esquilache in the Royal Palace, while his wife and daughters take refuge in the Salesas convent; the fact that the mob is persuaded not to burn the House of the Seven Chimneys, and does no more damage at Grimaldi's house than break a few windows; the spreading of disturbances to Zaragoza and other places; clashes between the crowd and the Walloons guarding the entrance to the Palace courtyard; the appearance of the king on a balcony with his confessor and courtiers; the involvement of a priest or friar as popular spokesman; the crowd flooding into the Plaza de la Armería, with a *calesero* as one of its leaders; the demands presented to the king; the conflicting views of his advisers; the king's intention to take Esquilache with him to Aranjuez; the reappearance of the king to announce his acceptance of the demands; evidence of Ensenada's role as an instigator of the uprising and provider of funds; reports that the crowds have cheered Ensenada during the rioting and at the Palace; Ensenada's surprise at receiving the order of banishment; the collection of Palm Sunday fronds for services of thanksgiving once the uprising has ended.

There is nothing in Buero's dramatization that directly contradicts the acknowledged facts. However, there is no such thing as pure, unmediated history, least of all in a literary text. The material is subjected to a careful process of selection, rearrangement and fictional elaboration, which constructs a particular interpretation of the events and the underlying historical processes.

One of the ways in which the material is re-worked for specific expressive purposes is compression of the true chronological sequence. There are three crucial instances of this. Firstly, the dramatically irresistible "no me da la gana" incident, reported by Ferrer (vol.2, p.14) as part of the skirmish in the Plaza de Antón Martín that sparked off the uprising on 23 March, is made use of in an earlier confrontation. This is a consequence of the fact that the main events of the popular uprising itself are not re-enacted on stage: the ambush at Antón Martín is being plotted at the end of Part 1; Part 2 begins in the aftermath of the attack on Esquilache's house; the march on the Palace and the negotiations in the courtyard are experienced by Esquilache and the audience only at a distance, through confused noises off and the reports of other characters. Concern for the practicalities of staging (as well as a characteristic reticence — Buero tends to avoid overtly spectacular scenes of violence and mass action) may have influenced these

decisions, but the effect is to produce an important shift of focus between the first and second halves of the play. The structure of the play will be discussed later in this introduction, but for the moment it is worth noting that in Part 1, we are able to feel that we are in touch with the development of events and with the motives of the people involved, enjoying a privileged view of both the street and the centres of power. At the opening of the second part, however, the clear perspectives established earlier are suddenly confused, the spatial divisions inverted. Much of this second part is set in the Palace. Our attention is focused mainly on Esquilache, but Fernandita becomes increasingly important: it is their response to events that is made the central point of interest, rather than the public dimension of the uprising itself.

The second instance of anticipation of later events occurs in the second conversation between Esquilache and the king in Part 2 (p.165). The king warns that there have already been disturbances in Zaragoza and other parts of the country, which he takes as evidence that the use of force against the rebels would lead to all-out civil war. In reality, the spirit of revolt spread more slowly and unevenly: the riots and demonstrations elsewhere all took place in April, and were almost all specifically concerned with the price of food. Most of these conflicts were resolved by local negotiation, but it is certainly conceivable that the popular mood — and the response of the authorities — would have been much more violent if the Madrid uprising had been crushed by force of arms and Esquilache had remained in office. Buero brings these other outbreaks forward in time and exaggerates the immediate threat they pose to the state in order to sharpen the dilemma described to Esquilache by the king: whether to concede a weakening of royal authority, sacrifice his most able minister and abandon crucial elements of a necessary programme of reform, or to use the power of the state and risk massive bloodshed.

There is some evidence that the king may have had no choice but to capitulate. José Navarro Latorre insists that historians have underestimated the extent to which the *motín de Esquilache* was a "military defeat" for Carlos's government. No-one took the warning signs seriously, no-one acted decisively when the uprising first broke out, and there were simply not enough troops stationed in Madrid to deal with the massive crowd that gathered around the Palace.[10] Evidence of this kind may not have been available to Buero (Danvila and Ferrer attribute the victory of the rebels to the benevolence of the king), but the impression given in the play that a military response from the Government would have had very serious consequences is evidently well founded.

The shifting forward of the spread of revolt to the provinces helps to prepare the ground for a crucially important piece of dramatic invention, for Buero has the king pass on the dilemma to Esquilache himself. Esquilache has to choose between imposing his will, whatever the cost in human life, and sacrificing himself to avoid bloodshed. His decision that the king should concede is clearly presented as a selfless and humanitarian act. Although few historians would be likely to credit Esquilache with such heroic self-sacrifice, certain details of Danvila's account provide some support for Buero's version: "His Majesty did not permit the use of military force

---

10   José Navarro Latorre, *Hace doscientos años: Estado actual de los problemas históricos del "Motín de Esquilache"* (Madrid: Instituto de Estudios Madrileños, 1966), p.21.

against the rebels, although it would have been easy enough to sweep them away in a few hours, and Squillace ordered that the insurrection be contained with the greatest possible restraint"; moreover, it was reported from Naples in May 1766 that Esquilache — inexplicably — saw his downfall as "a kind of triumph" (*Reinado de Carlos III*, pp.346 and 355).

The third instance of manipulation of the actual sequence of events is the device of having Esquilache deliver to Ensenada, on 24 March, the order banishing him to Medina del Campo. Both men assume at first that the document will offer Ensenada a return to power. The unpleasant surprise he receives on opening it prompts him to reveal his role in helping to instigate and finance the revolt, and Esquilache soon realizes that the king has brought about this confrontation deliberately. In reality, Ensenada did not receive the order of banishment until much later (according to Danvila, 18 April), and could not possibly have had it handed to him by Esquilache.

The basic dramatic function of this final encounter between the two men in the play is to confirm Ensenada's part in the insurrection. The king has presumably known about this for some time (and the audience may have suspected it), but the possibility has not occurred to Esquilache. Ensenada, relishing the ironic pleasure of receiving his call to office from the very man he has helped to overthrow, finds the irony turned against him. He admits that he has provided money to pay "the rabble" (p.171), and that he is motivated by jealousy of Esquilache, jealousy that has grown out of bitterness at having been replaced in power by a man he considers his inferior — and what is worse, a foreigner (p.173). Villasanta confirms that the person cheered by the crowds after the attack on Esquilache's house and at the Palace was Ensenada. This last detail appears to be the only substantial piece of evidence in the historical record implicating Ensenada (Ferrer, vol.2, p.49), although it was well known that he hoped to return to power, and the rumour that he had provided one and a half million *reales* for distribution amongst the rioters was widely believed (Ferrer, vol.2, p.51). However, no official reason for his exile was ever given: he received a letter from Roda, the Minister of Justice, assuring him that the king remained convinced of his loyalty (Danvila, p.395).

The question of Ensenada's involvement is one of several unsolved mysteries surrounding the *motín de Esquilache*, but Buero's version clearly identifies him as one of the chief conspirators.[11] The anticipation of his banishment and his admission of responsibility are indispensable components of a careful dramatic development that sets off the role of Ensenada against that of Esquilache, culminating in the final contrast between the former's cynical egoism and the latter's integrity and faith in the common people.

---

11   This was one of the aspects of the play that aroused fierce controversy after the première in 1958. Iglesias Feijoo reports that "after the first performance in Barcelona in January 1960, the 'Asociación de Hidalgos de España', deeply hurt by the portrayal of the Marquis of La Ensenada, resolved to establish a prize named after him for 'studies on our traditional aristocracy'" ('Introducción', Espasa Calpe edition of *Un soñador para un pueblo* (Madrid, 1989), p.24).

Public history, private dramas: the creation of character
These points at which public history intersects with private relationships are where the
creative interventions of the author are most decisive. The interactions between
individual characters are, necessarily, extensively fictionalized, yet never implausible.
The relationship between Esquilache and Ensenada may not in reality have been as
close or as significant as the play suggests, but there is evidence of a friendship (or at
least an alliance) which turned sour. Ferrer (vol.2, pp.50-1) writes that Ensenada was
well received by the king on his return from exile in 1760, and his friendship sought by
Esquilache; however, "Ensenada could not or would not conceal his desire for power,
which led to the king making it very clear that he did not wish to have him as an
adviser. [...] As time went by, Esquilache treated him more and more coolly, even
warily". Buero's treatment of their relationship acknowledges a certain cooling and
tension, and towards the end of the play Ensenada expresses scepticism about
Esquilache's claim to have pleaded with the king on his behalf, but the dramatic
development relies heavily on the prominence of the role of Ensenada, first as friend
and confidant of the protagonist, then as betrayer of that trust, and ultimately as catalyst
of Esquilache's full understanding and acceptance of what has occurred.

Another important character contrast is provided by the troubled relationship
between Esquilache and his wife. Once again, concrete details from the historical
sources are worked into a complex pattern of connections between the private life of the
protagonist and the public history of which the author makes him the focus. None of
the historians has a good word to say about Pastora Paternó. There is general
agreement on the portrayal of her as an arrogant, avaricious, brazenly corrupt social
climber. Ferrer, after enumerating some of the good points of the Marquis of
Esquilache's character and administration, condemns the damage done to his reputation
by "the corrupt conduct of his wife, doña Pastora, of whom it was said that she traded
royal favours so flagrantly that the only thing needed to complete the impression her
residence gave of being an auction house where public property was sold to the highest
bidder was the voice of the town crier" (Ferrer, vol.2, p.8). It seems to have been
widely believed that the marquis was equally grasping and unprincipled, yet Ferrer,
while acknowledging that he made full use of the resources available to him to buy
political support and enjoyed considerable favours from the sovereign, nevertheless
interprets his administrative reform programme (cuts in staff numbers, but higher
salaries) as a genuine attempt to establish principles of "morality and purity" in
government (vol.2, pp.6-7).

Buero seizes upon this hint of Esquilache as a fundamentally honest administrator
who has profited from a corrupt system in the past, is now determined to clean it up, but
is betrayed by the sleazy dealings in which his wife continues to engage behind his
back. The two revealing confrontations in Part 1 of *Un soñador para un pueblo* portray
their relationship as embittered and mistrustful, clearly blame Pastora for abuses of
power (including asking the king in her husband's name for the many favours bestowed
on their sons), and show the marquis's determination to make up for his past weakness
by setting a personal example of rectitude. Buero's treatment is not so simplistic as to
present Pastora as an outright villain, however. She is simply an opportunist who has
clawed her way up from nothing, and cannot see beyond the need to get what she can

from a system in which everyone else is doing the same (pp.61-3). Her cynicism runs parallel with that of Ensenada, in contrast to the idealism of her husband and the emotional honesty of Fernandita.

Esquilache's surprising friendship with Fernandita, which comes to be perhaps the most important relationship in the play, is entirely fictional. The circumstances of her initial encounter with the marquis, and the fact that he finds her chocolate soothes his intestinal pains more effectively than the brew usually served by his confectioner, may have been inspired by Fernán-Núñez's observation that "his stomach was the key to the Minister's moods" (*Vida de Carlos III*, vol.1, p.196). She is also linked with two figures briefly referred to in the history books: the *calesero* who played a prominent part in the insurrection (Bernardo) and the stable boy killed while resisting the assault on the House of the Seven Chimneys (Julián). Her relationship with Bernardo becomes a central element of the dénouement of the play, and her grief at the death of Julián sets up a significant contrast between her humanity and the casual brutality of the rioters. Moreover, some of the historical evidence about Esquilache's character adds to the plausibility of this empathy with his serving-maid. His own origins were relatively humble; it appears that he never won complete acceptance in court circles in Madrid, and had little reverence for established privileges; his manners were unrefined and his behaviour tended to be brusque and down-to-earth (Danvila, pp.302-4 and 356-7).

Whilst it is an emotional need that draws Esquilache to Fernandita in the first place, what she comes to represent for him is an encounter with the *pueblo* — a rediscovery of the interests of ordinary people and his own humanity. The common people feature in the historical accounts only in the form of the rebellious mob. Buero builds a crucial part of the play around assorted participants in and spectators of the popular uprising (Bernardo and his cronies, anonymous *embozados*, María and Claudia, the blind man, the *cesante*), but the individual experience and the emotional response of a typical passive victim of the historical circumstances can only be evoked through dramatic invention. The importance of Fernandita lies in the fact that she is individualized: part of the *pueblo*, yet separated from it, and given the chance to assess her position and make a decisive change in her life. She is less a representative of a social class than of the human consequences of the exercise of power. Her role is an essential component in the linking of the public and private domains in *Un soñador para un pueblo*, since she exemplifies the principle that every political decision must be considered in the light of its impact on individual human beings. Esquilache wins a kind of redemption at the end by learning the value of that link and acting upon it; Ensenada is condemned for failing to see it.

There are other characters similarly constructed on the basis of concrete historical details carefully integrated with the central dramatic development. King Carlos is first presented exactly as painted by Goya, and the allusions to his obsessive punctuality and dedication to hunting are based upon observations by Fernán-Núñez (vol.2, pp.46-7 and 52-3). The remark about washing children (p.105) is authentic, although according to Ferrer, it was uttered earlier than 1766, and was expressed more crudely: "It is well known that, in response to the outcry over the cleaning-up of Madrid, Carlos III said: 'The Spanish people are like children; they cry when the filth is washed off them'; although in fact he used a more graphic expression" (Ferrer, vol.1, p.268). In general, Buero's portrayal of the king is uncritical. Carlos comes across as an intelligent, fair-

minded ruler, genuinely interested in reform and modernization, yet realistic about the
practicalities of politics and the limits of his power.   Although there is certainly room
for scepticism about the extent of the real Carlos's commitment to Enlightenment ideals
and significant structural change, the positive portrayal in *Un soñador para un pueblo* is
based on substantial evidence in the primary historical sources.   Ultimately, the king is
not the main focus of the drama, and remains a rather insubstantial character, his main
function being to throw light on the evolution of the protagonist.   He recognizes
Esquilache's integrity and shares his ideals, but although his description of his favourite
minister as "a dreamer" denotes approval, it also implies a dangerous lack of
pragmatism (p.107). His actions towards the end of the play (making Esquilache decide
how to respond to the insurrection and allowing him to deliver the order of exile to
Ensenada) are more than just shrewd political manoeuvring.   He deliberately puts
Esquilache to the test, giving him the chance to turn political defeat into moral victory.
Danvila (pp.350-1) quotes a letter sent by Carlos to Naples on 1 April 1766, in which he
commends Esquilache's loyalty and competence, and remarks that "he has sacrificed
himself for me in these unhappy circumstances".   The dénouement of *Un soñador para
un pueblo* makes this considerably more complex: the hero's self-sacrifice is not
primarily for the sake of the person and authority of the sovereign, but rather for the
sake of Fernandita and others like her.   The king respects this, and perhaps
acknowledges that Esquilache has gained a kind of authenticity based upon
identification with the *pueblo* which his own necessarily remote position denies him.

     Another secondary figure, the cocky *calesero*, appearing in his red waistcoat as
described by Fernán-Núñez (vol.1, p.200), is clearly too picturesque a player to be left
out of a dramatization of the *motín de Esquilache*, but Buero ensures that he performs a
precise dramatic function.   In a superficial sense, he represents the people, as an
ordinary working man defending collective freedoms against the interference of an
authoritarian state. However, as the point of view of Esquilache increasingly conditions
the audience's response, while Bernardo comes to seem more and more bigoted and
ruthless, his status as potential folk hero crumbles.   His relationship with Fernandita
creates an ironic contrast between him and Esquilache, and strengthens the links
between the emotional lives of the characters and the events in which they are caught
up. Fernandita's revelation that she has been raped by Bernardo during the occupation
of the marquis's house has a profound effect on Esquilache's handling of the dilemma
put to him by the king. Bernardo is there in person, down below in the palace courtyard
leading the mob, while Fernandita whimpers in fear: suddenly, the private emotional
crisis of a young maidservant is thrown into the very centre of a major historical event.
Fernandita is pulled in two opposite directions: towards the destructive sexual power
and blind intolerance of Bernardo on the one hand, and towards the visionary
intelligence and understanding of Esquilache on the other.

     Villasanta is invented as a representative of two of the reactionary forces opposed to
Esquilache's policies: the established nobility, clinging to power and privileges
threatened by the processes of reform, and traditional Catholicism, alarmed by the
rationalist influence of the Enlightenment. Buero's protagonist is able to demonstrate
his intellectual and moral superiority over this social dinosaur, but the end of their long
conversation in Part 1 also serves to underline his vulnerability, as Villasanta
sarcastically congratulates him on the distinguished careers of his sons (p.89).

At the centre of this process of selection and elaboration of the historical source material is the figure of the Marquis of Esquilache himself, becoming increasingly complex in the course of the succession of encounters with Ensenada, Pastora, Fernandita, Villasanta and the king. The historians tend to give him credit for his energy and effectiveness in administration, but criticise him for his lack of both scruples and tact. Danvila quotes extensively from letters by the Neapolitan minister Tanucci: "relying upon a superficial grasp of things, speaking glibly, frequently about matters that he had not understood [...] he sacrificed everything to his ambition [...] he was prodigal with favours granted at the expense of the king to win friends [...] he gave jobs and pensions to inept people [...] he did all he could to enrich himself, and once a piece of business was successfully concluded, he would attempt to win public approval by spreading largesse" (Danvila, pp.302-4). Tanucci also claimed that there was hard evidence of the marquis's complicity in his wife's corrupt dealings (Danvila, p.356). Lynch, taking a wider perspective, recognizes Esquilache's energetic and constructive leadership, but implies that his most significant contribution was his encouragement of the careers of such reformers as Campomanes, Múzquiz and Moñino (later Count of Floridablanca).[12]

Buero decisively emphasises positive features in his portrayal of Esquilache, giving a clearly favourable slant to several controversial aspects of his character and conduct.[13] Before the protagonist appears on stage, a simplistic popular perception of his public image is offered in the conversation between Bernardo and his friends and in the text of the satirical poem that they recite, but it is clear that this impression is going to be substantially modified, since it is based upon crude exaggeration and absurd chauvinism. Fernandita's view is offered as a more sincere, thoughtful evaluation of Esquilache's practical achievements and, at the end, of his humanity. Insincere flattery is a convention all too familiar to the minister, but he soon realizes that her candour is genuine. She even unwittingly provides him with a justification for the ban on long capes and wide hats, seen from the point of view of a victim of crime rather than that of an enforcer of law and order (p.69).

Esquilache's lack of social graces and political finesse is repeatedly demonstrated in scenes with characters ranging in social status from his servants to his sovereign — even the harmless Fernandita is treated insensitively at first. In general, however, this is turned to his advantage. His directness and frankness seem refreshing in contrast to the calculating hypocrisy that prevails around him. He represents a new (albeit limited) form of social mobility, challenging the old, essentially feudal order, and his deflation of Villasanta's aristocratic pomposity is particularly impressive. The related allegation of hastiness and carelessness in decision-making is similarly converted by Buero into decisiveness: Esquilache's impatience is justified by the urgency of the work to be done. It turns out that his only real failing here is in underestimating the hostility of the forces plotting against him. He cannot believe that the people are not grateful for what he has done for them, and seems genuinely stunned when Ensenada's betrayal of his trust is

---

12 John Lynch, *Bourbon Spain, 1700-1808* (Oxford: Basil Blackwell, 1989), p.252.
13 Indeed, Buero concedes that his treatment of Esquilache may have been slightly too uncritical. In a conversation with me in 1991, he remarked that "le sublimé un poco" ("I overpraised him a little").

revealed. The "sly Italian" is thus presented as a surprising mixture of shrewdness and innocence. The apparently tough and ambitious politician is valued by the king as "an ingenuous dreamer, capable of showing the purest moral scruples" (p.107).

We have already seen how two of the key scenes contributing to the development of this character are based upon invented but highly believable incidents (taking the decision not to crush the rebellion, and handing the order of banishment to Ensenada). The scene in which Esquilache returns to his house on the night of the uprising, resulting in the episode in which he and Fernandita are stopped by a band of rebels, is also invented. Some accounts talk of his wife going into the house and later being stopped by rioters (Ferrer, p.17; Danvila, p.323), but it seems that the marquis himself —on his way back from San Fernando — went directly to the Palace as soon as he heard what was happening. The effect of this innovation is not only to add courage to the list of Esquilache's virtues. The point is that he risks his life for the sake of Fernandita: when she asks him why he has come back, he replies, "For you" (p.131). He puts his concern for another human being before his own safety and his public responsibilities as minister. A rash move, as Campos points out, but an important part of the lesson that this crisis is forcing him to learn.

The most serious accusation against Esquilache is perhaps the charge of corruption. Buero's version clearly blames Pastora for this, and suggests that such abuse of position is in fact the norm — something which even Esquilache has accepted and used in the past, but which he now determinedly opposes. He is therefore not entirely innocent in this respect, yet he is distinguished by having the honesty to admit this to himself and to act on that admission. Buero's invention of Esquilache's decision to ask the king to revoke his sons' privileges and allow him to separate from Pastora is an important part of the linking of public justice and private integrity. As the protagonist himself remarks, "you can't attempt to reform a country if you haven't been able to put your own house in order" (p.179). The public persona and political actions of men such as Ensenada and Villasanta are shown to be contaminated by very personal motives of self-interest and intolerance, just as the supposed patriotism of the defenders of traditional customs is shown to be driven largely by baser sentiments of chauvinism and xenophobia. Esquilache, by contrast, is engaged in a hopeless quest for ethical consistency in his public and private lives, at precisely the time when everyone else is intent on seeing his actions in the worst possible light. He accuses himself towards the end of being as much of an egoist as Ensenada, and yet Fernandita's predicament prevents him from wallowing in self-pity. She proves that both she and he have learned important lessons. His concern for the suffering of the individual has threatened to lead him into a deadly contradiction: he has been tempted for a moment to use the power of the state to suppress the revolt as a way of avenging the wrongs done to Fernandita but has seen that this would have been a hugely destructive act of selfishness. Ultimately, it is not the interests of Fernandita herself that matter most, but those of the people whom she represents. She confirms that he has "avoided massive suffering" (p.179), and in the closing moments of the play shows that he has empowered her to make her own decisions, to realize that she need not go on being a victim. He is finished, resigned to living out the rest of his life in bitterness and obscurity; she, by rejecting Bernardo, takes the first small step towards self-liberation.

Whose history? Differences of interpretation

It is clear, then, that *Un soñador para un pueblo* constructs a particular interpretation of a controversial historical episode. Esquilache is presented as an honest, progressive reformer, even something of a visionary: a condensation in one character of the energy and imagination of several ministers and administrators. Carlos III is intelligent and humane, and dreams of changes more radical than the measures that have been possible so far. The *motín* is sparked off by real popular grievances, but the scale of the revolt is out of proportion in relation to the specific issue of the capes and hats, for the common people are cynically used by powerful conspirators exploiting a distorted ideology of patriotism for political ends. Ensenada is identified as the leading conspirator, and he is shown to be motivated by personal ambition and resentment.

This interpretation differs markedly from some other versions of the events. The first official explanation of the uprising was produced by Campomanes's enquiry, which blamed the Jesuits for conspiring against the king and the Government and stirring up popular discontent. Unfortunately, the enquiry was conducted in secret and none of its evidence has survived. Several historians have doubted that the Jesuits were involved at all, arguing that the enquiry was manipulated to find a convenient scapegoat, and in some cases seeing the expulsion of the Order as an attack on religion in general.[14] In any case, Buero chose to avoid the Jesuit issue altogether. The influential position of the Catholic Church within the Franquist regime — and specifically its involvement in censorship — would have made this a dangerous issue. The author felt that, in the absence of reliable historical evidence, a reference to the Jesuit connection "would not have been worth the risk".[15]

Ferrer and Danvila are both well disposed towards Carlos III's administration, but as we have seen, tend to imply that Esquilache was to some extent guilty of provoking his own downfall. Neither of them comes to a firm conclusion on the causes of the insurrection. They agree on the assertion that the opposition to the ban on long capes and wide hats, although a genuine point of grievance amongst some citizens, was merely the catalyst for the popular uprising, and that other more powerful conspirators, intent on deposing Esquilache, either deliberately stirred up the capes and hats issue or capitalized upon it once it was already in motion. They identify the various groups who felt they had reason to be hostile to Esquilache, but avoid placing the blame definitively on Ensenada or the Jesuits. Danvila is particularly dismissive of the idea that the *motín* was the product of serious and legitimate popular grievances:

> No people ever had less cause for complaint, since food was plentiful and prices were moderate [...] but these very circumstances attracted to the capital a great number of low and contemptible people, who found the disguise of the long cape and floppy hat suited them very well. It was for the purpose of preventing this abuse that the decree was issued, to the consternation of these scoundrels, who began to foment rebellion, with the collaboration of others who took advantage of the freedom to give themselves over even more uninhibitedly to vice. (Danvila, p.346)

Vicente Rodríguez Casado emphasises the "counter-revolutionary" role of the aristocracy (without definitely singling out Ensenada). He argues that the common

---

14 For example: Constancio Eguía y Ruiz, *Los jesuitas y el motín de Esquilache* (Madrid, 1947).

15 From a conversation with me in 1991.

people were used by aristocratic opponents of Esquilache and middle-ranking members of the clergy, who carefully planned and led the uprising, and that the blaming of the Jesuits was a manoeuvre designed to avoid having to investigate the real responsibility of powerful nobles.[16]

Navarro Latorre, writing in 1966, takes a different line, insisting that what has sometimes been dismissed as a trivial local disturbance was a large-scale popular movement of major historical importance. He emphasises the seriousness of the issue of food prices, a factor given little importance in *Un soñador para un pueblo*, as well as the decisive factor of good old-fashioned chauvinism (and Navarro appears to accept this as natural, perhaps even commendable):

> But there is not the slightest doubt that the popular movement of March 1766 was also — above all — prompted by a deeply-rooted sense of xenophobic exasperation, since nationalist feeling is always to be found at the core of the Spanish soul. The replacement of what was considered [...] "national costume" by a style of dress regarded as foreign is enough to explain the violent, irritable reaction of the people, who were, moreover, goaded by the excesses of the agents of authority.
>
> (*Hace doscientos años*, pp.13-14)

Navarro finds no convincing evidence that either the Jesuits or the aristocracy had a significant role in instigating the revolt, and argues that they simply capitalized on an irresistible opportunity:

> The *Motín* was essentially a popular initiative at first. [...] Its unexpected initial success, encouraged by an almost universal attitude of acquiescence or passivity amongst all levels of Madrid society, [...] was exploited on the 24th [of March] by political groups hoping to gain power. The most well-organized and active of these was the "Ensenadista" faction [including leading Jesuits].   (p.50)

According to this argument, the Government ("in accordance with the mentality of the period") was not prepared to credit the common people with a legitimate sense of collective purpose, and consequently "excluded them from responsibility for the *Motín*, assuming them to have been seduced by other more politically sophisticated classes"; its retribution against Ensenada and the Jesuits is then a purely political move designed to secure its position while under severe pressure.

Pierre Vilar also focuses on the role of the ordinary people and discounts the theory of premeditated political conspiracy, although his emphasis is different from that of Navarro. He sees the insurrection as a spontaneous food riot: an example of a classic European phenomenon reflecting the kind of growth in mass political activity that culminated in the French revolution of 1789.[17]

Lynch, largely following Rodríguez Díaz,[18] takes a balanced view:

> It seems to have been a genuinely popular uprising, spreading out from the taverns under artisan leaders — one was a coach-maker, others were tailors — who refused to be bought

---

16   Vicente Rodríguez Casado, *La política y los políticos en tiempos de Carlos III* (Madrid: Rialp, 1962), pp.130-68.

17   Pierre Vilar, 'El motín de Esquilache y las crisis del Antiguo Régimen', *Revista de Occidente*, vol. 36, no. 107 (1972), pp.199-249.

18   Laura Rodríguez Díaz, 'The Riots of 1766 in Madrid', *European Studies Review*, 3 (1973), pp.223-42; 'The Spanish Riots of 1766', *Past and Present*, 59 (1973), pp.117-46; and *Reforma e Ilustración en la España del siglo XVIII: Pedro Rodríguez de Campomanes* (Madrid: Fundación Universitaria Española, 1975).

off. Protest was related to the high price of bread, a consequence of poor harvests, and the liberalization of the grain trade by Campomanes. But it was manipulated by others to become a direct attack on the reform policy of the government. Who, then, were the instigators of the riots? There were various candidates for the role. [...]
[Ensenada] still had political ambitions, kept himself in circulation, was a favourite with the mob, and apparently in good spirits throughout the riots. Ensenada in turn could embody the hopes of another sector hostile to Squillace, the higher nobility.
The nobility [...] saw the retrieval of *señoríos* announced by Campomanes in 1762 as a threat to their lands, rents and offices; and they resented the loss of political power, while upstarts and foreigners were being promoted to the highest appointments. [...] The other privileged sector, the Church, had been alienated or at least alerted by jurisdictional and financial losses since 1753; it was now further outraged by Campomanes's plan to disamortize its property; and some of the clergy genuinely sympathized with popular grievances. The replacement of Squillace by Ensenada would particularly satisfy the Jesuits, who had enjoyed the favour of the former minister [...]. For all these reasons it can be speculated that the riots were prepared by a group, or an alliance of groups, to call a halt to reform, warn off the government, and preserve existing privilege.

(*Bourbon Spain*, pp. 263-8)

On the general character of the reign of Carlos III, Lynch's view is more sceptical than Buero's, seeing more signs of absolutism than of Enlightenment. It was a period of substantial achievement, and he acknowledges a genuine desire for administrative rationalization and the reduction of traditional privileges, but reminds us that Carlos and his ministers were engaged in a long-term power struggle against the nobility and the Church: the intended beneficiary of much of the reform programme was the Crown, rather than the people. The primary objective was the enhanced effectiveness of centralized royal power, rather than the beginnings of democracy (pp.247-9).

Un soñador para un pueblo was written at a time when administrative and economic modernization was becoming a major policy objective. Franco's government was carrying out a major shift from the closed, rigidly controlled economy of the 1940s towards a more open, market-orientated system encouraging foreign investment and industrial development. Its propaganda was beginning to say less about order and tradition, and more about the achievements of a government giving its people economic well-being. This change was being directed by the new generation of administrators, the *tecnócratas*. They were capable and educated, committed to economic and administrative rationalization, but still loyal servants of an authoritarian regime determined to ensure its own survival. It is possible to draw a parallel between these technocrats and the reformers of Carlos III's reign, seeing both groups either as idealists democratizing dictatorship, or as cynics reinforcing it. Buero's portrayal of Esquilache and Carlos III could then be read as a defence of both eighteenth-century absolutism and the emerging new face of Franquism. Indeed, the play was criticized as "reactionary" by some advocates of an uncompromising literature of protest against the regime.

Buero himself resists such a parallel. He regards the Franquist *tecnócratas* as essentially conservative, fundamentally different from the genuinely progressive reformers of the eighteenth century.[19] His play draws attention to the frustration of

---

19   Conversation with me, 1991.

what could have been real progress in the past, and implies that such progress would be possible in the present if there were enlightened leaders prepared to challenge entrenched interests and established orthodoxies and, above all, to listen to the people. The reality of the 1950s was that very little was changing. Moreover, the point is that little had changed since the eighteenth century: "Many things in this country continue to resemble too closely those things which the king, Esquilache and the others thought it was necessary to struggle against".[20] If the text has anything specific to say about those in power in 1958, it is to contrast them with Esquilache, and to propose a warning rather than express approval: government, whether benevolent in its intentions or not, can be conducted without the consent of the people, but only at the cost of great human suffering. Esquilache realizes belatedly that his aim of improving the material conditions of the masses so as to allow them to "come of age" before they are given any real responsibility, although more constructive than Ensenada's cynical insistence that the *pueblo* is."always under age" (p.55), has underestimated the obstructive force of the established order and the potential capacity of the people for taking responsibility on their own terms. He resists the temptation to impose on them by force what he thinks they need, putting human lives above ideology and the interests of the state. Although no easy answers are offered, the implication is that real change requires a dismantling of established power structures as well as the genuine involvement of the people.

The aspect of *Un soñador para un pueblo* that seems to have caused Buero's left-wing critics most concern is the portrayal of the ordinary people. Fernandita is a positive character in personal terms, but, being a loyal servant of the ruling class who opposes a popular movement, she is of ambiguous value as a representative of the collective interests of the *pueblo*. The other representatives of the people are mostly boorish, bigoted layabouts incapable of seeing that they are being manipulated to act against their own interests. The legitimate grievances and political awareness of the populace are not taken seriously, and there is no sense of constructive collective purpose. One practitioner of "social theatre" asked indignantly: "Has the Spanish writer — the intellectual — really sunk so deep into pessimism about his own people?"[21] There is something in this argument, but it underestimates the impact of the figure of Fernandita. She cannot be dismissed as a mere lackey of the aristocracy, for Buero endows her with honesty, spirit, intelligence, compassion, and convincing personal reasons for respecting Esquilache and approving of his policies. At the end, she leaves behind her status as servant, turning down Esquilache's offer of a position in the royal household, and achieves a degree of independence by rejecting Bernardo. This is a very small step, and hardly a revolutionary one, but it is on the symbolic significance of this moment that the impact of the play depends. She has described Bernardo as representing "all the crudeness and brutality that I hate" (p. 161), while Esquilache's words have elevated her to the status of an embodiment of the positive potential of the people, and have explicitly linked her need to liberate herself from Bernardo with the hope that the people as a whole will one day "make it out of their grim darkness into the light" (p.181).

---

20   A statement by the author from an interview published in *Negro sobre Blanco*, 12 (1960), p.2, entitled 'Buero Vallejo nos habla de *Hoy es fiesta* y *Un soñador para un pueblo*'.

21   José María de Quinto, 'Crónica de teatro', *Insula*, 220 (1965), p.19.

Condemnation of *Un soñador para un pueblo* from a right-wing point of view also concentrated on the perceived injustice of the representation of the people as loutish riff-raff in contrast with an undeservedly favourable view of their rulers. A pair of articles by José María García Escudero written in response to the first production adopt a moderate tone, but clearly reflect the dominant ideology of the regime.[22] According to this view, the real historical stature of Carlos III and Esquilache provides no grounds at all for the idealization of them perpetrated by Buero, who is accused of gross over-simplification: "he sets up an opposition in his play between the touching paternalism of the official reformers and the obscurantism of a people on whose heads he pours the most vile abuse" ('Un soñador...'). Although some of the practical reforms of the period are accepted as useful, the real threat is secularism — a general anti-clerical ("if not heretical") tendency exemplified by the expulsion of the Jesuits. The play's "defence of what was known as 'the Enlightenment' is more unconditional and absolute than would be desirable, for the 'lights' of the Encyclopedia are as much a part of it as the lights on street corners; trimming capes, which is how it started, as well as throwing out cassocks, which is how it ended" ('Un pueblo...'). The essential identity of Spain — and by implication, of the *pueblo* — is equated with the Catholic tradition, founded in a mythical time of national unity and now threatened by heretical foreign influences: there were some who "desired not only reform, but also the total destruction of inner Spain, body and soul" ('Un pueblo...'). Buero is therefore accused of betraying a precious national spirit for the defence of which the rioters of 1766 should be celebrated: they rejected the capes and hats decree "more than anything because it was imposed by foreigners, which was not so unreasonable" ('Un soñador...'). This alleged landering of the Spanish people is not redeemed by the figure of Fernandita, "false from head to foot". Finally, García Escudero executes a disingenuous sidestep that brings him back to almost the same ground as the left-wing critics: "the play could easily be taken as a statement in praise of dictatorship".[23] This is because "the enlightened despotism of the 18th century may have been well-intentioned, but if it had one defining feature, this would be the fact that it functioned entirely without the involvement of the people", the Bourbon regime having lost the "fruitful contact that there had previously been between the people and their rulers" ('Un pueblo...'). Presumably, the implication is that the Franquist system had re-established this "fruitful contact" that characterized the Hapsburg empire of the seventeenth century (a myth comprehensively demolished by Buero's own *Las Meninas*).

Fortunately, García Escudero is right in some respects. *Un soñador para un pueblo* does go against the conservative, nationalist, rigidly Catholic values held sacred by Franco and his followers. These values are represented in the play by Villasanta, who is

---

22 José María García Escudero, 'Un soñador para un pueblo', *Ya* (27 December 1958), p.5, and 'Un pueblo para un soñador', *Ya* (1 January 1959), p.5. Luis Iglesias Feijoo points out that García Escudero was later appointed Director of Cinematography and Theatre in Franco's government, and mentions several other hostile reviews in a similar vein ('Introducción', *Un soñador para un pueblo*, pp.23-4).

23 The ambiguity of the Spanish is interesting: the definite article in "la dictadura" is necessary whether it means "the dictatorship" (i.e. Franco's) or "dictatorship in general". García Escudero evidently means the latter (the example he gives of a dictator is Khrushchov), but he may be attempting to embarrass Buero by implying support for the Government.

thoroughly discredited by the lucid arguments of Esquilache. The same reactionary values, embodied in Bernardo and the other rioters, are shown to be based on crude bigotry, driven by instincts all too easily distorted and manipulated. Buero's play, without being an overtly political protest, challenges such notions of national identity by asserting that neither rulers nor ruled need be like that: patriotism does not have to be nationalistic xenophobia; religion, government and human relationships can be based on tolerance, compassion and acceptance of change. The play's dedication to Antonio Machado is itself a significant part of this declaration of principle and hope. Machado and other members of the "Generation of 1898" were in some respects inheritors of the eighteenth-century spirit of reform, and were accordingly reviled by the regime and its followers. The poem from Machado's *Campos de Castilla* whose title, 'Una España joven', is included in Buero's dedication, ends with a radiant expression of faith in historical progress and the transforming energy of youth.[24]

Furthermore, the example of Esquilache's self-sacrifice implicitly questions the very legitimacy of Franco's government. The *Caudillo* and his followers insisted on the necessity of the war of 1936-39 and the rightness — indeed, holiness — of their cause. Total victory and the extermination of their enemies were required in order to cleanse Spain of contaminating influences, and once gained (at the cost of hundreds of thousands of lives), this victory conferred the unquestionable right to impose on the nation the rule and the ideology of the victors. The Esquilache of *Un soñador para un pueblo*, in contrast, decides that his cause, however rational, however necessary, cannot justify the massive suffering of a civil war. He admits that he is tempted by the intoxicating lure of military power, yet he resists the temptation and avoids bloodshed. The generals who claimed to be "saving Spain" in July 1936 let loose precisely the "hell on earth" that Esquilache envisages and prevents.

Buero's treatment of the historical material emerges as a complex, dynamic process. Elements are selected, reshaped and arranged in a fluid but intricate pattern of dramatic interactions. The historical recreation in itself stimulates a certain degree of interest, but it is neither purely factual documentary nor merely a colourful backdrop. The dramatic action is neither a mechanical working-out of the principles of the historical analysis nor an entirely ahistorical interplay of individual conflicts. The two dimensions are profoundly inter-dependent: history is made by human beings, and human beings are made by history. The fact that an uprising occurs in Madrid in March 1766 and leads to the departure of the Marquis of Esquilache is fixed, known in advance by the audience.[25] The audience can still be engaged, challenged, intrigued and surprised, however, by the interpretation of the causes and significance of the events, by the exploration of the motives and responses of the people involved, and, above all, by the relationship between the people and the events. The known factual

24 Antonio Machado, *Campos de Castilla* (Madrid: Cátedra, 1974), pp.169-70.
25 A typical member of the audience in Madrid in 1958 may have had only limited knowledge of this period of history, but would have been likely to have heard of the *motín de Esquilache*. An educated Spaniard in the 1990s might be slightly better informed, especially as the bicentenary of the death of Carlos III was marked in 1988 by a television series and numerous publications (Equipo Madrid, *Carlos III, Madrid y la Ilustración* (Madrid: Siglo XXI, 1988), for example).

outcome is the downfall of Esquilache and a setback for the reform programme. The dramatic climax consists not of the fact of the hero's defeat, but of the culmination of his painful acquisition of self-awareness and its effect on the audience.

The declaration made by Esquilache to Villasanta as a confident dismissal of the latter's backward-looking conservatism — "History does not stand still" (p.87) — becomes his consolation in defeat. He looks forward, in the hope that there will be other dreamers, other people of integrity and compassion who will make a difference (even if it takes centuries). One of the predictions he makes — "in a century or two from now, it won't occur to even the most intransigent of Catholics to burn someone for being a heretic" — will come true, but other injustices and cruelties will persist. History, full of disappointments yet illuminated by a few glimpses of real progress, will move on — has moved on — and the future awaited by Esquilache is suddenly the spectators' or readers' present, whenever that is, again and again. They too are both the products and the producers of history, challenged to assess their role in what has happened and in what is yet to happen.

"Ése eres tú": the spirit of tragedy

This discussion has concentrated largely on the process by which historical data and anecdotes are turned into the dramatic action of *Un soñador para un pueblo*. The question of the responses this action is designed to provoke in an audience has been emphasised, but further analysis of the specifically theatrical characteristics of the text is needed. After all, Buero's project is not simply to produce an alternative historical narrative or to make an explicit declaration of ideological principles. His declared aim is the creation of tragedy — a moving, thought-provoking, pleasurable, mysterious experience that works by means of a "direct aesthetic, rather than discursive, impression" ('La tragedia', p.67).

We have already seen that characterization is a factor of primary importance. Esquilache dominates the play: he is the nucleus of a carefully constructed series of interactions that gradually give the audience a convincing sense of being in touch with the complexity of the real man behind the public persona. The moment at which the hero resolves the central moral dilemma and commits himself to self-sacrifice comprises the climax of the play and the main focus of the classical tragic processes of *catharsis* and *anagnorisis*. Each of his relationships with the other main characters (Fernandita, Pastora, Ensenada, Campos, Villasanta and the king) adds a distinctive facet to this solid impression of believable personality, and each encounter strengthens the links between the public and private domains. Although these other characters serve mainly to contribute to the portrayal of Esquilache, each of them contains some element of surprise or change which confers a degree of individuality and complexity. Fernandita becomes the most important of the secondary figures, to the extent that at the end, she takes over from Esquilache the status of protagonist: his part is done, and he stands immobile in the shadows as she takes centre stage and performs a symbolic act of self-liberation. None of the other lower-class characters acquires the same measure of individuality: they tend to function as groups, and the men (some of them unnamed) are sometimes indistinguishable in their capes and hats. They represent the *pueblo*, but

in the form of a manipulable mass, without the individualizing awareness and will shown by Fernandita to be possible.

We are therefore encouraged to believe in these personalities, and to share something of the emotional crisis of the hero. At the same time, the symbolic function of each character is made perfectly clear. Each represents a political interest, a principle or a moral value, which in some cases is explicitly pointed out in the dialogue: for example, Esquilache concisely defines Villasanta's significance in their conversation in Part 1, and declares Fernandita to be the true representative of the people near the end. Esquilache himself becomes a condensation of humanist values: an archetypal bringer of enlightenment.

The bringer of the light of understanding to the people is also the bringer of light to the streets of Madrid. Esquilache and his reform project are associated with a pattern of verbal and visual symbolism centred on the streetlamps he has had installed.[26] Towards the end of the first part of the play, a lamp is lit outside Esquilache's window, illuminating him and Fernandita, just as he is saying: "We're like children lost in the dark" (p.119). It is unclear whether this remark refers only to himself and Fernandita or is a general pronouncement about the state of the nation, but when the gloom (literal and metaphorical) is suddenly relieved by the lamp outside, he makes clear the dual significance: "Look. The darkness is gone. Soon all the lamps in Madrid will be alight. Thanks to me, the grubbiest city in Europe is now the most beautiful. I can't believe that they're not grateful to me for that". A lamplighter lights the two lamps on stage, and a candelabra is brought into Esquilache's study. But the minister's optimism is misplaced. The glowing pools of light leave shadows, into which creep the caped conspirators. As Esquilache leaves Madrid, confident that the threatened disturbances will not happen, the first, highly symbolic, act of revolt against him is carried out: Bernardo and his accomplices smash the three lamps and the stage is plunged into darkness.

The scenes at the beginning of Part 2, showing the aftermath of the occupation of Esquilache's house on the following day, are then played out in gathering darkness. The streets are unlit and ruled by gangs of *embozados*. In the Royal Palace, Esquilache glumly observes that "Madrid isn't as lit up as it has been recently" (p.145), and Villasanta confirms that the mob has destroyed all the streetlamps in the city. Several key references in the final scenes consolidate and develop the light/darkness symbolism, linking it with a matching antithesis between seeing and blindness (or refusal to see the light), and deepening the ambiguity between private and public significance. A remark by the king about "the pigheaded blindness of a country infinitely less advanced than its rulers" (p.165) reinforces the notion that conservative opposition to reform (amongst both the common people and the aristocracy) is a wilful refusal to see, to let in the light. Esquilache, however, has begun to realize that his own vision has been inadequate. He prided himself upon his ability to see through the falseness of others, yet he has not perceived the true character of Campos or the threat

---

26   Several critics have emphasised the importance of symbolism of light and darkness in this
      and other plays by Buero. See, for example: Martha Halsey, '"Light" and "darkness" as
      dramatic symbols in two tragedies of Buero Vallejo', *Hispania*, 50 (1967), pp.63-8; and
      'More on "light" in the tragedies of Buero Vallejo', *Romance Notes*, 11 (1969), pp.17-20.

people of Madrid. He now finds himself powerless, virtually imprisoned in a room in the Palace, and is prevented from going out onto the balcony to see what is going on in the courtyard. Fearing the worst, he ruefully comments that "others see our destiny before we do" (p.157).

For Fernandita, on the other hand, Esquilache still represents light and vision (as a person and in his public achievements), in contrast to the darkness of the brutality and ignorance she has experienced and now fears in Bernardo: "I've tried to get away from all that darkness, all that horror... and I can't! I wanted to make myself better by finding a little light and a little human kindness. To escape towards you and everything you stood for!" (p.161). Thanks to the lesson offered by Fernandita, Esquilache sees, as he faces his supreme dilemma, that the personal and political levels of significance of the symbolism are inseparable. He is tempted to seize the power offered him by the king, so as to "continue shaping this beautiful land of Spain, and to bring a little light and a little joy... (*Looks towards the door at the right.*) to some suffering souls who deserve it" (p.165). He associates light with life and warmth, but this leads him to a vision of fire and of "hell on earth": the bearer of light could turn into a kind of Lucifer. He resists the temptation and puts out the flames. Although finally satisfied with his moral victory over Ensenada and over his own egoism, what he has learned above all is humility. He recognizes the limitations of the rational enlightenment he has pursued until now, and turns to Fernandita for a different kind of light. Recalling the blind peddler of almanacs, he says: "We know nothing. As blind as he is, all of us... (*He goes to* FERNANDITA *and takes her hands.*) Help me to see!" (p.179). She protests that she too is "blind", but she has already helped him decisively, without quite knowing how. What he still needs is a clearer and more hopeful vision of the future, and only Fernandita can give it to him. She has been regarding her weakness for Bernardo in spite of his brutishness as despicable but inevitable; Esquilache now persuades her that it is just another form of blindness that can be remedied: "the cruel blindness that's part of life. But you can open your eyes" (p.179). It is not easy for anyone to open their eyes and let in the light, but he insists that it can and must be done. And once again, a metaphor being applied to the personal crisis of an individual slides onto the general plane: "Maybe it'll be centuries before the people understand... They may never make it out of their grim darkness into the light... But it depends on you and on others who are like you! Is it possible? Will you make it possible?" (p.181).

Light is thus transformed from a mundane, realistic component of the situation into a powerful symbol — a condensation of a complex set of ideas and feelings of central significance. In a similar way, the series of dialogues required for the development of the character of the protagonist can be seen to be carefully arranged, so that the structure of the dramatic action itself acquires symbolic force. It was Robert Nicholas who first drew attention to the symmetrical arrangement of Part 1. He points out the alternation between interior and exterior, and identifies three sets of three encounters between Esquilache and another character:

> Each series of interior scenes is characterized by a downward progression from the highest to the lowest social class. The aristocrats, Villasanta, Ensenada and the king, precede Pastora, embodiment of the "nouveaux riche" [sic], who in turn comes before the peasant Fernandita. The good element of the lower class (Fernandita) is followed by and

contrasted with the evil segment of the lower class (in the street scenes). And the cycle begins again.[27]

Nicholas concludes that "the playwright has attempted to reflect the spirit of classicism, the dominant artistic mode of the epoch, in the symmetrical ordering of the action of his play" (p.64). This analysis can be elaborated to demonstrate precisely how controlled the text's structure is. The following scheme of Part 1 shows the links between exterior and interior locations (the main linking elements are marked with asterisks; silent action in one place during a scene in the other is shown by square brackets), and interior series of five scenes rather than three:

Part 1	Main Stage (street)	Platform (interiors)
A	Lights up;. B/S *pregón* 9 March (morning) Scene-setting: characters are introduced; public (opposition to Esquilache) & private (BER-FER relationship) themes initiated *Pregón* 9 March as B/S exits; ROQ & CRI comment as *ENS* passes; lights down	[Lights up; CAM in ESQ's study]
B	B/S crosses stage: *pregón* [Enter B/S; enter BER, then REL]	(9 March, immediately after A) 1. *ENS* with CAM, then ESQ 2. ESQ with ENS: politics 3. ESQ with PAS: ethics 4. ESQ with FER: feelings 5. ESQ with CAM: *order for 10 March* Lights down as ESQ & CAM go
C	B/S *pregón* *10 March* (next morning); lights up The *order* is posted, arouses hostility FER confronts BER FER picks up the crumpled *notice*; lights down as she goes	[MAY & CAM appear in study; lights up]

27 Robert L. Nicholas, *The Tragic Stages of Antonio Buero Vallejo* (Chapel Hill: University of North Carolina, 1972), p.62. This section of the book covers the same ground as an earlier article by Nicholas: 'The history plays: Buero Vallejo's experiment in dramatic expression', *Revista de Estudios Hispánicos*, 3 (1969), pp. 281-93.

	B/S *pregón* 11 March B/S sits on steps of platform; monologue [CES looks at protest poster] CES reads poster to B/S; *pregón* [Constables & *tailor* appear; <u>lights up</u>]	(11 March, next morning) 1. CAM with MAY, then ESQ (who has the *notice*); instruction about tailors 2. ESQ with VIL: politics & history 3. ESQ with PAS: ethics 4. ESQ with FER: trust 5. ESQ with CAM: *tailors*; <u>lights down</u>
E	(11 March, immediately after D) The *tailoring* operation, the authorities in control; shouts of "God save the *King*, death to Esquilache" as <u>lights down</u>	
F		<u>Spot on</u> the *KING* in **El Pardo** (some time between 11 & 22 March) 1. KING with ESQ: political & personal
	<u>Dim lights on</u>; B/S off: *pregón* 22 **March** [*Lamps* are lit on stage; *embozados* gather furtively]	(22 March, late afternoon) <u>Lights up</u> on the **study** 2. ESQ with CAM: Fernandita 3. ESQ with ENS: politics 4. ESQ with FER: growing intimacy (A *lamp* is lit outside)
G	(22 March, evening, immediately after F) Revolt is plotted; *lamps* are smashed <u>Lights out suddenly</u>; CURTAIN	[5. ESQ alone] <u>Light outside the window out suddenly</u>

This structure is remarkably fluid, balanced and orderly. There is a clear alternation between the street (A, C, E, G) and the interiors (B, D, F). Apart from interruptions by the Ballad-seller during some of the interior scenes, the two locations are kept separate (only Fernandita moves freely in both). The transitions from one setting to the other are achieved by means of deft overlapping of business and shifts of lighting. The interior scenes form a regular pattern: each series consists of three main dialogues, framed by shorter scenes involving Campos (with a slight variation in the third series). Connections are made, ideas are clarified — the mechanism works like clockwork, like a gavotte, with neoclassical elegance. The stage design itself contributes to this effect, thanks to the ingenuity of the device of the revolving platform. Esquilache dominates his own interior space — central, slightly elevated, geometrically as well as

decoratively elegant — and exercises (incomplete) control from a distance over the more open, irregular space outside. The audience too is allowed to feel in control, enjoying a privileged view of the two parallel areas of action.

However, this sense of order begins to break down at the end of the first part. Esquilache's study and the street are brought closer together by the lighting of the lamps (first outside his window, then on the main stage immediately afterwards). Esquilache finds this reassuring, but as soon as he leaves, the destruction of the lamps (again, in both places) foreshadows an invasion of his space. At the beginning of Part 2, everything is disordered, as the following scheme shows:

Part 2	MAIN STAGE (street)	PLATFORM (interiors)
A	(23 March, evening); getting dark Esquilache out of place & at risk Rebels dominate the street; they intimidate constables and ESQ BER shouts to REL, who appears here immediately after leaving the study	(Same time, overlapping); getting dark REL occupies ESQ's **study** In the **doorway**, FER & EMI try to move Julián's body, are interrupted by ESQ REL is woken by BER's voice, picks up the portrait & leaves
B	[Lights down completely]	(Later the same evening); lights up ESQ in the **Palace** with FER & CAM The KING reassures ESQ ESQ shows concern for FER VIL informs ESQ of destruction of lamps. Lights down
C	(Night **23-24 March**) MAR throws out slops; shouts off; lights up slowly as B/S crosses the stage (dawn)	
D		(24 March, morning); lights up ESQ loses control of events; clashes with CAM & VIL; feels abandoned ESQ is consoled by FER; she is horrified to see BER in the courtyard (noises off) The KING makes ESQ decide ESQ & FER judge ENS ESQ & FER console and help each other [ESQ stands alone by the balcony]

| E | (**24 March**, later the same day) Celebration of ESQ's fall (confirmed by B/S **pregón** off); FER rejects BER Same music as opening; SLOW CURTAIN | |

The inhabitants of the street occupy and disrupt the interior, while Esquilache risks the dangers of a city under mob rule. Business goes on simultaneously — almost confusingly — on the main stage and the platform, without the regular alternation of Part 1. There is then a change of rhythm as the action settles down in the Palace scenes. Esquilache finds himself in a space similar to his own study, but clearly not a vantage point from which to control events outside. He is isolated, virtually imprisoned, and prevented from seeing what is happening in the courtyard, as are the audience, who for long periods have nothing to watch on the main stage. At the end, Esquilache remains alone in the room in the Palace while our attention turns to Fernandita in the foreground.

The blind man who sells ballads, newspapers and the Piscator almanac has several crucial functions within this structure. He punctuates the action and marks the passage of days with his call. Esquilache obtains a copy of the almanac that appears to predict his fall, and is repeatedly unsettled by the blind man's call, which is barely noticed by the other characters inside the house. The rational, pragmatic minister begins to believe that the old man represents the power to see into the future: "That insignificant blind man held our destiny in his hands" (p.179). The ballad-seller's blindness seems to give him a mysterious kind of inner vision and, in a magical moment in Part 2, a special relationship with light: the stage direction calls for the lights to come up slowly as day breaks, and just as slowly, the blind man crosses the stage "as if it were he who was bringing in the new day" (p.147).[28] Esquilache moves from being troubled by this irrational enigma to celebrating it. He acquires not only humility and humanity, but also a touch of true spirituality. We are not asked to believe in destiny,[29] nor to accept that the old man has psychic powers; yet we should be struck by the sense of mystery that he evokes.

The play ends on a note of ambiguity, without complete resolution of the problems raised, but is in many ways deeply reassuring. Buero's texts, although always open-ended, guide their audiences' responses very firmly towards a coherent moral view. Heroism (albeit limited by human weakness) is possible; idealism is meaningful (even when it is doomed to fail); the cruel and the selfish are punished (even if only by their own consciences); society is perfectible (in certain ways, at certain times); human beings can learn to understand one another and express their fears and desires (if not calm or satisfy them).

---

28 Many of Buero's plays contain characters who are blind or deaf, but possess a mysterious sixth sense and special powers of perception or clairvoyance.

29 Buero argues that, even in classical tragedy, destiny is not an absolute force, nor an entirely superhuman one. He quotes Heraclitus's maxim that "Man's destiny is his way of thinking" ('La tragedia', p.69).

In other ways, however, this and other Buero plays are troubling rather than reassuring. Every member of the audience is challenged to examine their conscience, to see themselves in the imperfect characters on stage, to ask the "tremendous question" at the centre of *El tragaluz* — "¿Quién es ése?" ("Who is that?") — and realize that the answer is "Ése eres tú". In *El tragaluz*, the researchers of the future century present their reconstruction of the main story as if it were a history play, based upon reliable facts from the past, but condensed and reshaped in order to provide a moral lesson to their audience. One of them remarks at the end that the "experiment" will have failed if the spectators have not, just for a moment, felt as if they really were people from the twentieth century, victims or perpetrators of the crimes and errors they have seen, "observed and judged by some kind of future conscience", while at the same time seeing themselves as "beings from a future made present who sit in strict but merciful judgement on people from a remote past who are perhaps the same as you" (*El tragaluz*, p.106). The real audience, then, are being asked to pretend to be what they actually are. Ultimately, this is also what *Un soñador para un pueblo* and the other history plays do. They put in front of us remote, unknowable figures in antique costume; encourage us to ask who these figures are; suggest that we imagine that we are who they are; and finally make us realize that the point is not that we are pretending to be someone else, but that we are meant to be observing — and judging — ourselves.

The researcher in *El tragaluz*, speaking from a time in which human beings have found ways of living in peace and solidarity, suggests that "if all those who injured, tortured and trampled on others had thought, while they were doing so, that they themselves were the victims, they would not have done it" (p.88). Esquilache, a solitary dreamer in a time of violence and intolerance, begins to learn the significance for him of "ése eres tú": that neither the enlightened principles of reform (street lamps) nor patriotism and tradition (long capes and wide hats) justify the suffering of a single victim of war or torture or persecution. In the sharply polarized ideological context of the 1950s and 1960s, the political message of Buero's work may not have seemed in many people's eyes to be particularly radical. In the uncertain 1990s, with racism resurgent all over Europe and nations collapsing into warring tribes, the defence of human rights is the highest priority. The lesson of "ése eres tú" is more important and necessary than ever.

MICHAEL THOMPSON
University of Durham, November 1993

Fernando Fernán-Gómez as Esquilache and Ángela Molina as Fernandita in the film *Esquilache* (directed by Josefina Molina).

Portrait of Carlos III by Francisco de Goya, with kind permission from the Prado Museum, Madrid.

Antonio Buero Vallejo

A DREAMER FOR THE PEOPLE
Un soñador para un pueblo

A la luminosa memoria de DON
ANTONIO MACHADO, que soñó una
España joven.

*To the luminous memory of DON
ANTONIO MACHADO, who had a
dream of a new, young Spain.*

CAST (In order of appearance)

CIEGO DE LOS ROMANCES	The blind ballad-seller
LA CLAUDIA, Maja	A *maja*[1]
DOÑA MARÍA, Alcahueta	A procuress
FERNANDITA	
BERNARDO, El calesero	The cab driver[2]
MORÓN, Embozado	An *embozado*[3]
RELAÑO, Embozado	An *embozado*
ROQUE, Alguacil	A constable
CRISANTO, Alguacil	A constable
MAYORDOMO	Esquilache's steward
DON ANTONIO CAMPOS, Secretario Privado	Esquilache's private secretary
DON ZENÓN DE SOMODEVILLA	Marquis of LA ENSENADA
DON LEOPOLDO DE GREGORIO	Marquis of ESQUILACHE
DOÑA PASTORA PATERNÓ	Marchioness of ESQUILACHE
CESANTE	A *cesante*[4]
EL DUQUE DE VILLASANTA	
SASTRE	A tailor
EMBOZADO 1º	1st *embozado*
ALGUACIL 1º	1st constable
ALGUACIL 2º	2nd constable
EMBOZADO 2º	2nd *embozado*
EMBOZADO 3º	3rd *embozado*
EL REY	The King
DOÑA EMILIA	
LACAYO	A footman
(UN FIJADOR DE BANDOS, UN FAROLERO	A billposter and a lamplighter)

Madrid, during the month of March, 1766.
Carlos III is on the throne.

This play received its premiere on 18 December 1958 at the Teatro Español in Madrid, under the direction of José Tamayo.

EL DECORADO
Derecha e izquierda, las del espectador.

Rincón de Madrid cercano a la Casa de las Siete Chimeneas, donde tiene su morada el marqués de Esquilache. Un alto muro asoma apenas por el lateral izquierdo, dejando paso por el primero y el segundo término. Adosado a él y a buena altura, un farol se proyecta hacia la escena. En el lateral derecho, la estrecha fachada de una casa vieja muestra oblicuamente su chaflán y deja también paso por el primero y el segundo término. Un portillo misérrimo en ella y encima un balcón. En la esquina posterior de esa fachada y también hacia la escena, pero más bajo, otro de los faroles del alumbrado público que el marqués de Esquilache diera a la Villa y Corte.

Algo más atrás, una plataforma giratoria ocupa casi toda la escena y se eleva sobre ella mediante dos o tres peldaños. Está dividida en cuatro frentes: dos principales y dos secundarios. Los dos principales son también los mayores. Sus plantas, exactamente iguales. Opuestos diametralmente, la pared que los separa juega por sus dos caras para los dos decorados. Representan éstos un gabinete del palacio del marqués de Esquilache y otro del Palacio Real. Alargados frontalmente, los dos aposentos están limitados por la pared del fondo que les es común y otras dos laterales más pequeñas, oblicuas, que cortan en un tercio el perímetro de la plataforma.

Una estilizada arquitectura sin techo forma estos dos gabinetes. El de Esquilache tiene en la pared de la izquierda una puerta de una hoja; en la del fondo, hacia la derecha, puerta de dos hojas, y en la pared de la derecha, un ventanal, bajo el que luce una consola con un reloj. El ambiente es suntuoso: los muros están tapizados de damasco rojo y en el fondo, en rico marco dorado, osténtase un retrato de medio cuerpo que del marqués pintara Antonio Rafael Mengs. En el primer término y de frente al proscenio está la mesa taraceada con su sillón detrás. Sobre ella, escribanía, salvadera, campanilla de plata, carpetas y papeles. En su extremo izquierdo descansa la blanca maqueta de un edificio. Dos sillones a ambos lados de la consola y algunas sillas más completan el mobiliario.

Aunque de la misma planta, el gabinete opuesto se distingue del anterior por el color y las formas ornamentales: una armonía de tonos azulados que cortan los dorados brillos de las molduras y las medias cañas. En la pared de la izquierda está el balcón señorial, con poyete y balaustrada exterior; en la del fondo, la puerta de dos hojas (naturalmente, hacia la izquierda, pues juega la misma para los dos aposentos), y en la de la derecha, puerta de una hoja. Vemos aquí también una mesa, situada frontalmente a la derecha del foro, con su sillón detrás y una silla ante ella, ladeada. A la izquierda del primer término, una mesita y dos sillas. Alguna otra silla al fondo y diversos adornos completan el conjunto que, si bien tan lujoso como el anterior, tiene un aire más digno y más frío, como de habitación de poco uso. Junto a la puerta del fondo, el cordón de la campanilla.

THE SET
Left and right are from the spectator's point of view.

A corner of Madrid by the House of the Seven Chimneys, residence of the Marquis of Esquilache.[5] A high wall protrudes slightly from the wings at the left of the stage, providing entrances upstage and downstage. A street lamp is attached high up on the wall, projecting over the stage. At the right, the narrow façade of an old house can be seen at an angle, also leaving space for access to the stage in the foreground and background. It boasts a dingy-looking doorway and a balcony above. Projecting towards the stage from around the corner of this house, but lower than the first one, is another of the street lamps installed in the capital thanks to the Marquis of Esquilache.

Further back, a revolving platform takes up almost the whole width of the stage; two or three steps lead up from the main stage to this raised platform. The revolving stage is divided into four sections: two principal sections and two secondary. The principal sections are larger than the other two, and have exactly the same layout. They are diametrically opposite one another, with the wall that separates them forming the centrepiece of the set on each side. On one side there is a study in the Marquis of Esquilache's mansion, and on the other, a study in the Royal Palace. Each of these two rooms is formed from the long back wall between them and two shorter, angled walls meeting the edge of the platform.

The two studies are constructed in a stylized way without ceilings. Esquilache's has a single door in the wall at the left; a double door towards the right-hand end of the wall at the back, and a window in the wall at the right, under which is a console table with a clock. The room is sumptuously decorated: the walls are covered in red damask, and at the back, in a rich gilded frame, hangs the half-length portrait of the marquis painted by Antonio Rafael Mengs. In the foreground, facing the proscenium, is an inlaid desk with an armchair behind it. On the desk, writing materials, a small silver bell, portfolios and papers. At the left-hand end of it, there is a white model of a building. An armchair on each side of the console table and a few other chairs complete the furnishings.

Although it is laid out in the same way, the study on the other side differs from the first in its colours and ornamentation: a harmonious range of bluish tones setting off the glint of gold in the mouldings and columns. Set into the wall at the left is a grand balcony, with a step leading up to it and an exterior balustrade. In the back wall, there is the double door, towards the left-hand end, of course, since the same wall is shared by both rooms. And in the wall at the right, a single door. Here too we have a desk, situated face-on near the right-hand end of the back wall, with an armchair behind it and a chair in front of it, at an angle. Downstage left, there is a small side table with two chairs. One or two other chairs upstage and various ornaments complete the set, which, while just as luxurious as the other side, appears colder and more formal, with the air of a room not often used. Next to the door at the back there is a bell-pull.

Las cuatro pequeñas paredes laterales de estos dos gabinetes forman por su exterior los dos frentes secundarios del giratorio, asimismo iguales y opuestos entre sí. Cada uno de ellos está formado por dos paredes en ángulo entrante, que fingen la exterior mampostería de un edificio. Uno de estos ángulos, es claro, presenta una puerta en cada pared. Son las que juegan en los gabinetes y que aquí simulan dos puertas iguales a la calle. El ángulo opuesto presenta por su parte el exterior del balcón y el ventanal pertenecientes a los dos aposentos descritos.

En el fondo y entre los resquicios de toda la estructura se columbra un panorama urbano del Madrid dieciochesco. El resto es alto cielo.

Casa de las Siete Chimeneas, Madrid.

The four small side walls of these two studies also form the two secondary sections of the revolving stage. They are also diametrically opposite one another, and are both laid out in the same way. Each of them consists of the two walls meeting at an acute angle, made to look like the exterior of a building. In one of these angles, of course, there is a door on each side. These are the doors that lead out of the studies, and here serve as two identical doors opening onto the street. The balcony of the room in the palace and the window of Esquilache's study look out into the opposite angle on the other side of the platform.

In the background and through the gaps between the different parts of this structure can be glimpsed the skyline of eighteenth-century Madrid. The rest is open sky.

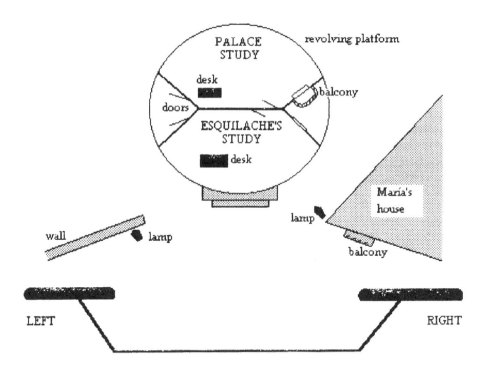

Plan of the Set

PARTE PRIMERA

El "Concierto de Primavera", de Vivaldi, inicia sus risueños compases antes de que el telón se alce.

Es de día. El giratorio presenta el gabinete de Esquilache solitario. El CIEGO DE LOS ROMANCES *se apoya contra la pared de la casa de la derecha. Un casacón astroso y un grasiento sombrero de tres candiles le malcubren. Bufanda, garrote. En los amplios bolsones de la casaca y bajo el brazo, cuadernillos y pliegos de aleluyas de los que exhibe alguno al que quiere pasar. De vez en vez patea el suelo y se sopla las manos: tiene frío. Sentado en los escalones de la plataforma,* MORÓN: *un embozado joven de gacho sombrero redondo y larga capa, prendas ambas bastante sucias. La música se pierde y deja de sonar.*

CIEGO ¡El Gran Piscator de Salamanca, con los pronósticos ciertos para este año de gracia de 1766!... (*Otra voz.*) También tengo el romance de la malmaridada y el espantable crimen de los tres portugueses... ¡Compren el Piscator Salmantino y verdadero Zaragozano de este año, por el licenciado don Diego Torres Villarroel!... El Diario... El Diario Noticioso, Curioso y Erudito para hoy, nueve de marzo...

Enmudece, aburrido. Por la segunda izquierda entró CLAUDIA *y cruza hacia la derecha. Es una maja no mal parecida, que viene de trapillo y trae una cesta y una vela envuelta en la mano. El balcón se abre y asoma una* VIEJA, *menuda y apajarracada.*

CLAUDIA ¡Apúrese, doña María, que no llegamos!
DONA MARÍA Ya estoy.

Se mete y cierra. La CLAUDIA *da unos paseítos mientras espera.*

CIEGO Cómprame el romance de la malmaridada, paloma.
CLAUDIA (*Da un respingo.*) ¡La lengua se le pudra en la boca, abuelo!
CIEGO (*Ríe.*) ¿Cuándo te vienes a vivir con la vieja? Siempre anda ella con esa copla.
CLAUDIA Y usté con la oreja en todos lados.
CIEGO Es mi manera de conocer... ¿Y tu hombre?
CLAUDIA Ricamente.

DOÑA MARÍA *aparece en su portal, muy pulcramente compuesta, y se santigua.*

PART ONE

The bright opening of "Spring" from Vivaldi's "Four Seasons" is heard before the curtain rises.

Morning. On the revolving platform we can see Esquilache's study, empty. The BLIND BALLAD-SELLER[6] *is leaning against the wall of the house on the right. He is poorly dressed in a shabby coat and a greasy three-pointed hat, with a scarf and a stick. In the capacious pockets of his coat and under his arm, there are pamphlets and sheets of* aleluyas, *some of which he attempts to show to passers-by. From time to time he stamps his feet and blows on his hands: he is cold. Sitting on the steps of the platform is* MORÓN, *a young man with his face covered by a round, floppy hat and a long cape, both of which are rather grubby. The music fades away.*

BALLAD-SELLER   The great Piscator of Salamanca, with all the most accurate predictions for this year of grace 1766!... (*In a different tone.*) I've got the ballad of the unfaithful wife and the terrible crime of the three Portuguese too... Buy the genuine Piscator of Salamanca and Zaragoza for this year, by the scholar don Diego Torres Villarroel!... Buy *The Journal* for all manner of news, novelties and erudition...[7] *The Journal* for today, the ninth of March...

He falls silent, out of boredom. CLAUDIA *has entered from upstage left, and crosses towards the right. She is an attractive* maja, *out in her everyday clothes carrying a basket and a candle wrapped in paper. The balcony opens and a small, birdlike old woman leans out.*

CLAUDIA   Hurry up, doña María, or we'll never get there in time!
MARÍA   I'm just coming.

She goes back inside and closes the balcony. CLAUDIA *paces up and down a little as she waits.*

BALLAD-SELLER   You'll buy the ballad of the unfaithful wife, won't you, love?
CLAUDIA   (*Taken by surprise.*) Keep that foul mouth of yours shut, you dirty old man!
BALLAD-SELLER   (*He laughs.*) When are you going to come and live with the old woman, eh? She's always droning on at you about it.
CLAUDIA   And your ears are always flapping at everybody else's business.
BALLAD-SELLER   I've got to find out what's going on somehow, haven't I? And how's your fella?
CLAUDIA   Fine.

DOÑA MARÍA *appears in her doorway, very daintily turned out, and crosses herself.*

CIEGO Le van a salir muchos años... Te deberías venir con la vieja.

DOÑA MARÍA (*En el tono meloso que prefiere para decirlo todo.*) No tan vieja, Matusalén... (*Toma a la* CLAUDIA *del brazo.*)

CIEGO (*Ríe.*) Punto en boca.

DOÑA MARÍA Pero razón sí que la tiene, Claudia... ¿Cuándo?...

CLAUDIA (*Elude su mirada.*) Ya me lo pensaré.

Caminan unos pasos.

DOÑA MARÍA (*Sigilosa.*) Esta noche no me faltes, ¿eh? Pero afila el ojo, que está el barrio muy vigilado desde que el marqués vino a vivir aquí. (*Toca la vela.*) ¿Qué es esto?

CLAUDIA Una vela para la Virgen de los Desamparados. A la que pasamos, se la pongo.

DOÑA MARÍA ¿Para que salga tu Pedro?

CLAUDIA (*Seca.*) Sí, señora.

DOÑA MARÍA (*Ríe.*) Milagros los hay, desde luego, pero... Calla. (*Y mira inquisitivamente, tratando de forzar sus fatigados ojos, a* FERNANDITA, *que entró por la segunda derecha y cruza. Es una muchacha muy joven, con discretos atavíos de azafata, que lleva una bolsa.*) ¡Vete con Dios, mujer!

FERNANDITA Buenos días nos dé Dios. (*Y sale, con la cabeza baja, por la segunda izquierda.*)

CLAUDIA ¿No es del servicio de la marquesa?

DOÑA MARÍA (*Asiente.*) Viene del Mesón de la Luna, de comprar chocolate.

CLAUDIA ¿Es ésta la que le gusta al calesero?

DOÑA MARÍA Y él a ella, pero... dificulto que lleguen a subir juntos a mi casa.

Caminaron mientras hablaban. Van a salir por la primera izquierda cuando entra por ella BERNARDO, EL CALESERO. *Es un majo de buen porte: blanco sombrero redondo, redecilla, chupetín encarnado y larga capa terciada. Dícenos la historia que era malagueño: tal vez la madrileña prosodia ha cubierto del todo su acento original.*

BERNARDO ¿A dónde van sus mercedes?

DOÑA MARÍA De ti parlábamos, mira. ¿Nos llevas en la calesa a Los Desamparados?

BERNARDO En cualquier otra ocasión, con mil amores. Pero a estas horas pasa por aquí cierta persona con la que tengo precisión de hablar.

DOÑA MARÍA (*Ríe.*) Tarde llegas. (*Mira hacia la segunda izquierda.*) Ahora mismo entra en el palacio.

BALLAD-SELLER   He's going to be inside for quite a few years... You ought to move in with the old woman, you know.

MARÍA   (*In the mellifluous tone she always uses.*) Not so much of the old, Methuselah... (*She takes* CLAUDIA *by the arm.*)

BALLAD-SELLER   (*Laughing.*) I'll say no more.

MARÍA   But he's right, you know, Claudia... When will you?...

CLAUDIA   (*Avoiding her gaze.*) I'll think about it.

They walk a few steps.

MARÍA   (*Confidentially.*) You won't let me down tonight, will you? But keep your eyes open: they've been putting a close watch on this neighbourhood ever since the marquis came to live here. (*She touches the packet containing the candle.*) What's this?

CLAUDIA   A candle: I want to light one for Our Lady Comforter of the Afflicted.[8] I'll pop in on the way past.

MARÍA   A prayer for Pedro to get out?

CLAUDIA   (*Curtly.*) That's right.

MARÍA   Well, I suppose miracles do happen, but... Shhh! (*And she peers myopically at* FERNANDITA, *who has come on upstage right and is crossing the stage. She is a young girl, sensibly dressed in clothes appropriate for a lady's maid, and carrying a bag.*) God be with you, Fernandita!

FERNANDITA   Good morning. (*And she goes off upstage left, looking down at the ground.*)

CLAUDIA   Isn't she one of the marchioness's servants?

MARÍA   (*She nods.*) She's just been at the Moon Inn to get some chocolate.

CLAUDIA   Is she the one the cab driver's taken a fancy to?

MARÍA   And she likes him too, but... I don't think they'll be coming up to my place together.

They have started walking while chatting. They are about to exit downstage left when BERNARDO, *the cab driver, appears.*[9] *He is a good-looking* majo, *well turned out in a round, white hat, a hairnet and a bright red waistcoat, his long cape folded open across his body. The history books tell us that he was from Málaga: perhaps the speech rhythms of Madrid have completely obscured his original accent.*

BERNARDO   Morning, ladies. May I ask where you're off to?

MARÍA   We were just talking about you, you know. Will you take us to Los Desamparados church in your cab?

BERNARDO   At any other time, with the greatest pleasure, madam. But there's a certain person I need to speak to, someone who'll be coming by here any moment now.

MARÍA   (*Laughing.*) You've got here too late. (*She glances towards where Fernandita went off, upstage left.*) She's just going into the house right now.

BERNARDO ¡Maldita sea! (*Se abalanza a la segunda izquierda para mirar, mientras ella ríe.*) ¡Un día le rajo el bandullo de un facazo a esa mula cansina de los diablos!

CLAUDIA Qué, ¿nos lleva?

BERNARDO (*De mal humor.*) ¡Vayan con Dios sus mercedes!

Las mujeres ríen y salen por la primera izquierda.

CIEGO (*Aburrido.*) El Gran Piscator de Salamanca, con todo lo que sucederá en este año de gracia de 1766...

BERNARDO ¡Chuzos de punta debían caer este año!

MORÓN Deja al viejo, Bernardo, que no tiene culpa.

BERNARDO (*Retrocede instintivamente un paso.*) ¿Quién es? (MORÓN *levanta el ala de su sombrero.*) ¡Vaya! ¡Mi compadre Morón!

MORÓN Siéntate conmigo.

BERNARDO ¿Para que el frío nos meta el cuerno?

MORÓN ¿Y qué vas a hacer? Está ya uno harto de no apañar. (*Se levanta, cansino, y va a su lado.*)

BERNARDO Vete a otro barrio.

MORÓN ¡El mío es éste! Y yo no le quito el pan a ningún compañero de industria en el suyo. ¡Tengo mi honrilla!

BERNARDO Pues te morirás con tu honrilla.

MORÓN (*Se sopla las manos.*) Sí, de frío... ¡Maldito sea Esquilache y quien lo trujo!

BERNARDO Amén.

RELAÑO, *otro pringoso embozado de larga capa y sombrero gacho, entra por la primera izquierda. Es hombre maduro.*

RELAÑO En cuanto que vi la calesa me lo he dicho: mi compadre Bernardo está de ronda.

BERNARDO Levante el ala.

RELAÑO (*La levanta.*) Soy Relaño. Desde Maravillas vengo huyendo del frío. Hogaño ha venido marzo muy traidor.

MORÓN Y que se siente más desde que empedraron.

RELAÑO (*Se arrebuja en el embozo.*) Si no fuera por la capa...

BERNARDO Pues pida a Dios que la conservemos.

MORÓN ¿Qué?

BERNARDO El rumor corre.

RELAÑO Pero ¿cuándo nos van a dejar tranquilos?

MORÓN ¡Esquilache lo habrá mandado, seguro! ¡Como el empedrado!

RELAÑO ¡Como todo lo malo!

BERNARDO   Damn! *(He rushes over to the left to have a look, while she laughs.)* That knackered old nag of mine! I'm going to slit her bloody belly open one of these days.

MARÍA   Well, will you take us?

BERNARDO   *(Ill-tempered.)* I'll... see you later!

The women laugh and go off downstage left.

BALLAD-SELLER   *(Bored.)* The great Piscator of Salamanca: everything that will happen in this year of grace 1766...

BERNARDO   All this "year of grace" needs to top it off is a good plague of locusts.

MORÓN   Leave the old man alone, Bernardo, it's not his fault.

BERNARDO   *(Instinctively steps back.)* Who is it? (MORÓN *lifts the brim of his hat.*) I'll be damned! It's my old mate Morón!

MORÓN   Sit down here with me.

BERNARDO   And get my bum frozen?

MORÓN   What else are you going to do? I'm fed up with not getting anything. *(He gets up wearily and goes across to BERNARDO.)*

BERNARDO   Go to another district, then.

MORÓN   This one's mine! And I'm not going to poach on anyone else's territory. I've got some honour, you know!

BERNARDO   Well, your honour won't keep you alive, will it?

MORÓN   *(Blowing on his hands.)* It's the cold I'll die of... God damn Esquilache and the man who brought him here!

BERNARDO   Amen to that.

RELAÑO, *another greasy rogue muffled in a long cape and a floppy hat, enters downstage left. He is older than the others.*

RELAÑO   As soon as I saw the cab I said to myself: Bernardo's out on his rounds.

BERNARDO   Let's see your face.

RELAÑO   *(Lifts up the brim of his hat.)* Relaño. I've come over from Maravillas trying to somewhere to get out of the cold.[10] March has really come in with a vengeance this year.

MORÓN   And you feel it more since they paved the streets.

RELAÑO   *(He wraps himself up more tightly in his cape.)* If it wasn't for our capes...

BERNARDO   Well, let's hope to God that we can keep them.

MORÓN   Why?

BERNARDO   There's a rumour going round.

RELAÑO   When are they ever going to leave us alone?

MORÓN   It'll be Esquilache who's behind that, for sure! Like the paving!

RELAÑO   Like everything bad!

MORÓN   ¡En su tierra se podía haber quedado, que para mí, que no será tierra de cristianos!

RELAÑO   ¡Paganos serán !

BERNARDO   *(Les pasa las manos por los hombros y baja la voz.)* Si se confirma, no faltarán esta vez buenos españoles que nos digan lo que hay que hacer.

RELAÑO   ¡Tú sabes algo!

BERNARDO   A su tiempo, que ahora es pronto.

MORÓN   *(Se separa, contrariado.)* ¡Bueno!

BERNARDO   *(Ríe.)* Vengan acá, que algo les diré a cambio... Hay letrilla nueva.

MORÓN   *(Vuelve.)* ¿De Esquilache?

BERNARDO   Escuchen sus mercedes:

> *Yo, el gran Leopoldo Primero,*
> *marqués de Esquilache augusto,*
> *rijo la España a mi gusto*
> *y mando a Carlos Tercero.*

RELAÑO   *(Ríe.)* ¡Está propia!

BERNARDO   Es más larga, pero no recuerdo el final.

CIEGO   *(Que no se ha movido.)*

> *Hago en los dos lo que quiero,*
> *nada consulto ni informo,*
> *al que es bueno le reformo*
> *y a los pueblos aniquilo.*
> *Y el buen Carlos, mi pupilo,*
> *dice a todo: me conformo.*

Se han ido acercando los embozados, entre risas contenidas que subrayan la letrilla.

MORÓN   ¡La verdad misma!

CIEGO   Si sus mercedes la quieren, se la llevan por un real.

BERNARDO   ¡Tráela!

El CIEGO mete su mano en un bolsillo.

RELAÑO   *(Que mira hacia la izquierda.)* ¡Chist! Guarda.

Por la segunda izquierda entran CRISANTO y ROQUE, alguaciles. Tricornio, golilla, espadín, corta capa negra. Al divisar el grupo, se detienen. La luz crece en el gabinete de Esquilache. Por la puerta de la izquierda entra DON ANTONIO CAMPOS con una carpeta en la mano y, de pie, ordena papeles sobre la mesa.

MORÓN   He could have stayed in his own country, couldn't he?   Spain's a place for
        decent Christians, not like where he comes from!
RELAÑO   I bet they're all heathens!
BERNARDO   (*Putting his hands around their shoulders and lowering his voice.*) If this
        turns out to be true, this time there'll be no shortage of good Spaniards who'll
        tell us what needs to be done.
RELAÑO   Ah, you know something!
BERNARDO   All in good time, it's early days yet.
MORÓN   (*Breaks away, put out.*) You don't trust us, eh?
BERNARDO   (*Laughs.*) Come here, and I'll tell you something else instead... There's a
        new rhyme.
MORÓN   (*Coming back.*) About Esquilache?
BERNARDO   Listen to this:

> *Leopoldo the First, that's me,*
> *Esquilache, the premier marquis.*
> *Spain does as I please,*
> *Charles the Third's on his knees,...*

RELAÑO   (*Laughing.*) That's just right!
BERNARDO   There's more of it, but I can't remember the end.
BALLAD-SELLER   (*Who has not moved.*)

> *And they both take their orders from me.*
> *I make my decisions alone,*
> *But virtue I cannot condone.*
> *The good I oppress,*
> *While King Charlie says yes,*
> *And lays down my law from his throne.*[11]

The men have been gathering around him, underlining the doggerel with barely-suppressed laughter.

MORÓN   Right on target!
BALLAD-SELLER   If you want a copy, you can have one for a farthing.
BERNARDO   Let's have it, then! (*The blind man puts his hand in his pocket.*)
RELAÑO   (*Looking towards the left.*) Pssst! The law.

Enter upstage left CRISANTO and ROQUE, the constables: tricorn hats, ruffs, foils and short black capes. They stop when they see the group of men. The light comes up on ESQUILACHE's study. DON ANTONIO CAMPOS comes into it through the door on the left carrying a portfolio and without sitting down, begins to arrange papers on the desk.

BERNARDO (*Disimulando.*) Vamos, amigos. Les llevo en la calesa.

Cruzan y salen por la primera izquierda. Los alguaciles los ven salir y miran al CIEGO; el CIEGO parece notarlo y rodea pausadamente la casa para salir por la primera derecha, mientras pregona.

CIEGO El Diario Noticioso, Curioso y Erudito para hoy, nueve de marzo...

Los alguaciles siguen hacia la segunda derecha. CRISANTO, que es el más viejo, se detiene de pronto.

ROQUE ¿Vamos?
CRISANTO Espera.

Entra por la segunda derecha un CABALLERO entrado en años, embozado en su capa. Tricornio galoneado, peluca antigua, espadín, medias de seda. Al cruzar, CRISANTO le cede el paso, se descubre y se inclina. El CABALLERO se detiene un segundo, desconcertado: saluda levemente y sale por la segunda izquierda.

ROQUE ¿Quién es?
CRISANTO (*Mira al hombre que se aleja.*) ¿Cómo no irá en su coche? ¡Mira! Entra en el palacio del señor marqués. Decían que estaban reñidos... Vámonos, Roque. Me da en la nariz que no quiere ser visto. (*Da unos pasos.*)
ROQUE Pero ¿quién es, Crisanto?
CRISANTO (*Baja la voz.*) Di mejor quién fue... Es el señor marqués de la Ensenada Vamos.

Salen por la segunda derecha. La luz del primer término se amortigua un tanto. La puerta del fondo del gabinete se abre y entra el MAYORDOMO.

MAYORDOMO Su excelencia el señor marqués de la Ensenada

Entra ENSENADA El MAYORDOMO sale. DON ANTONIO CAMPOS deja precipitadamente sus papeles para recibir al visitante. Este DON ANTONIO, secretario privado de ESQUILACHE, es un mozo de obsequiosa sonrisa y vivos ojos, que viste de oscuro. DON ZENÓN DE SOMODEVILLA, marqués de la Ensenada entra sin capa ni sombrero. Algo entrado en carnes, todavía se muestra erguido. Cuenta ya sesenta y cuatro años, pero su cara no ha perdido frescura: conserva aquella adolescente blandura de rasgos y aquella mirada, aguda y suave a la vez, que vemos en sus retratos. Es hombre de aire bondadoso, de irresistible simpatía física. Acaso por nostalgia de su pasado valimiento, usa todavía peluca de los tiempos de Fernando VI. Viste lujosa casaca bordada.

BERNARDO (*Covering up.*) Let's go, lads. I'll take you in the cab.

They cross the stage and go off downstage left. The constables watch them leave, then turn to the blind man; he seems to be aware of this, and walks slowly around the corner of the house and off downstage right, intoning his usual cry.

BALLAD-SELLER The *Journal* for today, the ninth of March...

The constables move upstage right. CRISANTO, *the older of the two, suddenly stops.*

ROQUE Are we going?
CRISANTO Wait a moment.

Enter upstage right an elderly gentleman, wrapped in his cape. He wears a braided tricorn hat, an old-fashioned wig, a foil and silk stockings. As he passes, CRISANTO *makes way for him, takes off his hat and bows. The gentleman pauses for a moment, disconcerted; then he nods his head and exits upstage left.*

ROQUE Who's that?
CRISANTO (*Watching the man walk away.*) I wonder why he hasn't come in his coach? Look! He's going into the marquis's house. I'd heard those two had fallen out... Let's go, Roque. I get the feeling that he doesn't want to be seen. (*He takes a few steps.*)
ROQUE But who is he, Crisanto?
CRISANTO (*Lowering his voice.*) More like who was he... The Marquis of La Ensenada. Let's go.

They go off upstage right. The lights on the foreground dim a little. The door at the back of the study opens and the STEWARD enters.

STEWARD His Excellency the Marquis of La Ensenada.

Enter ENSENADA. Exit the STEWARD. CAMPOS *hurriedly leaves the papers to receive the visitor. Don Antonio Campos is* ESQUILACHE's *private secretary: a young man with an obsequious smile and lively eyes, dressed in dark clothes.* DON ZENÓN DE SOMODEVILLA, *Marquis of La Ensenada, comes in without his cape and hat.*[12] *Although rather flabby, he still maintains an upright posture. He is sixty-four years old, but his face has not lost its freshness: he still has the adolescent softness of features and the gaze, at once penetrating and gentle, which can be seen in his portraits. He exudes generosity and affability. Perhaps out of nostalgia for his former importance, he still wears a wig in the style of the reign of Fernando VI. He wears a rich embroidered dress-coat.*

48   PARTE PRIMERA

CAMPOS (*Se inclina profundamente.*) Beso a vuecelencia las manos.

ENSENADA (*Leve inclinación.*) Bien hallado, mi señor don Antonio.

CAMPOS El señor ministro no ha vuelto aún de El Pardo, pero no puede tardar. Dígnese vuecelencia tomar asiento. (*Le ofrece un sillón junto a la consola.*)

ENSENADA Gracias. Hágame la merced de seguir en su trabajo, don Antonio. (*Se sienta.*)

CAMPOS (*Sonríe.*) Mi trabajo en este momento es servir a vuecelencia en cuanto se le ofrezca.

ENSENADA Se lo ruego.

CAMPOS Siendo así... Y por complacer a vuecelencia. (*Va a la mesa y permanece de pie, ordenando las carpetas.*) En realidad, ya había terminado... Sólo quedaba esta carpeta, que es la de las curiosidades... (*Mete en ella un memorial y la cierra.*) Y ya está lista. (*Escucha.*) Me parece que oigo la carroza del señor ministro...

ENSENADA ¿Por qué llama a esa carpeta la de las curiosidades?

CAMPOS Porque es la de... los proyectistas. El señor marqués lo estudia todo: dice que los aciertos se encuentran donde menos se piensa.

ENSENADA Y es muy cierto.

CAMPOS Hoy nos ha llegado un proyecto para erigir en Andalucía una ciudad exagonal: según el autor, una especie de cuartel para la reforma de criminales mediante las virtudes calmantes de la geometría.

ENSENADA Ese es un loco.

CAMPOS Pero ilustrado.

ENSENADA Sabe el son que se baila ahora. (*Ríen los dos.*)

CAMPOS Es fabulosa la cantidad de locos que da este país...

ENSENADA No. Es normal. El español es desequilibrado. En mi tiempo lo aprendí bie.: También me llegaban montones de cosas como ésa... (*Se encoge de hombros.*) ¿Qué se puede hacer con un pueblo así?

CAMPOS Nadie puede olvidar lo mucho bueno que con este pueblo supo hacer vuecelencia.

ENSENADA Se equivoca, don Antonio. Está ya olvidado. Nuestro país olvida siempre los favores: sólo recuerda los odios...

Se abre la puerta del fondo y entra, terminando de despojarse de la capa, ESQUILACHE. *Tras él, el* MAYORDOMO *con el tricornio en la mano.* DON LEOPOLDO DE GREGORIO *es un robusto anciano de sesenta y seis años. De bruscos ademanes, vivo y dinámico, se conserva esbelto. El amargo rictus de su cara denuncia, más que vejez, ocultas tristezas; y difícilmente calcularíamos su edad si no fuese porque tiene las cejas completamente blancas. Su vestido es rico, pero sobrio: en el cuello le brilla el toisón de oro.* CAMPOS *se inclina con respeto y* ENSENADA *se levanta y le dedica una cortés reverencia.* ESQUILACHE *tiende a* CAMPOS *la cartera que trae y que éste deja sobre la mesa.*

CAMPOS   (*With a low bow.*) At your service, my Lord.

ENSENADA   (*With a slight bow.*) A pleasure to see you, don Antonio.

CAMPOS   The minister has not yet returned from El Pardo[13], but he will not be long. Would your Excellency care to take a seat? (*He offers him an armchair next to the console table.*)

ENSENADA   Thank you. Please, don Antonio, do not let me disturb your work. (*He sits down.*)

CAMPOS   (*Smiling.*) My work at this moment is to be of service to your Excellency in any way that I can.

ENSENADA   No, I beg you.

CAMPOS   As you wish, my Lord. (*He goes to the desk and, standing next to it, continues to put the portfolios in order.*) In fact, I was just finishing... There was only this portfolio to be dealt with, the novelties file... (*He puts a document into it and closes it up.*) There, it's ready. (*Listening.*) I think I can hear the minister's carriage now...

ENSENADA   Why do you call that one "the novelties file"?

CAMPOS   Because it's the file for... Shall we say, "forward planning"? The marquis examines everything in detail: he says good ideas can be found where you least expect them.

ENSENADA   And that's very true.

CAMPOS   Today we received a proposal for the construction of a hexagonal city in Andalusia: according to the author, it would be a kind of barracks for the rehabilitation of criminals by means of the calming effects of geometry.

ENSENADA   He's a madman.

CAMPOS   But an enlightened one.

ENSENADA   He knows which way the wind is blowing. (*They both laugh.*)

CAMPOS   The number of madmen this country produces is fantastic...

ENSENADA   No. It's perfectly understandable. The Spanish are unstable. I came to learn that well in my time. I also used to receive piles of things like that... (*He shrugs his shoulders.*) What can you do with a people like ours?

CAMPOS   No-one can forget what you have done for them, my Lord.

ENSENADA   No, don Antonio, you're mistaken. It's already forgotten. Our country always forgets the favours it receives: it only remembers the hatred...

The door at the back opens and ESQUILACHE *comes in, taking off his cape. Behind him, the* STEWARD, *carrying his tricorn.* DON LEOPOLDO DE GREGORIO *is a robust old man of sixty-six.[14] He is lively and dynamic, his manner is brisk, and he keeps himself slim. The bitter twist of his mouth suggests a secret sadness, rather than old age; and it would be difficult to guess his age if it were not for the fact that his eyebrows are completely white. His clothes are expensive, but sober: around his neck glitters the insignia of the Order of the Golden Fleece.* CAMPOS *bows respectfully, and* ENSENADA *stands up and greets him courteously.* ESQUILACHE *hands* CAMPOS *a portfolio that he has brought with him;* CAMPOS *puts it down on the desk.*

ESQUILACHE Celebro verte, Zenón. Supongo que no te habré hecho esperar.
ENSENADA Has sido puntual, como siempre. (*El* MAYORDOMO *recoge la capa.*)
ESQUILACHE ¿Mucha gente en la antecámara?
MAYORDOMO Seis personas, excelencia.
ESQUILACHE ¿Don Francisco Sabatini entre ellas?
MAYORDOMO No, excelencia.
ESQUILACHE ¿Te apetece un chocolate, Zenón?
ENSENADA Gracias. Lo tomé ya.
ESQUILACHE A mí, sí. El viaje me ha despertado el apetito. (*Al* MAYORDOMO.)
  Avise en la cocina que me lo traigan. ¡Súbito! (*Lo despide con un gesto. El*
  MAYORDOMO *se inclina y sale, cerrando.*) Campos, ¿quiere dejarnos solos?
ENSENADA De ningún modo. Despacha antes tus asuntos. Yo estoy acostumbrado a
  esperar...
ESQUILACHE (*Le lanza una rápida ojeada.*) Como prefieras. ¡Pero toma asiento,
  hombre!
ENSENADA (*Se sienta.*) Gracias.
ESQUILACHE (*Va a la mesa.*) La firma. (*Se sienta.* CAMPOS *abre una carpeta,
  moja la pluma y se la ofrece. Después va recogiendo los documentos y
  rociándolos con la salvadera a medida que* ESQUILACHE *los firma.*) ¿Has
  visto la maqueta? Este Sabatini es admirable. El secreto del buen Gobierno
  son los buenos colaboradores. Pero no siempre se encuentran y hay que
  hacerlos... El mes pasado he concedido quince becas más. Jóvenes estudiantes
  de matemáticas, de botánica... Si Dios nos ayuda, a la vuelta de unos años el
  país tendrá gente apta para todo. ¡Sicuro!... (*A* CAMPOS.) ¿Qué es esto?
CAMPOS La aprobación de los créditos para la construcción de una fragata.

ENSENADA *se sobresalta: es su antigua tarea.*

ESQUILACHE Yo dije dos.
CAMPOS El Consejo de Hacienda ha recomendado retrasar la construcción de la
  segunda, excelencia.
ESQUILACHE ¡El ministro de Hacienda soy yo, y también el de Guerra! Los dos
  despachos están de acuerdo y esos señores no me van a enseñar a mí a hacer
  números. Nuestra estúpida guerra con Inglaterra nos ha costado barcos y hay
  que reponerlos. (*Ríe.*) Y si no, que se lo pregunten a Ensenada por quien
  España tiene hoy una flota.
ENSENADA Tu memoria me honra.
ESQUILACHE (*Aparta el documento.*) Firmaré cuando vengan los dos créditos: si
  firmo éste me duermen el segundo. (*Termina de firmar.*) Va bene. (*Deja la
  pluma.*)
CAMPOS Dentro de una hora le esperan en el Consejo de Castilla, excelencia.

ESQUILACHE   I'm delighted to see you, Zenón. I hope I haven't made you wait.
ENSENADA   You're punctual, as ever. (*The* STEWARD *takes* ESQUILACHE's *cape.*)
ESQUILACHE   Are there many people in the antechamber?
STEWARD   Six, your Excellency.
ESQUILACHE   Is don Francisco Sabatini one of them?[15]
STEWARD   No, your Excellency.
ESQUILACHE   Would you care for a cup of chocolate, Zenón?
ENSENADA   No, thank you. I've already had some.
ESQUILACHE   Well, I would. The journey has given me an appetite. (*To the* STEWARD.) Tell the kitchen to bring me some. *Súbito!* (*He dismisses him with a wave of his hand. The* STEWARD *bows and exits, closing the door behind him.*) Campos, would you leave us alone, please?
ENSENADA   Please, I wouldn't think of it. Finish your business first. I've become accustomed to waiting...
ESQUILACHE   (*Glancing briefly at him.*) As you prefer. But sit down, won't you?
ENSENADA   (*Sits down.*) Thank you.
ESQUILACHE   (*Going over to the desk.*) The documents for my signature. (*He sits down.* CAMPOS *opens a folder, dips a quill pen in ink and hands it to him. As* ESQUILACHE *signs the papers, he collects them and dusts them.*) Have you seen the model? Sabatini is brilliant. The secret of good government is to have good advisers. But you can't always find them, and you have to make them... Last month I awarded fifteen more scholarships. Young students of mathematics, botany... With God's help, in a few years the country will have people with the qualifications to do anything. *Sicuro!...* (*To* CAMPOS.) What's this?
CAMPOS   The approval of the funding for the construction of a frigate.

ENSENADA *starts: this used to be his job.*

ESQUILACHE   I said two.
CAMPOS   The Treasury Council has recommended that the construction of the second be delayed, my Lord.
ESQUILACHE   I'm the Minister of the Treasury, and of War! The departments themselves have agreed this, and those gentlemen are not going to give me lessons in arithmetic. Our senseless war against England has cost us ships and we need to replace them.[16] (*He laughs.*) And if they don't believe me, they should ask Ensenada: it's only thanks to him that Spain has a fleet at all these days.
ENSENADA   Your memory does me honour.
ESQUILACHE   (*Pushing the document aside.*) I'll sign when the funds for both ships are approved: if I sign this they'll lose the second one. (*He finishes signing the papers.*) *Va bene.* (*He puts down the pen.*)
CAMPOS   You are expected at the Council of Castile in one hour, your Excellency.

ESQUILACHE Bien. Déjenos ahora. Pero no se me aleje mucho: hay que dar curso a
    una Real Orden. (*Se levanta y se acerca a la maqueta mientras* CAMPOS *se
    inclina y sale por el foro con la carpeta de la firma.*) Mira qué hermosura,
    Zenón. (ENSENADA *se levanta y se acerca.*) *Molto bello,* ¿eh? Es un
    depósito de aguas. Sabatini es ingeniero y lo ha calculado admirablemente,
    pero, además, tiene buen gusto.
ENSENADA ¿Quién dijo aquello del fango y el mármol?
ESQUILACHE ¿Cómo dices?
ENSENADA La frase corre: el rey Carlos se encontró un Madrid de fango y lo ha
    dejado de mármol.
ESQUILACHE (*Ríe.*) Pero los descontentos lo comentan de otro modo: dicen que el
    rey tiene mal de piedra.
ENSENADA Tú eres el mal de piedra del rey..., gracias a Dios.
ESQUILACHE ¿Quieres adularme? Tú fuiste quien lo empezó todo.
ENSENADA (*Se aparta un poco, entristecido.*) Por favor, déjate de cumplidos. Yo he
    venido a saber algo concreto: no prolongues la humillación de sentirme como
    un pobre solicitante más de tu antecámara. Hemos estado distanciados pero
    ahora somos amigos otra vez, ¿no es así? Habla claro.

ESQUILACHE *baja los ojos. Se empieza a oír fuera de escena el pregón del* CIEGO,
que aparece inmediatamente por la primera derecha.

CIEGO El Gran Piscator Salmantino... (*Se detiene en el centro de la escena.*)
ESQUILACHE ¿Lo oyes?
ENSENADA ¿El qué?
CIEGO (*Reanuda su marcha.*) ... con todo lo que sucederá en este año de gracia de
    1766... (*Sale, lento, por la segunda izquierda.*)
ESQUILACHE (*Pensativo.*) ¿Has ojeado el Piscator de Salamanca? Ese calendario
    que escribe Torres Villarroel.
ENSENADA (*Suspira.*) ¡Por Dios santo, Leopoldo! Basta de disimulos.
ESQUILACHE (*Débil.*) No era disimulo... Es que, a veces, me preocupan cosas muy
    pequeñas... Soy un aprensivo. (*Se pasa la mano por la frente.*) Por cierto, que
    algo se me ha olvidado... Era algo pendiente con el mayordomo...
ENSENADA (*Frío.*) ¿Qué te ha dicho el rey?
ESQUILACHE (*Lo mira.*) Siéntate. (*Con un suspiro de impaciencia,* ENSENADA
    vuelve a sentarse. ESQUILACHE *pasea, irresoluto.*) Le he hablado a tu favor
    una vez más... y no ha dicho nada.
ENSENADA ¿Cómo, nada?
ESQUILACHE Sabes lo impenetrable que es a veces... Cuando oye tu nombre nunca
    dice nada. Yo le he recordado tus grandes méritos; le he dicho que eres de los

ESQUILACHE   Good. Leave us now. But don't go too far away: we have to draw up an Order in Council. (*He gets up and goes to stand by the model, while* CAMPOS *bows and goes out through the door upstage with the portfolio containing the papers that have been signed.*) Isn't this beautiful, Zenón? (ENSENADA *gets up and comes across to look.*) *Molto bello*, don't you think? It's a water reservoir. Sabatini is an engineer and he has calculated everything to perfection, but he has good taste as well.

ENSENADA   Who was it who came up with the remark about mud and marble?

ESQUILACHE   What do you mean?

ENSENADA   It's what people are saying: King Carlos has turned Madrid from a city of mud into a city of marble.

ESQUILACHE   (*With a laugh.*) Ah, but the malcontents are saying something different: that the king has "stone trouble".[17]

ENSENADA   You're the one who has brought on the king's "stone trouble",... thank God.

ESQUILACHE   You shouldn't be flattering me: it was you who started it all.

ENSENADA   (*Moves away a little, saddened.*) No compliments, please. I've come here to find out something specific: please don't keep me in suspense. It's humiliating enough to have to feel like just another wretched petitioner waiting in your antechamber. There have been differences between us, but we are friends now, aren't we? Speak frankly.

ESQUILACHE *looks down. We begin to hear the cry of the* BALLAD-SELLER *offstage, and he appears at once downstage right.*

BALLAD-SELLER   The great Piscator of Salamanca... (*He stops in the centre of the stage.*)

ESQUILACHE   Did you hear that?

ENSENADA   What?

BALLAD-SELLER   (*Walks on.*) ...all the events to come in this year of grace 1766... (*He goes off slowly upstage left.*)

ESQUILACHE   (*Pensively.*) Have you ever looked at the Piscator of Salamanca? The almanac that Torres Villarroel writes.

ENSENADA   (*With a sigh.*) For God's sake, Leopoldo, you know what I'm here for!

ESQUILACHE   (*Weakly.*) I wasn't trying to avoid the subject... It's just that, at times, I become preoccupied with very small things... I worry too much. (*He rubs his forehead.*) In fact, there is something that I've forgotten... It was something I was going to ask my steward...

ENSENADA   (*Coldly.*) What did the king say?

ESQUILACHE   (*Looks at him.*) Sit down, please. (*With an impatient sigh,* ENSENADA *sits down again.* ESQUILACHE *paces up and down, hesitating to speak.*) I have spoken to him on your behalf once again... and he said nothing.

ENSENADA   What do you mean, nothing?

ESQUILACHE   You know how inscrutable he is sometimes... When he hears your name, he never says anything. I've reminded him of your great talents; I've told

hombres que el país necesita hoy... En fin, todo. Que si perdiste el favor de su augusto hermano fue porque te negaste a la desmembración de Galicia en beneficio de Portugal: porque le avisaste a él mismo de éste y otros peligros antes de que ciñese la corona... (*Se detiene y lo mira.*) Preveo que te irás de aquí con la duda mordiéndote: ¿Le habrá hablado así al rey este italiano astuto? (*Lo mira fijamente.*) Ecco. Claro que lo piensas. ¿Qué puedo decirte? Te juro que he pedido al rey tu incorporación al Gobierno. Pero él ha callado. Como si no escuchase...

ENSENADA *baja la cabeza. Una pausa.*

ENSENADA   ¿En qué crees que puedo haberle disgustado?
ESQUILACHE   *¿Chi lo sá?*
ENSENADA   Pero algo supones.
ESQUILACHE   Lo visitabas demasiado al volver del destierro... Tal vez supuso que te creías indispensable... Un par de veces que te pidió consejo estuviste reservado y acaso creyó que así procurabas tu vuelta al Poder... En fin, no sé. El nada ha dicho. (*Pausa. Sonríe y va a la mesa para abrir la cartera que trajo, de la que saca un par de documentos.*) En cambio, he conseguido otra cosa que tú mismo me sugeriste. (*Toma uno de los dos papeles y se acerca.*) Mira.
ENSENADA   (*Sin levantar la cabeza, con una resignada sonrisa.*) Capas y sombreros.
ESQUILACHE   ¡Ecco! El bando que descubrirá las caras; el bando que evitará tanto crimen y tanta impunidad. Un buen tanto en la partida emprendida, ¿eh? Un poco más de higiene en los cuerpos y en las almas. Los madrileños parecerán al fin seres humanos, en lugar de fantasmones. (*Se sienta en el otro sillón. Confidencial:*) El Consejo de Castilla lo ha pretendido suavizar, retrasar... Alega que no es prudente violentar una costumbre, aunque sea mala. ¡Pero se ha intentado muchas veces, y ya es hora de demostrar a estos tercos que no sólo se exhorta, sino que se manda! ¿No crees? (*Un silencio.*) Perdona. Comprendo que el momento no es bueno para que te alegres de nada.

Se levanta y devuelve el papel a la mesa.

ENSENADA   Perdona tú. Has hecho perfectamente: esa medida se echaba de menos desde hace años, y ya es hora de aplicarla con mano dura. (*Se levanta y se acerca.*)
ESQUILACHE   Pero si no se trata de mano dura...
ENSENADA   No se puede reformar de otro modo. Recuerda nuestra divisa: "Todo para el pueblo, pero sin el pueblo." El pueblo siempre es menor de edad.

him that you are one of the men this country needs at this time... In short, everything. I said that if you fell out of favour with his illustrious brother, it was because you refused to agree to the dismembering of Galicia in favour of Portugal; because he himself was warned by you about this and other dangers before he came to the throne...[18] (*He stops and looks at him.*) I expect you'll leave here with a doubt gnawing at you: did this cunning Italian really say that to the king? (*Staring at him.*) *Ecco.* Of course you're thinking that. What can I say? I swear to you that I have asked the king to bring you back into the Government. But he hasn't said a word. As if he were not listening...

ENSENADA *bows his head. There is a pause.*

ENSENADA   In what way do you think I could have displeased him?
ESQUILACHE   *Chi lo sá*?
ENSENADA   But you must have some idea.
ESQUILACHE   You used to visit him too often when you returned from exile... Perhaps he got the idea that you considered yourself indispensable... Once or twice when he asked you for advice you were reticent, and perhaps he thought that it was a ploy of yours to attempt to get back into power... Anyway, I don't know. He hasn't said anything. (*Pause. He smiles and goes to the desk to open the portfolio that he brought, from which he takes a couple of documents.*) On the other hand, I have achieved something else that you yourself suggested to me. (*He picks up one of the two documents and takes it to him.*) Look at this.
ENSENADA   (*Without looking up, with a smile of resignation.*) Capes and hats, is it?
ESQUILACHE   *Ecco*! The decree that will uncover people's faces; the decree that will put a stop to so many crimes being committed with such impunity. A promising gambit, wouldn't you say? A little more cleanliness of bodies and souls. The people of Madrid will begin to look like human beings at last, rather than phantoms. (*He sits down in the other armchair. Confidentially:*) The Council of Castile has tried to tone it down, hold it up... They argue that it's unwise to interfere with a traditional custom, even if it is a bad one. But it has been tried many times before, and the time has now come to show these stubborn people that we don't just make appeals: we give orders. Don't you agree? (*A moment of silence.*) Forgive me. I can appreciate that at the moment you're not inclined to be overjoyed about anything.

He gets up and puts the paper back on the table.

ENSENADA   No, you must forgive me. You've done very well: this measure has been needed for years, and now is a good time to make it work, by force if necessary. (*He gets up and comes closer.*)
ESQUILACHE   It won't be a matter of using force...
ENSENADA   There is no other way of achieving reform. Remember our motto: "Everything for the people, but without the people". The people are always under age.

ESQUILACHE   (*Lo mira con curiosidad.*) No me parece que les des su verdadero sentido a esas palabras... "Sin el pueblo", pero no porque sea siempre menor de edad, sino porque todavía es menor de edad.

ENSENADA   (*Sonríe.*) No irás lejos con esas ilusiones. Yo las perdí hace veinte años. ¿Es que han dado nunca la menor muestra de comprender? ¿Te agradecen siquiera lo que haces por ellos? Les has engrandecido el país, les has dado instrucción, montepíos, les has quitado el hambre. Les has enseñado, en suma, que la vida puede ser dulce. Pues bien: te odian.

ESQUILACHE   (*Turbado.*) No.

ENSENADA   (*Paternal.*) ¿Aún no quieres reconocerlo? (*Sonríe y lleva su mano a la manga de la casaca.*) No debería enseñártelo... Podrías creer que es despecho por el mal resultado de tu gestión...

ESQUILACHE   ¿Otro libelo? Dámelo: no se puede gobernar sin saber lo que se dice en la calle. El pobre Grimaldi enferma cada vez que le llega un rumor adverso al despacho de Estado: ha prohibido que se lo digan. Pero yo no cierro los ojos. Trae. (*Le toma un papel que* ENSENADA *saca de su manga. Lee.*) "Yo, el gran Leopoldo Primero..."

Se le nubla la frente a medida que lee. Termina y se queda pensativo.

ENSENADA   No creí que te afectase tanto.

ESQUILACHE   Soporto aún mal que se me aborrezca sin razón.

ENSENADA   Ya ves que yo estaba en lo cierto.

ESQUILACHE   (*Reacciona.*) No. Este papel no demuestra nada: está impreso. No viene del pueblo, sino de nuestros enemigos: de todas las antiguallas que nos odian porque ocupamos puestos que ellos ya no se merecen.

ENSENADA   Pero es el pueblo quien lo propala...

ESQUILACHE   (*Tenaz.*) Unos pocos descontentos.

ENSENADA   (*Suspira.*) Te dejo con tus ilusiones, Esquilache. (*Da unos pasos hacia el foro.*)

ESQUILACHE   Te acompaño. (*Va a la puerta y la abre. Ríe.*) Y te prometo insistir con su majestad. Me haces falta en la tarea de educar al pueblo, aunque seas un escéptico...

Sale tras él y se pierde su voz. Golpecitos en la puerta de la izquierda, que se repiten. La puerta se abre y entra la MARQUESA DE ESQUILACHE. *DOÑA PASTORA PATERNÓ es una catalana arrogante, veinte años más joven, por lo menos, que su marido. Viene en traje de paseo. Al no ver a nadie, curiosea. Comenta con una sonrisa la maqueta de Sabatini; luego repara en la letrilla impresa, la toma y lee con expresión burlona y desdeñosa, volviéndola a dejar sobre la mesa.* ESQUILACHE *vuelve y cierra la puerta. Se miran.*

ESQUILACHE   (*Studies him curiously.*) I don't think you're giving those words their
true meaning... "Without the people", yes: not because they're always under
age, but because they're still under age.

ENSENADA   (*He smiles.*) You won't get very far with illusions like those. I lost them
twenty years ago.   Have the people ever shown the slightest sign of
understanding? Do they even give you any thanks for what you do for them?
You've made their country greater, you've given them education, Benefit
Societies, you've satisfied their hunger. All in all, you've shown them that life
can be sweet... And what do you get in return? They hate you.

ESQUILACHE   (*Disturbed by this.*) No, they don't hate me.

ENSENADA   (*Patronizingly.*) You still refuse to admit it? (*He smiles and reaches into
the sleeve of his coat.*) I shouldn't show you this... You might think that it's out
of resentment.

ESQUILACHE   Another libel? Let me have it: we can't govern without knowing what
they're saying in the street. Poor Grimaldi[19] falls ill every time an unfavourable
rumour reaches his office: he has given orders that he's not to be told from now
on. But I don't close my eyes to it. Let me see it, please. (*He takes the paper
that* ENSENADA *produces from his sleeve, and begins to read it.*) "Leopoldo
the First, that's me..."

His face darkens as he reads. When he has finished he looks thoughtful.

ENSENADA   I didn't think it would affect you so much.

ESQUILACHE   I still find it difficult to accept that people can hate me without reason.

ENSENADA   You can see that I was right, then?

ESQUILACHE   (*Regaining his self-assurance.*) No. This piece of paper doesn't prove
anything. It's a printed pamphlet. This isn't the real voice of the people: it has
been put out by our enemies, by all the relics of the old regime who hate us
because we have taken over the positions that they're no longer worthy of.

ENSENADA   But it is the common people who are distributing this stuff...

ESQUILACHE   (*Refusing to give way.*) A few trouble-makers.

ENSENADA   (*With a sigh.*) I'll leave you with your illusions, Esquilache. (*He takes a
few steps upstage.*)

ESQUILACHE   I'll see you out. (*He goes to the door and opens it. He laughs.*) And I
promise that I'll keep pressing His Majesty. I need you with me in this task of
educating the people, even if you are a sceptic...

*He follows him out and the sound of his voice fades. Someone taps on the door at the
left, and then taps again. The door opens and the Marchioness of Esquilache comes in.*
DOÑA PASTORA PATERNÓ[20] *is Catalan, arrogant, and at least twenty years
younger than her husband. She is dressed to go out. Finding the room empty, she
begins to look around. She smiles at Sabatini's model; then she notices the leaflet, picks
it up and reads it with a sardonic, scornful expression, before putting it back on the
desk.* ESQUILACHE *comes back in and closes the door. They glare at each other.*

ESQUILACHE   ¿Qué quieres?

DOÑA PASTORA   ¡Huy, qué humos!   Mal se levantó el día.   ¿Te ha dado hoy el dolor?

ESQUILACHE   No.

DOÑA PASTORA   Venía sólo a decirte que almuerzo fuera.

ESQUILACHE   (*Sardónico.*) ¡Qué novedad!   Para el banquete de esta noche podré contar contigo, ¿no?   Tenemos veinte invitados.

DOÑA PASTORA   (*Seca.*) Sabes que nunca falto a mis deberes de anfitriona.

ESQUILACHE   A ésos no, *è chiaro*.   Esos te gustan.   ¿Puede saberse dónde almuerzas?

DOÑA PASTORA   Naturalmente...

ESQUILACHE   Déjame adivinarlo...   ¿En la Legación de Holanda?   (DOÑA PASTORA *lo mira con desdén y se aparta.*) Mis más expresivos recuerdos a monsieur Doublet.

DOÑA PASTORA   Dios te guarde.   (*Va a salir por el foro. El se interpone.*)

ESQUILACHE   Un momento aún...   (*Va hacia la mesa, caviloso.*) Pero ¿qué es lo que se me está olvidando desde hace una hora?   (*Palmea en la frente.*) ¡Ecco!   (*Ríe y agita dos veces la campanilla.*) Sólo un minuto, *prego*.   No te entretengo nada.   (*Entra el* MAYORDOMO.) ¿Y mi chocolate?

MAYORDOMO   Ruego a su excelencia que me perdone.   Me informaré en seguida de la causa de esta demora.

ESQUILACHE   (*Se sienta a la mesa.*) Bene.

El MAYORDOMO *sale y cierra.*

DOÑA PASTORA   Me permito recordarte que tengo prisa.

ESQUILACHE   (*La mira fijamente.*) Ayer hablé con el rey... de nuestros hijos.

DOÑA PASTORA   (*Alegre.*) ¿Nuevas mercedes?

ESQUILACHE   (*Después de un momento.*) Cuando nombré al primero coronel y al segundo director de la Aduana de Cádiz, eran casi unos niños.   El tercero es ya hoy arcediano.   Todo se lo pedí al rey porque tú me insististe; pero no sólo por complacerte, sino porque quería que se convirtiesen en buenos servidores de su país.   Incurrí en esa costumbre, en esa mala costumbre de los poderosos, porque eran carne de mi carne y quería darles una buena ventaja inicial... que no han aprovechado.

DOÑA PASTORA   ¿Y qué más da?

ESQUILACHE   ¿Qué más da?   Unos petimetres; unos zascandiles de tertulias es lo que han resultado.   Ni siquiera puedo decir que los tenga: nunca los veo.

DOÑA PASTORA   Están fuera de Madrid...

ESQUILACHE   Cuando están en Madrid tampoco los veo.

DOÑA PASTORA   Porque siempre estás demasiado ocupado.

ESQUILACHE What do you want?

PASTORA Ooh, what a mood! Did you get out of the wrong side of the bed this morning, or something? Is it your pain?

ESQUILACHE No.

PASTORA I just came to tell you that I shall be going out for lunch.

ESQUILACHE (*Sarcastically.*) That's a novelty! You will be here for the banquet this evening, won't you? We'll have twenty guests.

PASTORA (*Coldly.*) You know that I never neglect my duties as hostess.

ESQUILACHE No, not those duties, *è chiaro.* You enjoy those. And may I ask where you are having lunch?

PASTORA Naturally...

ESQUILACHE Let me guess... The Dutch Legation? (PASTORA *looks at him with contempt and moves away.*) Please give my warmest regards to Monsieur Doublet.

PASTORA Goodbye. (*She sets off towards the door upstage. He blocks her way.*)

ESQUILACHE Wait a moment... (*He goes towards the table, preoccupied.*) What is it I've been trying to remember for the past hour? (*He smacks himself on the forehead.*) Ecco! (*He laughs and rings the bell twice.*) Just a minute, *prego.* I won't keep you long. (*Enter the* STEWARD.) Where is my chocolate?

STEWARD Forgive me, my Lord. I shall find out the cause of the delay at once.

ESQUILACHE (*Sitting down at the desk.*) Bene.

The STEWARD *leaves and closes the door behind him.*

PASTORA May I remind you that I'm in a hurry.

ESQUILACHE (*Staring at her intently.*) I spoke to the king yesterday... about our sons.

PASTORA (*Joyfully.*) More honours?

ESQUILACHE (*After a moment.*) When I made the eldest a colonel, and the second eldest head of Customs at Cadiz, they were virtually boys still. The third is already an archdeacon.[21] I asked the king for all of that because you insisted on it; not just to please you, though, but because I wanted them to become useful servants of their country. I followed the custom, that ugly custom of the powerful, because they were my flesh and blood and I wanted to give them an initial advantage... which they haven't made the most of.

PASTORA And what does it matter?

ESQUILACHE What does it matter? Pretentious fops, drawing-room layabouts: that's what they've turned into.[22] I can't even really say that they're my sons: I never see them.

PASTORA Well, they don't live in Madrid, do they?

ESQUILACHE I don't see them when they're in Madrid either.

PASTORA Because you are always too busy.

ESQUILACHE　Catorce horas de trabajo al día me parecen pocas para compensar la gandulería de esos inútiles. Por eso hace años que me he dicho: ¡No! Nunca volveré a pedirle al rey nada para ellos.

DOÑA PASTORA　(*Sonríe.*) Por fortuna el rey es menos escrupuloso que tú y nombró después al mayor mariscal de campo.

ESQUILACHE　(*Sombrío.*) Sí. Y tuve que aceptarlo... de mala gana. ¿Quién era yo para discutir la voluntad real?

DOÑA PASTORA　Claro.

ESQUILACHE　Claro. Además, que entonces no sabía que eras tú quien se lo había rogado.

DOÑA PASTORA　(*Inquieta.*) ¿Yo?

ESQUILACHE　(*Se levanta, iracundo.*) ¡Ese botarate es mariscal de campo porque tú se lo pediste a mis espaldas! (*Va hacia ella.*)

DOÑA PASTORA　¿Qué dices?

ESQUILACHE　¡Le contaste la repugnante mentira de que era mi mayor deseo y de que yo no me atrevía a pedírselo! Qué jugada, ¿eh? Sabes lo reservado que es. Supusiste que no me preguntaría nada y acertaste. Que su majestad pudiese despreciarme un poco desde entonces, eso no te importaba. ¡Sólo pensaste en atesorar para ti y para los tuyos, como siempre!... Ayer, por casualidad, se ha aclarado todo... y su majestad me ha dicho: "Me alegro de poder estimarte lo mismo que antes." (*Pausa.*) De ti no ha dicho nada. Pero puedes suponer lo que pensará de la marquesa de Esquilache, que miente a su rey.

DOÑA PASTORA　(*Se levanta.*) Pensará que es una madre que vela por sus hijos.

ESQUILACHE　¿No crees que todos tenemos ya más que bastante?

DOÑA PASTORA　¡No! ¡No lo creo! Pero ¿de qué te asombras? No sólo he conseguido cosas del rey, sino de tus compañeros de Gabinete. Y de tus subordinados. ¡De sobra lo sabes! ¿O es que tú, tan sagaz para otras cosas, vas a haber estado ciego como un topo para los pasos de tu mujer?

ESQUILACHE　(*Amargo.*) Más de lo que pensaba. (*Cruza.*)

DOÑA PASTORA　Pues debiste suponerlo. (*Ríe.*) ¿Crees que a nadie le gusta contrariar a la marquesa de Esquilache? ¡Cualquiera sabe si lo que pide es algo que su esposo desea!... De modo que todos resultan muy complacientes. Y también protejo a mucha gente... que sabe agradecérmelo. Podría contarte algunos asuntitos que te demostrarían lo buena discípula que es tu esposa; si tú sabes sacarle dinero al país para el rey, yo no me quedo atrás. Pero, más modesta, lo saco para nuestra casa.

ESQUILACHE　(*Frío.*) ¿Qué asuntos son ésos?

DOÑA PASTORA　Ya he hablado demasiado. Le temo a tu quijotismo. Por lo demás, no presumas tanto de idealista. Lo que pasa es que tienes miedo.

ESQUILACHE　¿Miedo?

DOÑA PASTORA　(*Levanta el papel de la letrilla.*) Sí, tú: "El gran Leopoldo Primero". Temes, como todos, perder el favor real. Y temes a los nobles, y a la Iglesia, y

ESQUILACHE   Fourteen hours' work a day seems a small price to pay to make up for the idleness of those good-for-nothings. That's why I said to myself years ago: No, never again will I go to the king to ask for anything for them.

PASTORA   (*She smiles.*) Fortunately, the king doesn't have the same scruples as you. He still promoted the eldest to field marshal.

ESQUILACHE   (*Gloomily.*) Yes. And I had to accept it... reluctantly. Who was I to question the royal will?

PASTORA   Of course.

ESQUILACHE   Of course. Besides, I didn't know at the time that it was you who had asked him.

PASTORA   (*Uneasily.*) Me?

ESQUILACHE   (*Getting up angrily.*) That idiot is a field marshal because you asked the king behind my back! (*He moves towards her.*)

PASTORA   What are you talking about?

ESQUILACHE   You told the king an odious lie: that it was what I most wanted and didn't dare ask him for. Quite a cunning move. You know how reserved he is. You guessed that he wouldn't ask me about it and you were right. It didn't matter to you that His Majesty would despise me just a little after that. You only thought about what you and your sons could get out of it, as always!... Yesterday, by chance, it all came out into the open... and His Majesty said to me: "I am glad that I can have the same faith in you as before." (*A pause.*) He said nothing about you. But you can guess what he must think of the Marchioness of Esquilache, who lies to the king...

PASTORA   (*Getting up.*) He'll think that she's a mother who looks after her children as best she can.

ESQUILACHE   Don't you think that we all have far more than we need already?

PASTORA   No! I don't think so! And anyway, what are you so surprised about? It's not only the king who has granted me things: there are the members of your Cabinet. And your subordinates. You know that very well! You're so shrewd about everything else: can you really have been so blind to what your own wife has been up to?

ESQUILACHE   (*Ruefully.*) More so than I thought. (*He moves across the stage.*)

PASTORA   Well, you should have guessed. (*She laughs.*) Do you think anyone can afford to deny the Marchioness of Esquilache anything? They don't know whether what she's asking for is something her husband wants!... So they all bend over backwards. And I protect a lot of people too,... people who have ways of showing their gratitude. I could tell you about a few little pieces of business that would prove to you what a good disciple of yours your wife has been; you know how to get money out of the country for the king, and I'm doing almost the same thing. But I'm not so ambitious: I just do it for our family.

ESQUILACHE   (*Coldly.*) And what pieces of business are those?

PASTORA   I've already said too much. Your quixotic pose alarms me. You shouldn't flaunt your idealism so much, anyway. The fact is, you're scared.

ESQUILACHE   Scared?

PASTORA   (*She picks up the piece of paper with the poem printed on it.*) Yes, "the great Leopoldo the First", scared. Like everyone else, you're afraid of losing

al pueblo. O si no, ¿a qué vienen esos banquetes, esas dádivas y esos favores
que prodigas y en los que gastas miles de peluconas, tú, el austero? Pues al
temor de que te derroten en la batalla de la vida. ¡No somos tan distintos!
(*Deja el papel sobre la mesa.*)

ESQUILACHE   Esto no va a quedar así, Pastora. (*Se acerca.*) Vete ahora con monsieur
Doublet. Lo que entre tú y él haya, no quiero saberlo...

DOÑA PASTORA   ¡No disparates! Es el cortejo. El chichisbeo, como ahora se dice.
Todas las damas lo tienen.

ESQUILACHE   No quiero saber lo que es. Hace tiempo que te perdí: tú aún eres joven
y yo ya no lo soy. Desisto de recobrarte. Desisto incluso de que comprendas.
Pero te ordeno...

DOÑA PASTORA   ¿Me ordenas?

ESQUILACHE   Te... ruego que te abstengas de minarme el terreno con tus
politiquerías. ¡En eso no te metas! De lo contrario...

DOÑA PASTORA   (*Seca.*) ¿Qué?

ESQUILACHE   (*Vuelve la cabeza.*) Nada. Puedes retirarte.

Una pausa.

DOÑA PASTORA   (*Perpleja, se acerca.*) ¿Cómo? ¿Los ojos húmedos?

ESQUILACHE   Hazme la caridad de retirarte.

DOÑA PASTORA   (*Se encoge de hombros.*) Siempre serás un niño... Pero tú también
tienes que comprender... Ya no estamos en nuestros primeros años, cuando nos
casamos en tu primera visita a España. Si todo se estropea, ¿qué le vas a
hacer?... Entonces me recitabas versos del Dante... Contigo comienza la vida
nueva, me decías... Pues bien, nunca hay vida nueva, los versos se olvidan, y tú
los habrás olvidado también. Pero no hay que hacer de eso una tragedia, sino
tomar lo que la vida pueda darnos aún... Aunque no sea más que dinero... o
poder. (*Golpecitos en el foro. DOÑA PASTORA se vuelve. Su marido no se
mueve. Después de mirar a su marido.*) ¡Adelante!

Entra el MAYORDOMO.

MAYORDOMO   Rogamos mil perdones a su excelencia... El repostero de su
excelencia se ha puesto repentinamente muy enfermo y ésa ha sido la causa del
retraso... La chocolatera de la señora marquesa lo ha preparado en su lugar y
aguarda fuera. Si su excelencia desea que le sirva yo mismo...

ESQUILACHE   Que pase ella. (*El* MAYORDOMO *va a salir.*) Espere... Lleve esa
maqueta al despacho grande.

El MAYORDOMO *la recoge, saluda y sale.* FERNANDITA *entra muy intimidada con
el servicio del chocolate y hace una genuflexión.*

the king's favour. And you're afraid of the nobility, and the Church, and the people. Why else would you, so proud of your austerity, spend so much on the banquets, the gifts, the favours that you spread around? It's because you're afraid of being defeated in the battle of life. We're not so different after all, you and I! (*She leaves the leaflet on the table.*)

ESQUILACHE You haven't heard the end of this, Pastora. (*Moving towards her.*) You can go and find your Monsieur Doublet now. Whatever there is between you, I don't want to know anything about it...

PASTORA Don't be ridiculous! It's just harmless courtship. Flirting, as they say nowadays. All the ladies are doing it.

ESQUILACHE I don't want to know what it is. I lost you some time ago: you're still young and I'm getting old. I'm not trying to win you back. I'm not even trying to make you understand. But I order you...

PASTORA You order me?

ESQUILACHE I... ask you to stop undermining my position with your politicking. Stay out of my business! Otherwise...

PASTORA (*Sharply.*) What?

ESQUILACHE (*Turning his head away.*) Nothing. You can go.

A pause.

PASTORA (*Puzzled, she moves closer to him.*) What's this? Tears?

ESQUILACHE Please, don't be cruel. Leave me now.

PASTORA (*Shrugging her shoulders.*) You'll always be a little boy... But you too need to understand a few things... Things aren't the same as they were in those early years, when we got married on your first visit to Spain. What can we do about it if everything turns sour?... You used to recite lines from Dante to me... Life is beginning again with you, you used to tell me... Well, there never are new beginnings, lines of poetry are easily forgotten, and I expect you've forgotten them as well. But there's no need to make a tragedy out of this: we should just get what we can out of life... Even if it's only money... or power. (*Someone knocks gently on the door upstage.* PASTORA *turns towards it. Her husband does not move. After glancing at him.*) Come in!

The STEWARD enters.

STEWARD A thousand pardons, your Excellency... Your Lordship's confectioner has suddenly fallen ill and that has caused the delay... One of her ladyship's maids has prepared your chocolate in his place and is waiting outside. If your Lordship would like me to serve you myself...

ESQUILACHE No, tell her to bring it in. (*As the STEWARD is about to leave.*) Wait... Take this model to the large office.

The STEWARD picks it up, bows and goes out. FERNANDITA enters very shyly with the chocolate tray and curtsies.

DOÑA PASTORA (*Después de mirar a su esposo, que está abstraído.*) Ponlo allí, hija mía. (*Por la consola.* FERNANDITA *lo hace.*) Te dejo, Leopoldo. Dios te guarde.

ESQUILACHE Vete con Dios.

DOÑA PASTORA *se encamina al foro.*

DOÑA PASTORA   Trátamelo bien, Fernandita... El señor marqués está ya muy delicado.

Envía una burlona mirada a su marido y sale mientras FERNANDITA *se inclina de nuevo. La puerta se cierra.* ESQUILACHE *está triste, turbado. Al fin se vuelve y ella, nerviosa, vuelve a inclinarse.*

ESQUILACHE   ¿De modo que te llamas Fernandita?
FERNANDITA   Para servir a su excelencia. (*Pensativo,* ESQUILACHE *va hacia la mesa.*) Si su excelencia quiere que le llene una jícara... Está muy calentito. (*Abstraído, él no contesta. Ha tomado la Real Orden de capas y sombreros y la ojea. Ella carraspea y eleva la voz.*) ¡Está muy calentito!
ESQUILACHE   ¿Eh?... Sí. Sírvemelo aquí mismo.

Sorprendida, ella se apresura a extender una servilleta sobre la mesa. El se sienta, cansado. Se oprime los ojos con los dedos. Ella vuelve rápida a la consola y llena una taza.

FERNANDITA   Me informé en la cocina y le he traído a su excelencia los bizcochos que prefiere... (*Le lleva la taza. Saca fuerzas de flaqueza.*) Me informé en la cocina y le he traído... (ESQUILACHE *se vence sobre la mesa con un gesto de dolor y gime sordamente.*) Señor marqués, ¿qué le pasa?... ¡Señor marqués!... (*Para sí.*) Yo llamo.

Va a tomar la campanilla, pero ESQUILACHE *extiende su brazo y se lo impide.*

ESQUILACHE   No, no... Es un dolor que a veces me toma el costado... Ya pasará.
FERNANDITA   ¿Quiere que baje en un vuelo? Yo sé buenos remedios... Puedo prepararle ruibarbo, o cristal tártaro... ¿Es el estómago?
ESQUILACHE   Ya... se pasa...
FERNANDITA   Para mí que no es el estómago... Es que su excelencia tiene demasiadas preocupaciones y le duelen los nervios. ¡Entonces, láudano! (*Y corre hacia la puerta.*)

PASTORA (*After looking at her husband, who seems withdrawn.*) Put it down there, my
   child. (*Pointing to the console table.* FERNANDITA *does so.*) I'll leave you
   then, Leopoldo. God be with you.
ESQUILACHE   Goodbye.

PASTORA *walks upstage towards the door.*

PASTORA   Look after him well, Fernandita... His lordship is feeling very delicate.

She directs a mocking glance at her husband and leaves, while FERNANDITA *curtsies
again. The door closes.* ESQUILACHE *looks sad and disturbed. At last he turns
towards her and she nervously curtsies again.*

ESQUILACHE   So your name is Fernandita?
FERNANDITA   At your service, my Lord. (*Pensively,* ESQUILACHE *goes towards
   his desk.*) Shall I pour you a cup, my Lord?... It's nice and hot. (*He is
   preoccupied and does not answer. He has picked up the decree about capes
   and hats and is looking it over. She clears her throat and raises her voice a
   little.*) It's nice and hot!
ESQUILACHE   What?... Ah, yes. Serve it to me here.

*She is taken aback, but hurriedly spreads a napkin on the desk. He sits down wearily.
He presses his fingers against his eyes. She goes quickly back to the console table and
fills a cup.*

FERNANDITA   I asked in the kitchen and I've brought some of the cakes that you
   like... (*She brings him the cup, plucking up her courage.*) I said, I asked in the
   kitchen and I've brought you... (ESQUILACHE *slumps forward onto the desk
   in pain and moans quietly.*) My Lord, what's the matter? My Lord!... (*To
   herself.*) I'd better ring for help.

As she is about to pick up the bell, ESQUILACHE *reaches out and stops her.*

ESQUILACHE   No, no... It's a pain that I get in my side sometimes... It'll soon go.
FERNANDITA   Shall I nip down to the kitchen to get you something? I know some
   good remedies... I can make you some rhubarb, or cream of tartar... Is it your
   stomach?
ESQUILACHE   It's all right... it's going now...
FERNANDITA   I don't think it is your stomach... I think it's because your Lordship
   has too much to worry about and your nerves are troubling you. Laudanum's
   what we need! (*And she runs towards the door.*)

ESQUILACHE (*Ya casi repuesto.*) ¡Quieta, criatura! (*Lleva su mano a la taza.*) Esto
   me caerá mejor. (*Sonríe.*) Pero sin mojar... Sólo una tacita. (*Bebe un sorbo.*)
   ¿Sabes que eres muy inteligente?
FERNANDITA ¡Qué va, excelencia!
ESQUILACHE (*Complacido por su naturalidad, ríe.*) ¡Sicuro! Los médicos se han
   empeñado en que vigile mis digestiones, pero saben menos que tú.
FERNANDITA Ruego a su excelencia que me perdone.
ESQUILACHE Al contrario, hija. Sé siempre natural. Yo tengo fama de tener malos
   modales, pero es que me harta la etiqueta... (*Bebe.*) ¿Qué le pasa a mi
   repostero?
FERNANDITA Que es un tragón y tiene un empacho de las comilonas que se atiza...
   ¡Ya le he dado yo una purga!
ESQUILACHE Tu chocolate es más suave...
FERNANDITA (*Sonríe.*) Es que yo tengo mi receta. ¿Le sirvo otra jícara?
ESQUILACHE No, gracias. (*El* CIEGO *de los romances aparece por la segunda
   derecha y va a recostarse contra su esquina habitual.* ESQUILACHE *está
   mirando a la muchacha con suma curiosidad. Ella retira taza y servilleta y las
   lleva a la consola.*) ¿Qué piensas?
FERNANDITA (*Lo mira, sorprendida.*) Nada, excelencia.
ESQUILACHE (*Ríe.*) ¡Eso no es posible! Dime qué pensabas. Pero con sinceridad,
   ¿eh?
FERNANDITA Pues... que el señor marqués debiera estar alegre y orgulloso de tantas
   cosas buenas que nos ha dado a los madrileños.

La fisonomía de ESQUILACHE *se endurece instantáneamente.*

ESQUILACHE ¡Hola! ¿También dominas la lisonja cortesana?
FERNANDITA (*Humilde, pero ofendida.*) No era lisonja, excelencia.

El se levanta y se recuesta en la mesa.

ESQUILACHE (*La observa, receloso.*) ¿Y qué cosas buenas son ésas, según tú?
FERNANDITA ¡Ah, pues muchísimas! Madrid es otra cosa desde hace seis años.
   ¡Antes era una basura!... Y un poblachón. Apestaba... Y a mí me gusta la
   limpieza.
ESQUILACHE (*Sonríe.*) No lo digas muy alto... No está de moda. ¿Eres madrileña?
FERNANDITA Sí, excelencia. Pero aunque fuese toledana. Toledana era mi madre.
ESQUILACHE ¿Era?
FERNANDITA Murió de aquellas fiebres que se llevaron a tanta gente en Madrid.
   Decían que si los aires... Pero aquello lo trajo la suciedad, seguro. Desde que

ESQUILACHE   (*Almost recovered now.*) No, wait! (*Reaching for the cup.*) This will do me more good. (*He smiles.*) But I won't have anything with it... Just one cup. (*He takes a sip.*) Do you know that you're very intelligent?

FERNANDITA   Oh, you're having me on, your Excellency!

ESQUILACHE   (*Delighted at her unaffectedness, he chuckles.*) *Sicuro!* The doctors have been nagging at me about my digestion, but they don't know as much as you do.

FERNANDITA   Forgive me, my Lord.

ESQUILACHE   No, on the contrary, my girl. You should always be yourself. I have a reputation for bad manners, but it's just that I can't stand etiquette... (*He takes another sip.*) What's the matter with my confectioner?

FERNANDITA   What's the matter with him is that he's a glutton and he's got indigestion from stuffing himself... I've given him something to clear him out!

ESQUILACHE   Your chocolate is smoother...

FERNANDITA   (*With a smile.*) Well, I've got my own recipe. Shall I pour you another cup?

ESQUILACHE   No, thank you. (*The blind* BALLAD-SELLER *appears upstage right and goes over to lean against his usual corner.* ESQUILACHE *is watching the young woman with considerable curiosity. She clears away the cup and the napkin and takes them to the console table.*) What are you thinking about?

FERNANDITA   (*She looks at him in surprise.*) Nothing, sir.

ESQUILACHE   (*He laughs.*) That's not possible! Come on, tell me what you were thinking. But honestly, all right?

FERNANDITA   Well... I was thinking that your Lordship ought to be happy and proud of all the good things you've given us in Madrid.

ESQUILACHE'*s face stiffens at once.*

ESQUILACHE   Well, well! So you know how to flatter like a courtier too, do you?

FERNANDITA   (*With deference, but genuinely hurt.*) It wasn't flattery, my Lord.

He gets up and leans on the desk.

ESQUILACHE   (*Watching her suspiciously.*) And what good things are those, according to you?

FERNANDITA   Oh, lots! Madrid's nothing like it was six years ago. Before, it was a dunghill!... A grubby little town. It used to stink... And I like things to be clean.

ESQUILACHE   (*With a smile.*) Don't say that too loudly... It's out of fashion to think like that. Were you born in Madrid?

FERNANDITA   Yes, my Lord. But I'd say the same even if I was from Toledo. My mother was.

ESQUILACHE   Was?

FERNANDITA   She died of one of those fevers that took so many people in Madrid. They used to say it was something in the air... But it must have been the filth

su excelencia mandó limpiar, está la gente mucho más sana y con mejores colores. Antes estaban... ¡verdes!

ESQUILACHE   Y tu padre, ¿vive?

FERNANDITA   (*Baja la cabeza.*) Había muerto ya... Lo mató un embozado.

ESQUILACHE   ¿Qué?

FERNANDITA   Nadie supo quién era, pero yo sí. Era muy pequeñita, pero ya me daba cuenta de todo... Lo mató él, seguro.

ESQUILACHE   ¿Quién es él?

FERNANDITA   Era... También se lo llevó Pateta cuando la peste, y muy bien llevado. Era un chispero que perseguía a mi madre. A mí me recogió mi madrina, que es bordadora, y que me recomendó a la señora marquesa.

ESQUILACHE   (*Frío, la considera.*) ¿Has oído tú algo de un bando que voy a lanzar?

FERNANDITA   No, excelencia.

ESQUILACHE   Pues se comenta.

FERNANDITA   Abajo tampoco he oído nada. Julián me lo habría dicho.

ESQUILACHE   ¿Tu novio?

FERNANDITA   (*Sonríe.*) Es el mozo de mulas del señor marqués. Me corteja, pero yo no le quiero.

ESQUILACHE   ¿Porque quieres a otro?

FERNANDITA   (*Desvía la vista.*) No, excelencia. Yo no quiero a nadie. (*Por la primera izquierda entra BERNARDO, embozado. Da unos pasos y se detiene, mirando hacia la invisible entrada del palacio, como en espera. Ella se exalta.*) ¡Y menos, a uno de esos majos de malas entrañas!

ESQUILACHE   (*Irónico.*) ¿Para quién te reservas entonces?

FERNANDITA   (*Deja de mirarlo.*) No sé.

ESQUILACHE   (*Después de un momento, con frialdad.*) Eres una niña encantadora. Me recuerdas a otra niña encantadora que conocí hace veinte años... Me pregunto si serás como ella.

FERNANDITA   ¿Cómo era?

ESQUILACHE   (*Sonríe con melancolía y soslaya la pregunta.*) Yo le recitaba versos de un gran poeta de mi país... Versos que no he olvidado. ¿Sabes italiano?

FERNANDITA   (*Sonríe.*) ¿Yo, excelencia?

CIEGO   (*Aburrido.*) El Gran Piscator de Salamanca, con los pronósticos de todo el año...

ESQUILACHE *levanta la cabeza. Ha oído.* BERNARDO *mira un momento al* CIEGO *y vuelve a su postura.*

ESQUILACHE   ¿Sabes siquiera lo misterioso que es el ser humano? A lo mejor, cuando ya le vence la edad y está lleno de temores, recuerda esas futesas de su

that did it. Ever since your Excellency ordered the place cleaned up, people are much healthier, they look much better. Before, they looked... well, green! [23]

ESQUILACHE   And your father, is he alive?

FERNANDITA   (*Lowering her head.*) He'd already died before that... He was murdered.

ESQUILACHE   Murdered?

FERNANDITA   The killer had his face covered by his cape, so nobody ever knew who he was, except me. I was just a little girl, but I knew what was going on... There's no doubt about it, he killed him.

ESQUILACHE   Who is he?

FERNANDITA   Was... The Devil took him off as well in the plague, and a good thing too. He was one of the local *majos*, and he was after my mother. I was taken in by my godmother: she does embroidery, and she recommended me to her ladyship.

ESQUILACHE   (*Observing her coolly.*) Have you heard anything about a decree that I'm about to issue?

FERNANDITA   No, my Lord.

ESQUILACHE   People are talking about it.

FERNANDITA   I haven't heard anything downstairs either. Julián would have told me.

ESQUILACHE   Is he your boyfriend?

FERNANDITA   (*She smiles.*) He's the lad who looks after your Lordship's mules. He's courting me, but I'm not in love with him.

ESQUILACHE   Because you're in love with someone else?

FERNANDITA   (*Looking away.*) No, my Lord. I'm not in love with anybody. (*Enter* BERNARDO *downstage left, muffled in his cape. After a few steps he stops and looks towards the entrance to the palace offstage, as if waiting for someone. She is becoming agitated.*) And certainly not with one of those heartless crooks!

ESQUILACHE   (*With an ironic tone.*) Who are you saving yourself for, then?

FERNANDITA   (*Looking away from him.*) I don't know.

ESQUILACHE   (*After a moment, he speaks coldly.*) You're a delightful girl. You remind me of another delightful girl I knew twenty years ago... I wonder if you'll turn out like her.

FERNANDITA   What was she like?

ESQUILACHE   (*With a melancholy smile, he avoids the question.*) I used to recite her some lines of verse by a great poet from my country... Lines that I've never forgotten. Do you know any Italian?

FERNANDITA   (*With a smile.*) Me, sir, know Italian?

BALLAD-SELLER   (*In a bored voice.*) The Great Piscator of Salamanca, predictions for the whole year...

ESQUILACHE *looks up. He has heard the* BALLAD-SELLER's *cry.* BERNARDO *looks at the blind man for a moment, then resumes his watch on the palace.*

ESQUILACHE   Do you have any idea of how mysterious human beings can be? Perhaps, when they grow old and begin to feel afraid, they look back on those

juventud, y se ríe de sí mismo, porque comprueba que... no es más que un niño envejecido... Un niño que todavía quisiera confiar en los demás... ¿Sabes tú de esas cosas? ¿Qué sabes tú? ¿Qué buscas tú?

FERNANDITA   (*Herida, sin saber bien por qué.*) ¿Yo, excelencia...?

ESQUILACHE   Calla. Y escucha:

> *Mostrasi si piacente a chi la mira,*
> *che da per gli occhi una dolcezza al core,*
> *che 'ntender non la puó chi non la prova.*
> *E par che della sua labbia si mova*
> *un spirito soave pien d'amore,*
> *che va dicendo all'anima: sospira.*

Un silencio. FERNANDITA *baja la vista.*

FERNANDITA   No los entiendo bien, pero... conmueven.

ESQUILACHE   (*Brusco.*) Son ridículos. (*Deja de mirarla y agita dos veces la campanilla. Dice, muy seco:*) Gracias por todo, Fernandita. (FERNANDITA *se inclina y va a recoger su bandeja. Entra el* MAYORDOMO. RELAÑO, *embozado, aparece por la primera izquierda y se recuesta sobre el muro.*) Don Antonio Campos. Y mi carroza.

MAYORDOMO   Sí, excelencia.

Sale el MAYORDOMO. FERNANDITA *va a salir con la bandeja, después de inclinarse.*

ESQUILACHE   (*Con la hiriente frialdad de un "ilustrado".*) ¿Sabes leer, Fernandita?

FERNANDITA   (*Avergonzada.*) No, excelencia. Perdón, excelencia...

Sale, y entra CAMPOS. ESQUILACHE *le tiende la Real Orden.*

ESQUILACHE   Don Antonio, una copia de esto a la Imprenta Real. Doble cantidad que otras veces. Debe ser fijado mañana por la mañana. Estamos a nueve, ¿no?

CAMPOS   Sí, excelencia.

ESQUILACHE   *Ecco.* Mañana, diez de marzo. (*Le da otro papel.*) Esta instrucción contra infracciones del bando al señor Corregidor y para todos los alcaldes del barrio, con copia de la Real Orden.

CAMPOS   Sí, excelencia.

ESQUILACHE   *Andiamo.*

little things that bothered them so much when they were young, and they laugh
at themselves, because they realize that... they are no more than aging
children... Children who still want to trust other people... Do you know
anything about such things? What do you know? What are you searching for?
FERNANDITA (*Hurt, but without quite knowing why.*) Me, sir...?
ESQUILACHE Be quiet. And listen:

> *Mostrasi si piacente a chi la mira,*
> *che da per gli occhi una dolcezza al core,*
> *che 'ntender non la puó chi non la prova.*
> *E par che della sua labbia si mova*
> *un spirito soave pien d'amore,*
> *che va dicendo all'anima: sospira.*[24]

A moment of silence. FERNANDITA *lowers her eyes.*

FERNANDITA I don't understand it very well, but it's... moving.
ESQUILACHE (*Brusquely.*) It's ridiculous. (*No longer looking at her, he rings the
    bell twice. Very curtly, he says:*) Thank you for everything, Fernandita.
    (FERNANDITA *curtsies and goes to collect her tray. The* STEWARD *comes
    in.* RELAÑO, *wrapped up in his cape, appears downstage left and leans
    against the wall.*) Get me don Antonio Campos. And get my carriage ready.
STEWARD Yes, my Lord.

Exit the STEWARD. FERNANDITA *heads for the door with the tray, after curtsying.*

ESQUILACHE (*Impersonal and patronizing.*)[25] Can you read, Fernandita?
FERNANDITA (*Embarrassed.*) No, sir. Excuse me, sir...

She leaves, and CAMPOS *comes in.* ESQUILACHE *hands him the Order in Council.*

ESQUILACHE Don Antonio, a copy of this to the Royal Print. Twice the usual
    quantity. To be posted tomorrow morning. Is it the ninth today?
CAMPOS Yes, sir.
ESQUILACHE *Ecco.* Tomorrow, then, the tenth of March. (*Handing him another
    document.*) These instructions for dealing with infractions of the decree are to
    go to the Mayor and all the deputy mayors, together with a copy of the Order in
    Council.
CAMPOS Very well, my Lord.
ESQUILACHE *Andiamo.*

Sale por el foro. CAMPOS *se inclina y sale tras él, cerrando, en tanto que el* CIEGO *pregona.*

CIEGO   El Noticioso, Curioso y Erudito para hoy, diez de marzo...

La luz se amortiguó en el gabinete y crece en el primer término. Acompañado de CRISANTO *y* ROQUE, *entra por la segunda izquierda un menestral de sombrero apuntado que lleva un tarro de engrudo y un rollo de bandos bajo el brazo.* BERNARDO *se vuelve lentamente, viéndolos cruzar. Llegan a la esquina posterior de la casa de la derecha y, tras ella, el hombre mima los gestos del que pega un cartel. El balcón se abre y* DOÑA MARÍA, *peinándose las greñas, asoma, intrigada. Un* CESANTE *(media edad, redingote, tricornio) entra por la primera izquierda y se acerca lentamente a mirar. Terminada su faena, el fijador de bandos y los dos alguaciles avanzan para salir por la primera derecha.* BERNARDO *se acerca al* CESANTE, *que está leyendo.*

BERNARDO   Lea en voz alta.

El CESANTE *lo mira, intimidado, y carraspea.*

CESANTE   Pues dice... Um... (RELAÑO *se va acercando al centro de la escena mientras lee.* DOÑA MARÍA *le hace pabellón a la oreja.)* ... "No habiendo bastado para desterrar de la Corte el mal parecido y perjudicial disfraz o abuso del embozo con capa larga, sombrero chambergo o gacho, montera calada, gorro o redecilla, las Reales Ordenes de los años dieciséis, diecinueve..."
BERNARDO   ¡Al grano!
CESANTE   Pues... "Mando que ninguna persona, de cualquier calidad, condición y estado que sea, pueda usar..." Um... "del citado traje de capa larga y sombrero redondo para el embozo; pues quiero que todos usen precisamente de capa corta, que a lo menos le falte una cuarta para llegar al suelo, o de redingote o capingote y de peluquín o pelo propio y sombrero de tres picos de forma que de ningún modo vayan embozados ni oculten el rostro...". Um... "Bajo la pena por primera vez de seis ducados o doce días de cárcel..." "Por la segunda, doce ducados o..."
BERNARDO   ¡Basta ya!

Un silencio.

DOÑA MARÍA   (*Le arranca al peine la broza y la tira a la calle.*) ¡En Madrid ya no hay valientes!...

BERNARDO *le lanza una viva mirada. Ella se mete y cierra.*

He goes out upstage. CAMPOS *bows and follows him out, closing the door behind him, while the* BALLAD-SELLER *starts up his cry again.*

BALLAD-SELLER   The *Journal* for today, the tenth of March...

The lights have come down on the study and up on the foreground. Accompanied by CRISANTO *and* ROQUE, *a workman enters upstage left. He wears a hat stitched up into three corners, and carries a pot of paste and a roll of notices under his arm.* BERNARDO *turns slowly as he watches them cross the stage. They reach the rear corner of the house on the right and, just behind it, the workman mimes the actions of pasting up a poster. The balcony opens and* DOÑA MARÍA, *in the middle of combing her unruly hair, leans out, intrigued. A* CESANTE *(middle-aged, in a double-breasted coat*[26]*and tricorn hat) enters downstage left and comes slowly across to watch. When he has completed the job, the billposter heads off downstage right with the two constables.* BERNARDO *goes up to the* CESANTE, *who is reading the notice.*

BERNARDO   Read it aloud, then.

The CESANTE *gives him an intimidated look and clears his throat.*

CESANTE   Well, it says... Umm... (RELAÑO *moves towards the centre of the stage as he reads.* MARÍA *cups her hand around her ear.*) ... "In view of the continuing abuse of the objectionable custom of concealing the face by means of long capes, broad-brimmed hats or caps, and other indecorous headgear in contravention of the Orders in Council of seventeen sixteen, seventeen nineteen..."
BERNARDO   Get to the important bit!
CESANTE   Let's see... "I hereby decree that no man, of whatever rank or position, shall make use of..." Umm... "the aforementioned long cape with round hat for the purposes of concealment. Indeed, it is my wish that all men shall wear short capes which clear the ground by at least one quarter of their length, or redingotes, together with short wigs or natural hair and three-cornered hats, so that no man may disguise himself or hide his face..." Umm... "The penalty for a first offence is a fine of six ducats or twelve days' imprisonment"... "For the second offence, twelve ducats or..."[27]
BERNARDO   That's enough, dammit!

A moment of silence.

MARÍA   (*She pulls the comb out of her hair and flings it down into the street.*) There aren't any real men in Madrid any more!

BERNARDO *glances at her sharply. She goes back inside and closes the balcony.*

CESANTE   En enero hicieron lo mismo con los empleados públicos... Tuve que malvender mi capa para comprarme esto... Luego no me sirvió de nada, porque Esquilache redujo el personal... Yo era recomendado del señor duque de Medinaceli, pero no lo tuvieron en cuenta... Ahora como de su pan.

Suspira. De repente, BERNARDO *se abalanza al bando y lo arranca furiosamente, haciendo con sus restos una pelota que tira al suelo.*

RELAÑO   ¡Los corchetes están cerca!

BERNARDO   ¡Que vengan si se atreven! ¡En Madrid va a haber gresca y tararira porque le da la gana a Bernardo el calesero! ¡Y el que quiera demostrarle a ese italianini con quién se la juega, que me lo diga a mí, que yo sé donde tenemos que apuntarnos todos!

RELAÑO   ¡Pues aquí tienes a un hombre y de otros sé que también querrán!

BERNARDO   ¡Pues ya tardamos! (*Le toma del brazo.*)

CESANTE   (*Tras él.*) ¿De qué apuntamiento habla su merced?

BERNARDO   (*Se vuelve.*) A su merced le apuntaron ya... el sombrero: ya es gallo capón. Esto es para gente más entera. Pero pregúntele a su señor el duque: a lo mejor, él sabe algo...

El CESANTE *lo mira y opta por salir aprisa por la primera derecha.* BERNARDO *ríe.* FERNANDITA *apareció con su bolsa de compras por la segunda derecha y se ha parado para ver lo que ocurre.* BERNARDO *la ve ahora y deja de reír.*

RELAÑO   ¿Qué esperamos?

BERNARDO   Aguárdame en la calesa. (*Lo empuja.* RELAÑO *sale por la primera izquierda.* BERNARDO *se acerca a* FERNANDITA, *que baja los ojos.*) Dios te guarde, Fernandita... Las horas me paso rondándote y sin verte... Tan ricamente que nos iba y, de pronto, me huyes... ¿Qué te he hecho? (*Un silencio.*) ¿Di, qué te he hecho? ¿Así tratas a un hombre de ley que te quiere? ¿Por qué? ¿Por algún mal pájaro de esa casa, quizá? ¿Algún hijo del marqués?...

FERNANDITA   (*Ofendida.*) ¡Bernardo!

BERNARDO   ¡A todas os ciega el mismo brillo! Y tú vives en mala escuela: la marquesa es una golfa y golfa te hará a ti.

FERNANDITA   ¿Y qué puede importarte, si tú también me quieres para eso?

BERNARDO   ¿Cómo?

FERNANDITA   ¿Qué te va con que me hagan una golfa, si tú también me quieres hacer una golfa?

BERNARDO   (*Titubea.*) ¡Sabes que no son ésas mis intenciones!

CESANTE   They did the same to us civil servants in January... I had to get what I could for my cape so that I could buy this... In the end it didn't do me any good, because Esquilache cut the staff... I had a recommendation from the Duke of Medinaceli, but they took no account of that... Now I'm having to rely on his charity.

He sighs. Suddenly, BERNARDO *rushes to the poster, furiously tears it off the wall and crumples it up into a ball, which he throws to the ground.*

RELAÑO   Watch out! The constables aren't far away!
BERNARDO   They can come if they've got the guts! One word from Bernardo the cabby and there'll be all hell let loose in Madrid. And anybody who wants to show that Italian ponce who he's up against, just let me know! I know where to sign up for this kind of operation.[28]
RELAÑO   Here's one man who's with you, and I know there'll be plenty more!
BERNARDO   Let's get on with it, then! (*Taking hold of his arm.*)
CESANTE   (*Scurrying along behind him.*) What operation is this you're talking about signing up for?
BERNARDO   (*Turning towards him.*) You, sir, have already had the operation, on your hat, at least: they've gelded you. This business is for men who've still got everything where it's supposed to be. Anyway, you could try asking your friend the duke: maybe he knows something...

The CESANTE *looks at him and decides to leave rapidly downstage right.* BERNARDO *guffaws.* FERNANDITA *has appeared upstage right with her shopping bag and has stopped to see what is going on.* BERNARDO *sees her at this point and stops laughing.*

RELAÑO   Well, what are we waiting for?
BERNARDO   Wait for me in the cab. (*He gives him a push.* RELAÑO *exits downstage left.* BERNARDO *goes towards* FERNANDITA, *who looks down at the ground.*) Good morning, Fernandita... I keep waiting for hours around here without seeing you... We were getting along so nicely, and all of a sudden, you're avoiding me... What have I done wrong? (*Silence.*) Tell me, what have I done? Is this any way to treat a good man who loves you? Why are you doing this? Maybe someone in that house has turned you against me, eh? Maybe one of the marquis's sons has taken you under his wing?...
FERNANDITA   (*Offended.*) Bernardo!
BERNARDO   Oh, come on! Women just can't resist a bit of glitter. And you're not exactly being set a good example: the marchioness is a tart and she'll make you one too.
FERNANDITA   And why should that bother you, if that's all you want me for?
BERNARDO   What?
FERNANDITA   Why should you care if they make a tart of me if that's what you want me to be anyway?
BERNARDO   (*Faltering.*) You know that's not what I want!

FERNANDITA (*Triste.*) No quise verte más desde que supe que eras casado.

BERNARDO ¿Qué? (*Improvisa, vacilante.*) ¡Chiquilla, eso es un infundio! ¡Yo te juro...!

FERNANDITA (*Desgarrada.*) ¡No jures más!... (*Levísima pausa.*) Tu mujer, tus dos hijos, nunca te ven... Te gastas lo que ganas con mujerzuelas y en los garitos... Te pasas la vida mintiendo y engañando... Y a mí... (*Se le quiebra la voz.*) has querido engañarme también.

BERNARDO (*Le aferra una muñeca.*) ¡Yo sabré quién te ha contado eso! ¡Caro le va a costar!

FERNANDITA (*Con un alarido, se suelta y cruza.*) ¡Déjame!

BERNARDO (*Retrocede, jadeante.*) ¡Esto no va a quedar así, Fernandita! Tú me quieres.

FERNANDITA (*Llorando.*) ¡No!

BERNARDO Casado o soltero, me quieres... ¡Y serás mía!

FERNANDITA ¡Rufián!...

BERNARDO (*Con maligna sonrisa.*) ¡Nos veremos!

Sale, brusco, por la primera izquierda. Angustiada, FERNANDITA le mira alejarse. Luego recoge la pelota de papel, la estira un poco, la vuelve a arrugar, asustada, y sale, llevándosela, por la segunda izquierda. Entretanto entraron al gabinete por el fondo el MAYORDOMO y CAMPOS, éste con una carpeta que dejó sobre la mesa. El MAYORDOMO ha permanecido junto a la puerta mientras el secretario ordena unos papeles. Inicióse un leve oscurecimiento en el primer término y, al salir FERNANDITA, crece la luz en el gabinete.

CAMPOS Cierre. (*El MAYORDOMO lo hace.*)

CIEGO El Noticioso, Curioso y Erudito para hoy, once de marzo...

CAMPOS ¿Cuántas veces la llamó desde ayer?

MAYORDOMO Esta es la cuarta, don Antonio.

CAMPOS ¿Dónde están?

MAYORDOMO (*Señala a la izquierda.*) Le ha servido el desayuno ahí dentro.

CAMPOS mira hacia la puerta en el momento mismo en que ésta se abre.

CAMPOS ¡Chist!

Disimulan ambos. ESQUILACHE entra en bata, estudiando un papel que trae en la mano. Levanta los ojos y los mira.

ESQUILACHE (*A CAMPOS.*) ¿Novedades?

CAMPOS Nada grave, excelencia.

FERNANDITA   (*Sadly.*) I haven't wanted to see you again ever since I found out you
        were married.
BERNARDO   Eh? (*Clumsily attempting to bluff his way out of this.*) That's a lie,
        sweetheart! Honestly, I swear...!
FERNANDITA   (*In anguish.*) Don't swear anything!... (*A slight pause.*) Your wife,
        your two children, they never see you... You spend everything you earn on
        womanizing and gambling... You go through life lying and cheating... And me
        too,... (*Her voice breaks.*) you tried to deceive me as well.
BERNARDO   (*Grabbing her by the wrist.*) Just wait till I find out who told you that!
        I'll get my own back!
FERNANDITA   (*With a scream, she tears herself free and runs across the stage.*) Let
        go of me!
BERNARDO   (*Steps backwards, panting.*) This isn't the end of it, Fernandita! You
        love me.
FERNANDITA   (*In tears.*) No, I don't!
BERNARDO   Married or not, you love me... And you'll be mine!
FERNANDITA   You're a thug and a bully and a pimp!
BERNARDO   (*With a malevolent grin.*) We'll be seeing each other again!

*He storms off downstage left. In distress, FERNANDITA watches him go. Then she
picks up the ball of paper, opens it out, crumples it up again in alarm, and goes off with
it upstage left. In the meantime, the STEWARD and CAMPOS have come into the
study through the door at the back; CAMPOS has brought with him a portfolio, which
he leaves on the desk. The STEWARD has been standing by the door while the
secretary arranges some papers. The lights have begun to fade in the foreground, and
as FERNANDITA leaves, they come up on the study.*

CAMPOS   Close the door. (*The STEWARD does so.*)
BALLAD-SELLER   The Journal for today, the eleventh of March...
CAMPOS   How many times has he called for her since yesterday?
STEWARD   This is the fourth time, don Antonio.
CAMPOS   Where are they now?
STEWARD   (*Pointing towards the left.*) She's served him breakfast in there.

CAMPOS *looks towards the door just as it opens.*

CAMPOS   Shhh!

*They both pretend to be busy. ESQUILACHE enters in his dressing gown, reading a
piece of paper in his hand. He looks up at the two men.*

ESQUILACHE   (*To CAMPOS.*) Any new developments?
CAMPOS   Nothing serious, my Lord.

ESQUILACHE   ¿De veras? (*Va a la mesa y deja el papel.*) ¿Es que no hay informes de
     la Policía?

CAMPOS   (*Inmutado.*) No me pareció oportuno distraer a vuecelencia con simples
     cosas de trámite.

ESQUILACHE   *¡Santa Madonna!* Cosas de trámite. (*Seco.*) ¿Qué ocurre con el
     bando?

CAMPOS   (*Vacila.*) Pues...

ESQUILACHE   Yo le diré lo que ocurre con los bandos. (*Saca del bolsillo de la bata
     la pelota que recogió* FERNANDITA *y la extiende ante los ojos del
     secretario.*) ¡Los están arrancando todos!

CAMPOS   (*Abre su carpeta.*) Aquí están los informes de la Policía.

ESQUILACHE   ¡Tarde me los da! (*Le arrebata los papeles y se sienta.*) Felizmente, yo
     soy más rápido. (*Deja a un lado los informes y recoge el papel que traía al
     entrar.*) Esta es una orden para el señor Corregidor. Séllela y que un oficial de
     mi antecámara la lleve en el acto: ha de empezar a cumplirse esta misma
     mañana. (*Se la tiende.*) Puede leerla.

CAMPOS   (*La repasa.*) ¿Sastres?

ESQUILACHE   ¿Qué le asombra? El bando tiene que cumplirse. Llévela
     inmediatamente y vuelva.

CAMPOS   Sí, excelencia. (*Sale por el foro.*)

ESQUILACHE   ¿Alguien en la antecámara?

MAYORDOMO   El señor duque de Villasanta, excelencia.

ESQUILACHE   (*Se sobresalta.*) ¿Desde cuándo?

MAYORDOMO   Desde hace una hora, excelencia.

ESQUILACHE   (*Da un golpe en la mesa y se levanta, irritado.*) ¿Por qué no me ha
     avisado?

MAYORDOMO   Como su excelencia estaba ocupado.... creí...

Un silencio. ESQUILACHE *mira a la puerta de la izquierda, pasea y lo mira de
soslayo.*

ESQUILACHE   Yo no había dado ninguna orden.

MAYORDOMO   Ha sido un error, excelencia, que deploro con toda mi alma.

ESQUILACHE   Ya. Un error más. (*Golpecitos en la puerta entreabierta.*) ¡Adelante!
     (*Entra* CAMPOS. *Al* MAYORDOMO:) Mi casaca. *¡Súbito!*

Se despoja de la bata y queda en chupa. El MAYORDOMO *la recoge y va hacia la
puerta de la izquierda.*

CAMPOS   La orden acaba de salir, excelencia.

ESQUILACHE   Really? (*He goes to the desk and puts down the paper he was carrying.*) Are there no police reports?

CAMPOS   (*His face falls.*) I did not think that this was a suitable moment to disturb you with unimportant details, my Lord.

ESQUILACHE   *Santa Madonna!* Unimportant details, he says. (*Businesslike.*) What's happening about the decree?

CAMPOS   (*Hesitantly.*) Well...

ESQUILACHE   I'll tell you what's happening about the decree. (*He takes out of the pocket of his dressing gown the ball of paper that* FERNANDITA *picked up and opens it out for his secretary to see.*) They're tearing down the posters, that's what!

CAMPOS   (*Opening his folder.*) Here are the police reports.

ESQUILACHE   You should have brought them sooner! (*He snatches the papers from him and sits down.*) Fortunately, I work more quickly. (*He pushes the reports aside and picks up the document he was carrying when he came in.*) This is an order for the Mayor. Seal it and have one of my staff deliver it to him at once: it must be put into effect this morning. (*Handing it to him.*) You may read it.

CAMPOS   (*Glancing over it.*) Tailors?

ESQUILACHE   Why so surprised? The decree must be carried out. Take it straight away and come back.

CAMPOS   Yes, sir. (*He goes out upstage.*)

ESQUILACHE   Is there anyone waiting in the antechamber?

STEWARD   The Duke of Villasanta, sir.

ESQUILACHE   (*With a start.*) How long has he been there?

STEWARD   An hour, sir.

ESQUILACHE   (*He bangs the desk in irritation and gets to his feet.*) Why didn't you tell me?

STEWARD   As your Lordship was busy..., I thought...

A moment of silence. ESQUILACHE *glances towards the door at the left, begins to pace up and down, and looks out of the corner of his eye at the* STEWARD.

ESQUILACHE   I gave no instructions to that effect.

STEWARD   A mistake that I regret deeply, your Excellency.

ESQUILACHE   Quite. Yet another mistake. (*Someone taps at the door, which has been left ajar.*) Come in! (*Enter* CAMPOS. *To the* STEWARD:) My coat. *Subito!*

He takes off his dressing gown and waits in his waistcoat. The STEWARD *takes the dressing gown and goes towards the door at the left.*

CAMPOS   The order has just gone out, my Lord.

ESQUILACHE *saca su reloj y lo mira. Se vuelve al* MAYORDOMO, *que titubea ante la puerta, y le dice con voz suave.*

ESQUILACHE   ¿Y mi casaca?
MAYORDOMO   Ahora mismo, excelencia.

Abre la puerta y sale, bajo la mirada de ESQUILACHE.

ESQUILACHE   ¿Se introdujeron las nuevas cuadrillas en el empedrado de la plaza Mayor?
CAMPOS   Desde ayer. Ahorraremos un mes de trabajo.
ESQUILACHE   ¿Qué hay de Ensenada?
CAMPOS   Le pasé dos veces recado. Parece que no está en Madrid.
ESQUILACHE   ¿Dónde se habrá metido?... (*El* MAYORDOMO *vuelve y cierra.*) Ah... (*Mientras se pone la casaca que le trae.*) ¿Está en casa la señora marquesa?
MAYORDOMO   Ha salido, excelencia.
ESQUILACHE   Si vuelve, que me haga la merced de venir.
MAYORDOMO   Bien, excelencia.
ESQUILACHE   Haga pasar al señor duque de Villasanta. O si no, iré yo mismo. Retírense de aquí.

Sale por el foro. EL MAYORDOMO *se inclina. La luz va creciendo suavemente en el primer término: es como un rayo de sol que fuese rompiendo nubes.*

CAMPOS   ¿Sigue ahí?
MAYORDOMO   Sentada en una silla... Se ha puesto colorada al verme entrar. (*Se disimulan mutuamente la sonrisa.*)
CAMPOS   Salgamos. (*Salen los dos por el foro. Una pausa.*)
CIEGO   (*Da unos pasos hacia el centro de la escena y se detiene. Tanteando, se sienta en los peldaños del giratorio, bajo la mesa de* ESQUILACHE. *Habla para sí.*) Ya puede uno sentarse en la calle... (*Ríe débilmente.*) Marzo tiene estas sorpresas: frío, ventisca... Y, de pronto, un sol muy dulce. ¿Será dulce este marzo en Madrid?... Para mí al menos, que soy ya como un perro a quien sólo le importa el sol y la pitanza...

Enmudece, arrebujándose en su casacón. ESQUILACHE *y* VILLASANTA *se hacen una reverencia ante la puerta del foro. Entra el* DUQUE *y* ESQUILACHE *cierra la puerta. El* DUQUE DE VILLASANTA *es un noble español de edad indefinida, chapado a la antigua. La peluca, como la de* ENSENADA, *pasada de moda. Sobre la cerrada casaca lleva bordada la verde venera de Alcántara. Viene claramente molesto.* ESQUILACHE *extrema sus sonrisas de amabilidad.*

ESQUILACHE *takes out his watch and looks at it. Turning to the* STEWARD, *who is hesitating at the door, he addresses him gently.*

ESQUILACHE   My coat?
STEWARD   At once, your Excellency.

He opens the door and goes out, watched by ESQUILACHE.

ESQUILACHE   Have the new teams of labourers been put to work on the paving of the Plaza Mayor?
CAMPOS   Yes, since yesterday. We'll save a whole month's work.
ESQUILACHE   Any news of Ensenada?
CAMPOS   I've sent him a message twice. He doesn't seem to be in Madrid.
ESQUILACHE   Where can he have got to?... (*The* STEWARD *comes back in and closes the door behind him.*) Ah... (*As he puts on the coat that has been brought to him.*) Is her ladyship at home?
STEWARD   She has gone out, my Lord.
ESQUILACHE   If she returns, ask her to be so good as to come and see me.
STEWARD   Very well, my Lord.
ESQUILACHE   Show in the Duke of Villasanta. No, I'll go myself. Leave this room, both of you.

He goes out through the door at the back. The STEWARD *bows. The lights come up smoothly on the foreground: rather like a ray of sunlight gradually breaking through clouds.*

CAMPOS   Still there, then?
STEWARD   Sitting on one of his chairs... She blushed when she saw me come in. (*They exchange a furtive smirk.*)
ESQUILACHE   Come on, let's go. (*They go out upstage. There is a pause.*)
BALLAD-SELLER   (*Takes a few steps towards the centre of the stage and stops. Feeling his way, he sits down on the steps of the revolving platform, just below* ESQUILACHE's *desk. He talks to himself.*) It's good to be able to sit out in the street... (*Laughing faintly.*) You get these surprises in March: cold, blizzards... And suddenly, lovely sunshine. I wonder if this March will turn out to be lovely in Madrid?... I hope it will be for me, anyway: these days I'm just like a dog that doesn't care about anything except for getting a bit of sun and a bite to eat every day...

He lapses into silence, wrapping himself up in his coat. ESQUILACHE *and* VILLASANTA *bow to one another outside the door at the back of the stage.* ESQUILACHE *follows the duke into the study and closes the door. The* DUKE OF VILLASANTA[29] *is an aristocrat of the old school. His age is difficult to guess. His wig, like* ENSENADA's, *is of an outmoded style. He wears his coat buttoned up; on it is embroidered the green scallop shell of the Order of Alcántara. He is clearly very annoyed.* ESQUILACHE *overflows with amiability.*

ESQUILACHE   No sé cómo desagraviarte, querido Villasanta. Mi mayordomo es un
    imbécil. Dígnate tomar asiento... (*Le indica un sillón.*)
VILLASANTA   (*Glacial.*) Gracias.

Se sienta en el sillón de la derecha y ESQUILACHE *ocupa otro, junto a la consola.*

ESQUILACHE   Creo que es la primera vez que cruzamos la palabra...
VILLASANTA   Así es.
ESQUILACHE   Me harás feliz si puedo servirte en algo. ¿A qué debo el honor de tu
    visita?
VILLASANTA   Poca cosa. Y sin ninguna dificultad, creo, para vuecelencia.

ESQUILACHE *tuerce el gesto al advertir el tratamiento.*

ESQUILACHE   Me encantará complacerte. Pero aunque vengas a hablar al ministro, el
    tratamiento sobra, ¿no crees?
VILLASANTA   Muy reconocido a la deferencia de usía.

ESQUILACHE *lo mira, se levanta y va a la mesa. Pensando en otra cosa examina*
algún papel.

ESQUILACHE   ¿Debo pedir perdón? Creí que entre nobles se acostumbraba el tuteo.
VILLASANTA   Es a mí a quien debe disculpar si no logro hacerme a esa costumbre.
ESQUILACHE   (*Se vuelve y lo mira. Decide atacar, aunque sonriente.*) Sobre todo,
    con ciertos títulos recientes, ¿no? (*Va hacia él.*) Si yo fuese el sinuoso italiano
    que dicen que soy, dejaría pasar esto sin comentario. Pero da la casualidad de
    que no soy tan prudente como dicen. ¿Prefiere que nos tratemos de usía? Bien.
    Pues yo he visto a usía tutear a otros nobles. (*Ademán de hablar de*
    VILLASANTA.) ¡Ya, ya sé que eran títulos de dos o tres siglos! ¡Los famosos
    tres siglos! Yo he remediado en el breve término de tres años los abusos en
    España y en América de esos tres siglos, muy gloriosos pero muy mal
    administrados. Es así como se ganan los títulos, ¿no? Usía debe saberlo por la
    historia de sus abuelos. Los gobernantes de esta hora no solemos tener abuelos
    linajudos. Somos unos advenedizos que saben trabajar y eso es imperdonable
    para la antigua nobleza, que ya no sabe hacerlo. (*Ríe.*) Usía es muy agradable,
    de veras: le cuesta trabajo disimular sus sentimientos y a mí me ocurre lo
    mismo. Esto aumenta mi deseo de complacerle. ¿De qué se trata?

ESQUILACHE   I cannot apologize enough, my dear Villasanta. My steward is an imbecile. Please, take a seat... *(Pointing towards an armchair.)*
VILLASANTA   *(Frostily.)* Thank you.

He sits in the armchair on the right, and ESQUILACHE *takes another, next to the console table.*

ESQUILACHE   I believe this is the first time we have spoken to each other...
VILLASANTA   It is.
ESQUILACHE   I shall be delighted if I can help you in any way. To what do I owe the honour of this visit?
VILLASANTA   A small matter. And one that I am sure your Excellency will be able to resolve without difficulty.

ESQUILACHE *frowns at the formality with which the duke addresses him.*

ESQUILACHE   I shall be happy to do what I can for you. You may have come to talk to me in my position as minister, but there's really no need to address me so formally, is there?
VILLASANTA   Your Lordship is very gracious.

ESQUILACHE *looks at him, gets up and goes across to the desk. He examines a piece of paper while clearly thinking about something else.*

ESQUILACHE   Do I owe you an apology? I had the idea that between noblemen it is customary to treat one another with some familiarity.[30]
VILLASANTA   Why no, it is I who must apologize for being unable to get used to it.
ESQUILACHE   *(Turning to look at him. He decides to attack, but with a smile.)* It's particularly difficult with certain recently-acquired titles, isn't it? *(Moving towards him.)* If I were really the devious Italian they say I am, I would let this go without saying anything. But I happen not to be as careful as people say. Would you prefer me to address you as your Grace? Fine. But I've seen you dealing on more familiar terms with other noblemen. (VILLASANTA *is about to say something.*) Yes, I know that their titles go back two or three centuries! The famous three centuries! Well, in three short years I've put right in Spain and America the abuses of those three centuries. Very glorious centuries they may have been, but they were incompetently administered. That's where titles come from, isn't it? Your Grace should know all about that from the history of your ancestors. The men who are running things now tend not to come from illustrious families. We're just upstarts who don't mind hard work, and that is something the ancient nobility can't put up with, because they no longer know how to work. *(He laughs.)* I think you and I get on very well, your Grace: you find it difficult to hide your feelings, and I have the same trouble. That makes me all the more anxious to do something for you. What were you going to ask me?

VILLASANTA   (*Se levanta.*) No suelo pedir... Ignoro sin duda por eso la manera de
    hacerlo. Olvide mi visita.
ESQUILACHE   De ningún modo. Usía debe exponerme su asunto. (*Vacilación de*
    VILLASANTA.) ¿Tendré que recordarle que está en mi casa?

Le indica el sillón.

VILLASANTA   (*Suspira y se sienta.*) Se trata de una reposición. El hijo del capataz de
    mi finca de Extremadura prestaba sus servicios en el despacho de Hacienda y le
    echaron en la última reducción de personal. Se había casado aquí... Era su
    único medio de vida...
ESQUILACHE   ¿No podría usía facilitarle algún otro en Extremadura?
VILLASANTA   Usía dijo que deseaba atender mi petición.
ESQUILACHE   (*Se sienta.*) Consideremos el asunto, duque. La reducción del personal
    era una medida necesaria. Las oficinas públicas se ahogaban bajo el peso de
    tanto... protegido. Son gentes que nunca debieron salir de sus pueblos. Usía
    pensará que se puede hacer una excepción, pero habría que hacer tantas... Casi
    todos los expulsados eran... protegidos.
VILLASANTA   De modo que se niega usía.
ESQUILACHE   Lo deploro sinceramente.
VILLASANTA   (*Después de un momento.*) He debido recordar que en estos tiempos
    los favores se reservan para otros. A nosotros se nos dedican ya solamente
    bellas palabras fingidas.
ESQUILACHE   (*Ríe levemente.*) ¿Me acusa de hipócrita? (*Se levanta y pasea.*) Pues
    bien, *è vero*. Pero ¿qué es un hipócrita? Pues un desdichado que sólo acierta a
    tener dos caras. En el fondo, un ser que disimula mal, a quien insultan con ese
    epíteto los que disimulan bien. El hipócrita Esquilache tiene que mentir, pero
    miente mal y es detestado. No es uno de esos hombres encantadores que tienen
    una cara para cada persona: él sólo tiene dos y se le transparenta siempre la
    verdadera... (*Grave.*) La verdadera es la de un hombre austero que, si entra en
    el juego de las dádivas y de los halagos, nada quiere para sí. La de un hombre
    capaz de enemistarse con toda la nobleza española si tiene que defender
    cualquier medida que pueda aliviar la postración de un país que agonizaba.
VILLASANTA   Y que tiene que afrancesarse para revivir, ¿no?
ESQUILACHE   Por desgracia, es verdad. ¿Cree que soy enemigo de lo español? He
    aprendido a amar a esta tierra y a sus cosas. Pero no es culpa nuestra si sus
    señorías, los que se creen genuinos representantes del alma española, no son ya
    capaces de añadir nueva gloria a tantas glorias muertas...
VILLASANTA   ¿Muertas?
ESQUILACHE   Créame, duque: no hay cosa peor que estar muerto y no advertirlo. Sus
    señorías lamentan que los principales ministros sean extranjeros, pero el rey nos

VILLASANTA (*Getting up.*) I am not used to asking favours... That must be why I am
    unsure of how to go about it. Please forget that I have been here.
ESQUILACHE By no means. I insist that you put your case. (VILLASANTA
    hesitates.) Must I remind you that you are a guest in my house?

He gestures towards the armchair.

VILLASANTA (*Sits down with a sigh.*) It's a matter of getting someone his job back.
    The son of the foreman on my estate in Extremadura had a post at the Treasury
    and was sacked in the last purge of civil servants. He had got married here in
    Madrid... It was his only way of earning a living...
ESQUILACHE Couldn't you find him a position in Extremadura?
VILLASANTA You said that you were anxious to help.
ESQUILACHE (*Sitting down.*) Let's look at this carefully, shall we, your Grace? The
    reduction in personnel was necessary. Government departments were
    foundering under the weight of so many... protégés. They are people who
    should never have left their villages. You might say that we could make an
    exception in a case like this, but we would end up having to make so many...
    Almost all of those who were fired were... protégés.
VILLASANTA So you refuse, then?
ESQUILACHE With great regret.
VILLASANTA (*After a moment.*) I should have remembered that these days the
    favours are reserved for others. All we are offered now are fine but empty
    words.
ESQUILACHE (*With a slight laugh.*) Are you accusing me of hypocrisy? (*He gets up
    and begins to walk around.*) Well, *è vero*. But what is a hypocrite, anyway?
    Simply an unfortunate who only manages to have two faces. Basically,
    someone who is bad at pretending, called a hypocrite by those who are good at
    it. Esquilache the hypocrite has to lie, but he lies badly and is detested. He's
    not one of those charming fellows with a different face for everyone: he only
    has two, and his real one always shows through... (*Solemnly.*) The real one is
    the face of an austere man who, if he plays the game of favours and
    backscratching, wants nothing for himself. The face of a man prepared to make
    enemies of the whole of the Spanish aristocracy, if that is what it takes to
    defend any policy that can alleviate the agony of a country in crisis.
VILLASANTA A country that must turn French in order to revive itself. Is that it?
ESQUILACHE Unfortunately, it's true. Do you think I'm against Spanishness itself?
    I've learned to love this land and its customs. But it's not our fault if your
    lordships, you who consider yourselves the true representatives of the soul of
    Spain, are no longer capable of creating any new glories on top of so many dead
    ones...
VILLASANTA What do you mean, dead?
ESQUILACHE Believe me, your Grace: there is nothing worse than being dead and
    not realizing it. The nobility complain that the most important ministers are
    foreigners, but the fact is that the king brought us with him from Italy because

trajo consigo de Italia porque el país nos necesitaba para levantarse. Las naciones tienen que cambiar si no quieren morir definitivamente.

VILLASANTA   ¿Hacia dónde? ¿Hacia la Enciclopedia? ¿Hacia la "Ilustración"? ¿Hacia todo eso que sus señorías llaman "las luces"? Nosotros lo llamamos, simplemente, herejía.

ESQUILACHE   (*Se estremece.*) No hay hombre más piadoso que el rey Carlos y usía sabe que no toleraría a su lado a quien no fuese un ferviente católico.

VILLASANTA   Sin duda por eso han apagado sus señorías las hogueras del Santo Oficio.

ESQUILACHE   (*Después de un momento.*) Hemos apagado (*Recalca.*) cristianamente las hogueras del Santo Oficio porque nuestra época nos ha enseñado que es monstruoso quemar vivo a un ser humano, aunque sea un hereje. El infierno es un misterio de Dios, duque: no lo encendamos en la Tierra.

VILLASANTA   Blanduras, marqués. Blanduras tras las que se agazapa la incredulidad, y que nos traerán lo peor si no lo cortamos a tiempo.

ESQUILACHE   ¿Lo peor?

VILLASANTA   (*Se levanta.*) La desaparición en España de nuestra Santa Religión.

ESQUILACHE   (*Ríe.*) Mal confía en ella si cree que puede desaparecer tan fácilmente. Le aseguro que dentro de uno o dos siglos, a los más intransigentes católicos no se les ocurrirá ni pensar en quemar por hereje a un ser humano. Y no por eso la religión habrá desaparecido. Puede que esos católicos se crean sucesores directos de sus señorías; pero en realidad serán nuestros sucesores. Y ése es todo el secreto: nosotros marchamos hacia adelante y sus señorías no quieren moverse. Pero la Historia se mueve.

VILLASANTA   Es fácil hablar del futuro sin conocerlo.

ESQUILACHE   Como usía, aventuro mis pronósticos. ¿Quiere que le dé otro?

VILLASANTA   (*Leve inclinación irónica.*) Será un placer.

ESQUILACHE   El que no quiera cambiar con los cambios del país se quedará solo.

VILLASANTA   (*Ríe.*) No será otro acto de hipocresía, marqués...

ESQUILACHE   ¿Por qué iba a serlo?

VILLASANTA   Vamos, señor ministro. Supongo que no ignora que el pueblo está arrancando los bandos de capas y sombreros. No parece que quiera cambiar mucho...

El CESANTE *entra por la segunda derecha y va a pasar de largo. Repara en algo que hay en la pared donde pegaron el bando y se vuelve a leerlo, muy interesado. El* CIEGO *no se mueve, pero sonríe.*

ESQUILACHE   (*Después de un momento.*) El pueblo sabe aún muy poco... Y quizá es ahora fácil presa de perturbadores sin ocupación... Tal vez de protegidos sin trabajo, (*Se miran fijamente.* ESQUILACHE *agita dos veces la campanilla y*

the country needed us to pull it back together. Nations must change if they are not to fade away forever.

VILLASANTA   Change in which direction, though? Towards the Encyclopaedia?[31] Towards the "Enlightenment"? Towards what you call "reason"? We call it, quite simply, heresy.

ESQUILACHE   (*Quivering slightly.*) There is no-one more pious than King Carlos, and you know that he would not want anyone at his side who was not a fervent Catholic.

VILLASANTA   Is that why you have put out the fires of the Holy Inquisition, then?[32]

ESQUILACHE   (*After a pause.*) Yes, we have, with a Christian (*Underlining the word.*) sense of compassion, put out the fires of the Inquisition, because these times have taught us that it is monstrous to burn human beings alive, even if they are heretics. Hell is part of the mystery of God, your Grace: let's not try to re-create it on earth.

VILLASANTA   That's just faint-heartedness, my Lord. Behind that faint-heartedness lurks disbelief, and I fear the worst if we don't stamp it out in time.

ESQUILACHE   What do you mean by "the worst"?

VILLASANTA   (*He stands up.*) The disappearance from Spain of our great religion.

ESQUILACHE   (*He laughs.*) You must have very little confidence in it if you think it can be made to disappear so easily. I'm sure that in a century or two from now, it won't occur to even the most intransigent of Catholics to burn someone alive for being a heretic. And that won't mean that religion will have disappeared. Those Catholics may think of themselves as direct inheritors of your tradition; but in reality they will be our successors. And that is the real secret: we are moving forward while you and your kind are refusing to move. But History does not stand still.

VILLASANTA   It's easy to talk about the future when one doesn't know what it will be like.

ESQUILACHE   Like you, I'm simply putting forward my predictions. Would you like me to give you another one?

VILLASANTA   (*With a slight, ironic bow.*) I'd be delighted.

ESQUILACHE   Anyone who will not change as the country changes will end up alone.

VILLASANTA   (*He laughs.*) Not just another act of hypocrisy, my Lord...?

ESQUILACHE   Why should it be?

VILLASANTA   Come, come, Minister. You must know that the people are tearing down your notices about capes and hats. They don't seem very willing to change...

The CESANTE *enters downstage right, and is about to pass by when he notices something on the wall where the notice was posted earlier. He stops to read it, with great interest. The blind* BALLAD-SELLER *does not move, but smiles.*

ESQUILACHE   (*After a moment's pause.*) The people are still ignorant... And at the moment they may be easy prey for agitators with time on their hands... Some of those hangers-on who've lost their jobs, perhaps? (*They stare at each other.*)

dice secamente:) Siento no poder atender a su petición, duque. No sería honesto.

VILLASANTA *enrojece y se dirige al foro. Allí se vuelve.*

VILLASANTA ¿Puedo, antes de retirarme, felicitar a usía por las brillantes carreras de sus hijos? (ESQUILACHE *se estremece. Ha sido tocado.*) Creo que el mayorcito es ya mariscal de campo... (*El* MAYORDOMO *entra.*) Es admirable, tan joven... Sin duda en el Ejército faltan generales: ha hecho muy bien usía en ascenderlo. (ESQUILACHE *se muerde los labios: no puede contestar.*) Siempre a sus pies, señor ministro.

Se inclina y sale. El MAYORDOMO *sale tras él y cierra.* ESQUILACHE *se recuesta sobre la mesa, profundamente turbado.*

CIEGO ¿Qué dice ese papel?
CESANTE (*Lo mira.*) ¿Eh? ¿Cómo sabe...?
CIEGO He notado que se paraba.
CESANTE (*Se rasca la cabeza y da unos pasos hacia el* CIEGO.) Pues dice... que se levantarán tres mil españoles contra Esquilache si no retira la orden... Muchos me parecen.
CIEGO Usté sabe que serán más. ¿O es que no le dice nada el señor duque de Medinaceli?
CESANTE (*Retrocede, asustado.*) ¿Eh?
CIEGO (*Ríe.*) No se asuste... Le recuerdo por la voz.

ESQUILACHE *mira hacia la puerta de la izquierda y se dirige lentamente hacia ella. Va a abrir, pero se detiene, dudoso.*

CESANTE Yo no sé nada. Yo no me meto en nada. Quede con Dios.

Sale, rápido, por la segunda izquierda. El CIEGO *ríe y pregona.*

CIEGO ¡El Gran Piscator de Salamanca, con los augurios para este año!

ESQUILACHE, *que iba a abrir la puerta, levanta la cabeza y escucha. Se pasa la mano por la frente tratando de sacudir su inquietud. Golpecitos en el foro.* ESQUILACHE *da unos pasos y alisa su casaca.*

ESQUILACHE Adelante.

Entra DOÑA PASTORA y cierra.

ESQUILACHE *(Rings the bell twice and says curtly:)* I regret that I cannot respond favourably to your petition, your Grace. It would not be proper.

VILLASANTA *reddens and sets off upstage. At the door, he turns around.*

VILLASANTA   Before I leave, will you allow me to congratulate you on the brilliant careers of your sons? (ESQUILACHE *twitches. This has hit home.*) Your biggest boy's already a field marshal, isn't he? (*The* STEWARD *comes in.*) So young, and he's done very well... I suppose they must be short of generals in the army: you were right to promote him. (ESQUILACHE *bites his lip: there is nothing he can say.*) Your servant, sir.

He bows and goes out. The STEWARD *follows him out and closes the door.* ESQUILACHE *leans on his desk, deeply troubled.*

BALLAD-SELLER   What does it say, then, that piece of paper?
CESANTE   *(Staring at him in surprise.)* Eh? How did you know...?
BALLAD-SELLER   I noticed that you stopped.
CESANTE   *(Scratches his head and moves a few steps towards the blind man.)* Well, it says... that there'll be three thousand Spaniards who'll rise up against Esquilache if he doesn't withdraw his decree... Sounds a lot to me.
BALLAD-SELLER   There'll be even more, you know that. Or doesn't your Duke of Medinaceli tell you anything?
CESANTE   *(Recoiling, startled.)* What?!
BALLAD-SELLER   *(With a laugh.)* Don't be so jumpy... I recognized you from your voice.

ESQUILACHE *looks towards the door at the left of the stage and walks slowly towards it. As he is about to open it, he hesitates.*

CESANTE   I don't know anything. I don't get involved in anything. Goodbye.

He goes off rapidly upstage left. The BALLAD-SELLER *laughs and begins again with his cry.*

BALLAD-SELLER   The Great Piscator of Salamanca, with all the predictions for this year!

ESQUILACHE, *on the point of opening the door, raises his head and listens. He rubs his forehead as if attempting to wipe away his troubles. Someone taps on the door at the back of the stage.* ESQUILACHE *takes a few steps towards it and straightens his coat.*

ESQUILACHE   Come in.

PASTORA *comes in and closes the door behind her.*

DOÑA PASTORA ¿Me has llamado?

ESQUILACHE Sí. ¿Quieres sentarte?

DOÑA PASTORA Déjame antes preguntarte una cosa: ¿Es cierto que has ordenado el pase a tu servicio de Fernandita?

ESQUILACHE (*Titubea.*) Pensaba decírtelo ahora. Supongo que no te costará trabajo sustituirla.

DOÑA PASTORA (*Se sienta.*) No es tan fácil. Tiene manos primorosas para los dulces.

ESQUILACHE Por eso mismo... He notado que los de ella no me despiertan el dolor.

DOÑA PASTORA Puedes quedártela. Al fin y al cabo, no me agradaba.

ESQUILACHE ¿Por qué?

DOÑA PASTORA Demasiado natural con sus superiores. Pero yo creo que es una hipócrita.

ESQUILACHE *desvía la vista.*

ESQUILACHE Tal vez.

DOÑA PASTORA ¿Qué me querías? (*Un silencio.* ESQUILACHE *saca sus espejuelos y se acerca para mirar un broche que la marquesa lleva en el pecho.*) ¿Te gusta mi broche? ¿Verdad que es bonito?

ESQUILACHE Nunca te lo vi.

DOÑA PASTORA Lo acabo de comprar. Y muy barato, no creas, porque...

ESQUILACHE (*La interrumpe.*) Celebro que lo lleves puesto, pues así te ahorras un paseo a tus habitaciones. Dámelo.

DOÑA PASTORA (*Intenta levantarse.*) ¿Qué?...

ESQUILACHE (*Violento, la obliga a permanecer sentada.*) ¡Dame ese broche!

DOÑA PASTORA ¡Es mío!

ESQUILACHE (*Mordiendo la palabra, echa mano al broche.*) ¡Dámelo!...

DOÑA PASTORA (*Forcejea.*) ¡No me pongas la mano encima! (ESQUILACHE *se lo arranca y se aparta, agitado, mientras ella se levanta, iracunda.*) ¡Eres repugnante!

ESQUILACHE, *que miraba el broche con detenimiento, le lanza una ojeada. Luego deja el broche sobre la mesa.*

ESQUILACHE El pobre imbécil me estuvo mareando durante todo el banquete con ese cargo que desea en las Indias. Pero cometió la torpeza de insinuarme que te había enviado ya un regalo... Mi Policía ha hecho lo demás. Esta mañana tenía yo la descripción de la joya que había comprado para ti: ésta. (*Un silencio.*) Un regalo más que aceptas a mis espaldas, y con un descaro que no quiero comentar, porque tú no ibas a interceder por él: te lo tengo prohibido. (*Un silencio.*) Hay mujeres en la Galera por cosas así, pero con la diferencia de que

PASTORA Did you call for me?

ESQUILACHE Yes, I did. Won't you sit down?

PASTORA Let me ask you something first. Is it true that you've had Fernandita transferred to your personal staff?

ESQUILACHE (*Hesitantly.*) I... I was going to tell you now. Surely you'll be able to replace her easily enough.

PASTORA (*Sits down.*) Well, it's not that easy. She's very good with confectionery.

ESQUILACHE That's why I need her... I've found that the things she makes for me don't bring on my pain.

PASTORA You can keep her. In any case, I've never really liked her.

ESQUILACHE Why not?

PASTORA She can be too familiar with her betters. But I think she's a hypocrite.

ESQUILACHE *looks away.*

ESQUILACHE Possibly.

PASTORA What was it you wanted me for? (*A moment of silence.* ESQUILACHE *takes out his glasses and goes up to his wife in order to take a closer look at a brooch she is wearing on her bosom.*) Do you like my brooch? Pretty, isn't it?

ESQUILACHE I haven't seen it on you before.

PASTORA I've only just bought it. And it didn't cost much, you know, because...

ESQUILACHE (*Interrupting her.*) I'm glad you've got it on. That saves you from having to go your rooms to get it. Give it to me.

PASTORA (*Tries to get up.*) What?...

ESQUILACHE (*Roughly, he forces her down onto the chair.*) Give me that brooch!

PASTORA It's mine!

ESQUILACHE (*Snarling as he grabs hold of the brooch.*) Give it to me!...

PASTORA (*Struggling.*) Get your hands off me! (ESQUILACHE *rips it off and moves away, panting agitatedly, while she jumps to her feet in a rage.*) You're despicable!

ESQUILACHE, *after examining the brooch carefully, glances at her. Then he puts the brooch on the desk.*

ESQUILACHE The poor fool was pestering me through the whole of the banquet about that post he's after in the West Indies. But he made the mistake of hinting that he'd already sent you a present... My police did the rest. By this morning I had a description of the jewel he'd bought you: this one. (*A pause.*) Yet another gift accepted behind my back, and this time with a brazenness that I won't bother to comment on, since you weren't going to be able to intercede on his behalf: I forbid it. There are women in prison for doing this kind of thing, the only difference being that they've swindled on a smaller scale than you.

han estafado menos. (*DOÑA PASTORA va a cruzar.*) ¡Aguarda! Contéstame antes de salir a una pregunta: ¿Debo yo darle a ese aprovechado el cargo que quiere para robar a manos llenas, o debo dejar en mal lugar a mi esposa y devolverle el broche?... ¿Callas?... El broche será devuelto con una excusa cortés.

DOÑA PASTORA ¿Puedo ya retirarme?

ESQUILACHE (*Suspira.*) Aún no, Pastora... Debo decirte algo muy grave y te aconsejo que vuelvas a sentarte.

DOÑA PASTORA Estoy bien de pie.

ESQUILACHE (*Cansado.*) ¿Sí? Yo no... (*Se sienta, con cara de malestar.*) Y debo decírtelo... (*Sonríe en medio de un rictus doloroso.*) ¡Este estúpido dolor que me toma cuando menos falta hace... no lo va a impedir! (*Jadea, sin poder hablar.*)

DOÑA PASTORA (*Con una vengativa sonrisa.*) Estoy esperando.

ESQUILACHE Tú eres la culpable... de mi mala fama... Entre tú y nuestros hijos... se destruye mi obra entera todos los días... Y ya no hay solución... Ya sólo queda... un remedio.

DOÑA PASTORA ¿Cuál?

ESQUILACHE *se incorpora un poco y suspira.*

ESQUILACHE ¡Ah!... Ya se pasa. (*La mira.*) He decidido pedir al rey la renovación de todos los cargos de nuestros hijos...

DOÑA PASTORA ¿Qué has dicho?

ESQUILACHE (*Voz llena.*) Y nuestra separación.

DOÑA PASTORA (*Grita.*) ¿Estás loco?

ESQUILACHE ¡Ni una palabra, te lo ruego! Mi decisión es firme.

DOÑA PASTORA (*Roja de ira.*) ¡No te atreverás a cometer semejante desatino, imbécil! ¡No destruirás tu hogar, porque también es el mío! ¿Lo oyes? ¡Y si te atreves a...!

ESQUILACHE (*Fuerte.*) ¡Cállate!

DOÑA PASTORA ¡No me levantes la voz!

ESQUILACHE (*Grita.*) ¡Silencio he dicho! Es tarde ya para que pronuncies una sola palabra. Retírate.

DOÑA PASTORA ¡No te saldrás con la tuya! (*Y se encamina, rápida, hacia la izquierda.*)

ESQUILACHE ¡Pastora! (*Ella se vuelve.*) Por allí. (*Señala al foro.*)

DOÑA PASTORA (*Reanuda su marcha.*) Voy a mi tocador.

ESQUILACHE ¡Por ahí, no!

DOÑA PASTORA ¿También me vas a prohibir en mi casa que vaya por donde quiera?

Va a la puerta de la izquierda y la abre, antes de que él pueda impedirlo.

(PASTORA *sets off across the stage.*) Wait! Before you go, just answer one question. What should I do: give that crook the post he wants so that he can line his pockets, or embarrass my wife by sending the brooch back?... Well? No answer?... The brooch will be sent back with a polite excuse.

PASTORA   May I go now?

ESQUILACHE   (*With a sigh.*) Not yet, Pastora... I've something very serious to say to you, and I'd advise you to sit down again.

PASTORA   I'm fine standing up.

ESQUILACHE   (*Wearily.*) Are you? I'm not... (*He sits down, showing discomfort.*) And I must tell you this... (*Grimacing as he winces with pain.*) This damned pain that hits me at the most awkward moments... is not going to stop me! (*He pants, unable to speak for a moment.*)

PASTORA   (*With a vengeful smirk.*) I'm waiting.

ESQUILACHE   You're to blame... for the damage that's being done to my reputation... Every day, you and our sons between you... are ruining everything I've achieved... And it can't go on... There's only one thing for it now.

PASTORA   And what's that?

ESQUILACHE *sits up and takes a deep breath.*

ESQUILACHE   Ah!... Now it's going. (*He looks at her.*) I've decided to ask the king to remove our sons from all their official positions...

PASTORA   What did you say?

ESQUILACHE   (*Now speaking perfectly clearly.*) And to allow us to separate.

PASTORA   (*Shouting.*) Have you gone mad?!

ESQUILACHE   Not a word, please! My decision is final.

PASTORA   (*Red with rage.*) You fool! You wouldn't dare do something so stupid! You're not going to break up your home, because it's mine too! Do you hear me? And if you dare to...!

ESQUILACHE   (*Loudly.*) Shut up!

PASTORA   Don't shout at me!

ESQUILACHE   (*Bellows at her.*) I said hold your tongue! It's too late for you to try to say anything. Get out.

PASTORA   You won't get away with it! (*And she heads rapidly towards the left.*)

ESQUILACHE   Pastora! (*She turns around.*) This way. (*Pointing upstage.*)

PASTORA   (*Continuing on her way.*) I'm going to my dressing room.

ESQUILACHE   Not that way!

PASTORA   So now you're going to tell me where I can and can't go in my own house, are you?

She goes to the door at the left and opens it, before he can stop her.

ESQUILACHE (*Da unos pasos tras ella.*) ¡Pastora!

DOÑA PASTORA *se ha parado en seco al mirar al interior. Despacio, vuelve a cerrar y se enfrenta con su marido.*

DOÑA PASTORA (*Con maligna sonrisa.*) Debí comprenderlo antes.

ESQUILACHE (*Se aparta, irritado.*) No hay nada que comprender.

DOÑA PASTORA (*Tras él.*) El señor marqués sueña a la vejez con una vida nueva, ¿verdad? Quizá no ha olvidado aún los versos del Dante. (*Ríe.*) ¡Ah, cómo te conozco!

ESQUILACHE ¡Cállate!

DOÑA PASTORA Pero claro: el senor marqués es muy honesto. Antes hay que repudiar a la mujer y a los hijos. ¡Todo el equipaje por la borda!

ESQUILACHE ¡Sal inmediatamente!

DOÑA PASTORA (*Ríe.*) Descuida... Me guardaré de intervenir en tu idilio con esa intrigante. (*Con la mano en el pomo de la puerta del fondo.*) Pero cuídate... (*Ríe.*) Ya no eres un mozo... (*Dura.*) Y guárdate de mí.

Abre y sale, cerrando de golpe. ESQUILACHE *permanece inmóvil, muy turbado, mirando hacia la izquierda. Al fin se decide, va a la puerta y la abre.*

ESQUILACHE Puedes retirar el servicio, Fernandita. (FERNANDITA *entra con la bandeja del chocolate y se encamina al foro. El no la pierde de vista.*) Un momento... (*Ella se vuelve y aventura una sonrisa.*) Deja eso allí. (*Ella deja la bandeja en la consola.*) Y siéntate.

FERNANDITA (*Vacila.*) Señor marqués...

ESQUILACHE (*Brusco.*) ¡Vamos, siéntate! ¿Qué esperas?

FERNANDITA (*Turbada.*) Con su permiso, señor. (*Se sienta, muy envarada.*)

ESQUILACHE *está junto a la mesa. La considera un momento, enigmático; toma el broche y se acerca a ella.*

ESQUILACHE ¿Te gusta?

FERNANDITA ¡Oh!... ¡Qué hermosura!

ESQUILACHE (*Ríe.*) ¡Dejarías de ser mujer si no te gustase!

FERNANDITA (*Ingenua.*) No, señor. Es que es muy bonito.

ESQUILACHE (*Entre risas.*) ¡Ah! ¡La terrible, la irresistible ingenuidad!

FERNANDITA No comprendo.

ESQUILACHE (*Baja la voz.*) ¿Te gustaría que te regalase este broche?

FERNANDITA (*Asombrada.*) ¿A mí?

ESQUILACHE ¿Te gustaría?

ESQUILACHE (*Taking a few steps after her.*) Pastora!

PASTORA *has stopped dead as soon as she looks into the room. Slowly, she closes the door again and turns to face her husband.*

PASTORA (*With a malicious smile.*) I should have realized sooner what was going on, shouldn't I?

ESQUILACHE (*Moves away, annoyed.*) There's nothing going on.

PASTORA (*Following him.*) His lordship is fantasizing about a new life in his old age, isn't he? Perhaps he still hasn't forgotten those lines from Dante. (*She laughs.*) Oh, I know you so well!

ESQUILACHE That's enough!

PASTORA But of course his lordship is ever so scrupulous. He has to ditch his wife and children first. Toss everything overboard!

ESQUILACHE Get out of here at once!

PASTORA (*Laughing.*) Don't worry... I'll stay out of the way of your little idyll with that scheming bitch. (*With her hand on the handle of the door at the back of the stage.*) But do be careful... (*Another snigger.*) You're not as young as you were... (*Harshly.*) And don't underestimate me.

She opens the door and sweeps out, slamming it behind her. ESQUILACHE *is left standing still, very upset, looking towards stage left. He finally makes up his mind, goes to the door and opens it.*

ESQUILACHE   You can clear away the chocolate things now, Fernandita. (FERNANDITA *comes in with the tray and heads upstage. He does not take his eyes off her.*) Just a moment... (*She turns towards him and smiles faintly.*) Leave that there. (*She puts the tray down on the console table.*) And sit down.

FERNANDITA (*Hesitates.*) My Lord...

ESQUILACHE (*Brusquely.*) Go on, sit down! What are you waiting for?

FERNANDITA (*Unsettled.*) Begging your pardon, sir. (*She sits down, very stiffly.*)

ESQUILACHE *is standing next to his desk. He observes her for a moment with an enigmatic expression; then picks up the brooch and goes over to her.*

ESQUILACHE Do you like it?

FERNANDITA Oh!... It's beautiful!

ESQUILACHE (*With a chuckle.*) You wouldn't be a woman if you didn't like it!

FERNANDITA (*Innocently.*) It's not that, sir. It's just that it's very nice.

ESQUILACHE (*With an ironic laugh.*) Ah, that terrible, irresistible innocence!

FERNANDITA I don't know what you mean.

ESQUILACHE (*Lowering his voice.*) Would you like me to give you this brooch?

FERNANDITA (*Astonished.*) Give it to me?

ESQUILACHE Would you like me to?

FERNANDITA   (*Después de un momento, baja los ojos.*) No. señor. Esas cosas no se han hecho para muchachas como yo.

ESQUILACHE   (*Va a la mesa y tira el broche sobre ella.*) Dime una cosa, Fernandita: ¿Crees que te he ofrecido el broche de verdad?

FERNANDITA   (*Compungida.*) A mí me parece... A mí me gustaría creer... que era una broma de su merced.

ESQUILACHE   Y... ¿con qué cara me dices tú eso? ¿Lo has rechazado de corazón? Yo me he pasado la vida tratando de leer tras las caras... Es difícil.

FERNANDITA   (*Después de un momento.*) Su merced desconfía de mí.

ESQUILACHE   Y tú de mí. ¿No?

FERNANDITA   (*Llorosa.*) Yo... no sé...

El se acerca. Le levanta la barbilla.

ESQUILACHE   Lágrimas. He visto muchas lágrimas.

FERNANDITA   Permítame su merced que me retire.

ESQUILACHE   Si tú lo quieres... (*Se aparta. Ella se levanta.*) Pero no desconfíes de mí. (*Ella va hacia la consola.*) Aunque te llame constantemente...

FERNANDITA   Me llama cuando necesita que le sirva algo...

ESQUILACHE   No. Lo hago porque quiero tenerte cerca. (*Ella baja los ojos.*) Aunque sin ninguna mala intención. ¿Puedes tú comprender eso?

FERNANDITA   Sí, señor.

ESQUILACHE   (*Suspira.*) Pero no debo hacerlo más... Que se piense mal de mí es inevitable, pero no tengo derecho a que a ti te difamen. (*Suspira.*) Ahora retírate.

FERNANDiTA *recoge la bandeja y va al foro. Allí se vuelve.*

FERNANDITA   (*Con un extraño anhelo.*) A mí no me importan las habladurías... ¡Si a su merced le agrada llamarme, no deje de hacerlo!...

ESQUILACHE   (*Que vuelve a desconfiar.*) Retírate ahora. (*Agita una vez la campanilla. La puerta se abre y entra el* SECRETARIO. *Ella se inclina y sale.*) Recoja esa carpeta: vamos al Consejo de Hacienda. (CAMPOS *lo hace.* ESQUILACHE *se encamina al foro. Se detiene, pensativo, y saca su reloj.*) Si el señor Corregidor se ha movido, estarán ya instalando puestos en todos los barrios. ¿Quiere mirar si hay ya alguno en la plaza?

CAMPOS   Sí, excelencia. (*Se acerca al ventanal.*) No veo nada... Pero por Infantas desembocan ahora cuatro alguaciles y un paisano.

ESQUILACHE   Ellos deben de ser. *Andiamo presto.*

Sale, seguido de CAMPOS, *que cierra. Inmediatamente después de las palabras de éste, han aparecido por la segunda derecha* CRISANTO *y* ROQUE, *seguidos de un*

FERNANDITA   (*After a moment, she lowers her eyes.*) No, my Lord. Things like that
    are not meant for girls like me.

ESQUILACHE   (*Goes to the desk and tosses the brooch onto it.*) Tell me something,
    Fernandita. Do you think I was really offering to give you the brooch?

FERNANDITA   (*Chastened.*) Well, I suppose... I'd like to think that... that your
    Lordship was just playing a joke on me.

ESQUILACHE   And... I wonder what sort of face it is that you put on to say that? Did
    you really not want it? I've spent my whole life trying to read what lies behind
    people's faces... It's very difficult.

FERNANDITA   (*After a moment's pause.*) You don't trust me, do you, my Lord?

ESQUILACHE   Nor you me. Am I right?

FERNANDITA   (*Beginning to break down into tears.*) I... I don't know...

He goes up to her, and lifts her chin.

ESQUILACHE   Tears. I've seen a lot of tears.

FERNANDITA   Please, sir, let me go.

ESQUILACHE   If that's what you want... (*He moves away from her. She gets up.*) But
    don't distrust me. (*She goes towards the console table.*) Even if I do keep
    calling for you constantly...

FERNANDITA   You call for me when you need me to bring you something...

ESQUILACHE   No. I call for you because I want to have you near me. (*She looks
    down.*) But no more than that, I promise you. Can you understand that?

FERNANDITA   Yes, my Lord.

ESQUILACHE   (*He sighs.*) But I shouldn't do it any more... It's inevitable that they
    should think badly of me, but I've no right to let them throw mud at you. (*Sighs
    again.*) Now you may go.

FERNANDITA *picks up the tray and goes upstage. When she gets there, she turns
around.*

FERNANDITA   (*With surprising eagerness.*) I don't care what people say... If your
    Lordship likes to call for me, then you should!

ESQUILACHE   (*Distrustful again.*) You may go now. (*He rings the bell once. The
    door opens and* CAMPOS *comes in.* FERNANDITA *curtsies and goes out.*)
    Take that portfolio. Let's go to the Treasury meeting. (CAMPOS *does so.*
    ESQUILACHE *walks upstage. He stops, thoughtfully, and takes out his
    watch.*) If the Mayor has done his job, they should be setting up their stalls all
    over the city by now. Would you see if there's one down in the square yet?

CAMPOS   Of course, your Excellency. (*He goes over to the window.*) No, I can't see
    anything...   But wait: there is someone coming down Infantas with four
    constables right now.

ESQUILACHE   That must be them. *Andiamo presto.*

Exit, followed by CAMPOS, *who closes the door behind them. Just after* CAMPOS's
remark that he could see them coming, CRISANTO *and* ROQUE *have appeared*

PAISANO *con un capacho y dos* ALGUACILES *más.* CRISANTO *se dirige en seguida al portal y entra en él.* ROQUE *repara en el pasquín, lo arranca y permanece junto a la esquina. El* PAISANO *aguarda en medio de la escena. El* ALGUACIL 1º *se dirige al* CIEGO *y el* 2º *se sitúa estratégicamente a la izquierda.*

ALGUACIL 1º   Váyase de aquí, abuelo.
CIEGO   ¿Por qué?
ROQUE   (*Alto.*) ¡Puede caerle algún golpe!
CIEGO   (*Se levanta, risueño.*) Los golpes llueven sobre quien menos se lo piensa, seor alguacil.
ALGUACIL 1º   Por eso mismo debe irse.
CIEGO   ¡Lástima! ¡Con el sol tan rico que cae ahora! Gracias de todos modos por el aviso. Y que Dios le guarde.

Sale por la segunda izquierda y el ALGUACIL 1º *se sitúa en ella después de verle marchar.* CRISANTO *sale del portal.*

CRISANTO   Ya tiene mesa y silla dispuesta, maestro. (DOÑA MARÍA *se asoma al balcón, muy intrigada.*) ¡Pero no se canse! Los sombreros, con alfileres, y a las capas, la tijera.
PAISANO   (*Se encamina al portal.*) ¡Vaya chapuza!
ROQUE   ¡No rechiste!
CRISANTO   ¡Calma!...

El PAISANO *entra en el portal.*

DOÑA MARÍA   (*A* CRISANTO) Seor alguacil, ¿qué ocurre?
ROQUE   ¡Métase para dentro!
CRISANTO   ¡Déjala, hombre!   Está en su casa.   (DOÑA MARÍA *se mete refunfuñando, pero atisba tras los visillos. Una pausa. De pronto, el* ALGUACIL 1º *sisea y señala a la primera derecha. Por ella entra un* HOMBRE *del pueblo, embozado, que cruza.*) ¡Eh, paisano! (*El embozado mira a los alguaciles y se baja el embozo.*) ¿No ha leído el bando?
EMBOZADO 1º   Precisamente me lo iba diciendo: en cuanto llegue a casa le digo a la parienta que me recorte la capa y me apunte el sombrero.

Con una muda risita, ROQUE *se va acercando a él.*

ROQUE   (*Le pone la mano encima y le empuja hacia el portal.*) Aquí, salvo la multa, te lo hacemos de balde.
EMBOZADO 1º   ¿Qué?
ROQUE   Verás qué guapo te dejamos.

upstage right, followed by a man with a basket and two other constables. CRISANTO *immediately goes towards the house at the right of the stage and through the door.* ROQUE *notices the poster on the wall, tears it down and remains by the corner. The* TAILOR *waits centre stage. The* 1ST CONSTABLE *goes over towards the* BALLAD-SELLER, *while the* 2ND CONSTABLE *takes up a strategic position at the left.*

1ST CONSTABLE You'd better move on, old man.
BALLAD-SELLER Why?
1ST CONSTABLE (*Loudly.*) You might get hurt.
BALLAD-SELLER (*Gets to his feet, grinning.*) It's the people who least expect it who can get hurt, isn't it, constable?
1ST CONSTABLE Right. So you'd better get out of the way.
BALLAD-SELLER What a shame! Just when I was nicely settled here in the sun. Anyway, thanks for the warning. God be with you.

Exit upstage left. The 1ST CONSTABLE *stations himself on the corner around which the blind man has gone.* CRISANTO *emerges from the door of the house.*

CRISANTO (*To the* TAILOR.) There's a table and chair set up for you in there. (DOÑA MARÍA *pokes her head out at the balcony, very intrigued.*) And keep at it! You know what to do: pins for the hats, scissors for the capes.
TAILOR (*Heading towards the door.*) Bloody marvellous line of work I've got myself into here!
ROQUE Shut your mouth and get on with it!
CRISANTO All right, keep calm!

The TAILOR *goes in through the door.*

MARÍA (*To* CRISANTO.) Hey, constable, what's going on?
ROQUE Get back inside!
CRISANTO Leave her alone! She's in her own house. (MARÍA *withdraws, muttering to herself, but spies through the lace curtains. There is a pause. Suddenly, the* 1ST CONSTABLE *hisses and points downstage right. A man wrapped in a long cape appears and begins to cross the stage.*) Hey, you! (*The man looks at the constables and uncovers his face.*) Haven't you read the decree?
1ST EMBOZADO You know, I was just saying to myself: as soon as I get home, I'll get the wife to snip a bit off my cape and pin my hat up.

Smirking, ROQUE *sneaks up behind him.*

ROQUE (*Gets hold of him and pushes him towards the door.*) You can get it done here for nothing, except for the fine you'll have to pay.
1ST EMBOZADO What?
ROQUE We'll leave you looking a treat, just you wait and see.

EMBOZADO 1º Le juro, seor alguacil, que ahora mismo llego a casa y...
ROQUE   ¡Entra! (*Lo empuja y sale tras él.*)
ALGUACIL 1º ¡Allí se escurre otro! (*Señala.*)
ALGUACIL 2º ¡Deja, yo lo cazo!

Corre a la segunda izquierda y sale al punto empujando a otro embozado que, cosa rara, no trae sombrero, sino tan sólo la redecilla.

ALGUACIL 1º ¡Je! ¿Dónde se dejó usté el chambergo?

El EMBOZADO *lo mira y no contesta.*

ALGUACIL 2º   ¡Trae la capa!
EMBOZADO 2º (*Se resiste.*) ¡Es mía!
CRISANTO Toda no, buen mozo. Su majestad quiere una cuarta.

El ALGUACIL 2º *le quita la capa. El* EMBOZADO *oculta a la espalda el sombrero.*

ALGUACIL 1º (*Señala.*) ¡Mira qué sombrerito más lindo aparece por ahí!

El ALGUACIL 2º *vuelve al* EMBOZADO *para verlo.*

ALGUACIL 2º ¡Y qué redondito! (*Risas.*) ¿Es que le está chico, paisano?
EMBOZADO 2º No, señor.
ALGUACIL 2º Si no se lo pone se va a constipar. Venga conmigo.

Lo lleva al portal, donde aparece el EMBOZADO 1º *con la capa al brazo. Tras él,* ROQUE. *Los dos embozados se miran.*

CRISANTO ¿Pagó la multa?
ROQUE   ¡Pues claro! (*El* EMBOZADO 2º *y el* ALGUACIL 2º *entran en el portal.*
        ROQUE *tira de la capa del* EMBOZADO 1º.) ¿No te la pones?
EMBOZADO 1º No tengo frío. (ROQUE *le encasqueta el chambergo, al que le han
        apuntado los tres candiles con alfileres, y el* EMBOZADO *se lo quita al
        punto.*)
ROQUE   ¡Anda a tus asuntos!

El EMBOZADO 1º *sale, furioso, por la segunda izquierda.*

ALGUACIL 1º ¡Recuerdos a la parienta! (*Risas de* ROQUE.)
CRISANTO Sin ofender... (*Las risas cesan.*) Atención, que ahí viene otro. Y muy
        tranquilo. (*En efecto: por la primera izquierda entra otro* EMBOZADO *de*

1ST EMBOZADO   No, honestly, constable, I was just on my way home and...
ROQUE   Get in there! (*He shoves him through the door and follows.*)
1ST CONSTABLE   There's another one trying to get away! (*Pointing.*)
2ND CONSTABLE   All right, I'll get him!

He dashes off upstage left and returns at once pushing in front of him another man in a cape, who, unusually, is not wearing a hat, only his hairnet.

1ST CONSTABLE   Ha! Where did you leave your hat, then, mate?

The man glares at him without answering.

2ND CONSTABLE   Let's have that cape!
2ND EMBOZADO   (*Struggling.*) No, it's mine!
CRISANTO   Not all of it, my friend. His Majesty wants a quarter of it.

The 2ND CONSTABLE *pulls the cape off him. The man was hiding his hat underneath it, on his back.*

1ST CONSTABLE   (*Points at the hat.*) Well, well, look what's turned up under here!

The 2ND CONSTABLE *turns him around so that he can have a look.*

2ND CONSTABLE   Nice and round, isn't it? (*They snigger.*) What's the matter with it, a bit small for you?
2ND EMBOZADO   No.
2ND CONSTABLE   Well, if you don't put it on you'll catch your death of cold. Come along with me.

He drags him to the door, out of which emerges the 1ST EMBOZADO *with his cape over his arm.* ROQUE *comes out behind him. The two victims look at each other.*

CRISANTO   Did he pay the fine, then?
ROQUE   Of course he did! (*The* 2ND EMBOZADO *and the* 2ND CONSTABLE *go through the door.* ROQUE *tugs at the* 1ST EMBOZADO's *cape.*) What, not putting it on?
1ST EMBOZADO   I'm not cold. (ROQUE *puts his hat on for him, now pinned up into three points, but he whips it off again at once.*)
ROQUE   Go on, get out of here!

The man storms off upstage right.

1ST CONSTABLE   Give my regards to your missus! (*Guffaws from* ROQUE.)
CRISANTO   Don't overdo it, lads... (*The laughter stops.*) Watch out, here comes another one. Cocky too, by the looks of him. (*Sure enough, another man*

andares despaciosos y petulantes. Mira con descaro al ALGUACIL 1º, *después a los otros y, contoneándose, da unos pasos hacia el centro de la escena.*) Alto, paisano. ¿No leyó el bando?

EMBOZADO 3º   (*En jaque.*) ¡Velay!

CRISANTO   ¿Velay? ¿Y qué es velay?

EMBOZADO 3º   ¡Que sí! ¡Que lo he leído!

CRISANTO   ¿Y por qué no lo cumple!

EMBOZADO 3º   ¡Porque no me da la gana!

ROQUE   ¡Bocazas!

Va hacia él. El ALGUACIL 1º *se adelanta también. El* EMBOZADO *retrocede rápido y saca una mano armada de temible facón.* DOÑA MARÍA *asoma a su balcón y sigue el incidente con expresivos gestos de simpatía por el embozado.*

EMBOZADO 3º   ¡Quietos! ¡Al que se acerque, lo ensarto!

ROQUE   (*Mientras desenvaina.*) ¡Vas a probar ésta, bergante!

CRISANTO   (*Se acerca.*) ¡Rodéalo! (*El* ALGUACIL 1º *lo rodea.*) ¡No resista, que le costará caro! (*Desenvaina.*)

EMBOZADO 3º   ¡A ver quién es el guapo!

El ALGUACIL 1º *lo sujeta por detrás. Los otros dos caen sobre él.*

CRISANTO   ¡Suelta eso!

ROQUE   ¡Gran bestia!

EMBOZADO 3º   ¡Atrás! (*Su mano dibuja con la faca temibles molinetes.*)

ALGUACIL 1º   ¡Ah!... (*Gime. Le han herido. El* ALGUACIL 2º *aparece en el portal.*)

CRISANTO   ¡Aquí, aprisa! (*El* ALGUACIL 2º *corre a ayudarlos.*)

EMBOZADO 3º   ¡Dejadme! ¡Soltadme! ¡Me caso en...!

Pero logran reducirlo. CRISANTO *sujeta al* ALGUACIL 1º, *que desfallece.*

ROQUE   ¡Trae! (*Le arrebata el facón al embozado.*)

CRISANTO   (*Mientras pasa el brazo del* ALGUACIL 1º *por su cuello.*) Llevadlo. (*Al herido.*) Vamos al portal.

Lo lleva despacio mientras los otros dos empujan y golpean al embozado.

ROQUE   ¡A galeras vas a ir!

ALGUACIL 2º   ¡En la cárcel te pudrirás!

El embozado se resiste: lo golpean.

muffled in a cape enters downstage left, swaggering slowly and provocatively. He casts an insolent eye over the 1ST CONSTABLE, *then the rest of them, and struts towards the middle of the stage.*) Halt! Haven't you read the decree?

3RD EMBOZADO   (*Very cavalier.*) Why-aye!³³

CRISANTO   Why-aye? What's that supposed to mean?

3RD EMBOZADO   Yes, I've read it, man! So?

CRISANTO   And why aren't you doing what it says?

3RD EMBOZADO   Because I don't feel like it!

ROQUE   Cheeky bugger!

ROQUE *moves towards him, as does the* 1ST CONSTABLE. *The man darts back a few steps and draws a long, vicious-looking knife.* DOÑA MARÍA *leans out at her balcony and follows the incident with obvious gestures of support for the man in the cape.*

3RD EMBOZADO   Stay where you are! Come near me and you'll be mincemeat!

ROQUE   (*Drawing his sword.*) You'll get a taste of this first!

CRISANTO   (*Closing in.*) Surround him! (*The* 1ST CONSTABLE *moves behind him.*) Don't resist, it's not worth it! (*Draws his sword.*)

3RD EMBOZADO   Come on, then, let's see if you've got the guts!

The 1ST CONSTABLE *grabs him from behind. The other two rush at him.*

CRISANTO   Drop it!

ROQUE   Got you, you bastard!

3RD EMBOZADO   Get off me! (*His hand traces fearsome swirls with the long, curved blade.*)

1ST CONSTABLE   Aaagh!... (*He groans. He has been wounded. The* 2ND CONSTABLE *appears in the doorway.*)

CRISANTO   Over here, quick! (*The* 2ND CONSTABLE *runs across to help.*)

3RD EMBOZADO   Get off me! Let me go, you bastards!

But they manage to subdue him. CRISANTO *supports the* 1ST CONSTABLE, *who is collapsing.*

ROQUE   Give me that! (*He grabs the knife from the man's hand.*)

CRISANTO   (*Putting the* 1ST CONSTABLE's *arm around his neck.*) Take him away. (*To the wounded man.*) Come on, let's get you inside.

He helps him slowly to the door, while the other two shove and punch the prisoner.

ROQUE   We're going to lock you up, mate!

2ND CONSTABLE   In the clink till you rot!

The man struggles against them: they beat him.

ROQUE ¡Vamos!

DOÑA MARÍA ¡No le peguen!...

EMBOZADO 3º ¡Viva el rey!... ¡Pero muera Esquilache!

ROQUE (*Puñetazo.*) ¡Camina!

EMBOZADO 3º ¡Muera Esquilache!... (*Salen por la segunda derecha, mientras* CRISANTO *mete en el portal al* ALGUACIL *herido. La voz desesperada del embozado se va perdiendo. La luz se amortigua.*) ¡Muera Esquilache! ¡Muera Esquilache!

El giratorio se desliza y presenta el ángulo de las dos puertas, oculto ahora por dos tapices donde se representan escenas venatorias. La escena se sume en total oscuridad, al tiempo que crece un alto foco blanco que ilumina, ante los tapices, a una curiosa figura. Es un hombre alto y enjuto de unos cincuenta años: la nariz prominente y derribada, la boca sumida y risueña, los ojos melancólicos. Viste sobrio atavío: un tricornio negro sin galón ni plumas, una casaca sin bordados, color corteza, chupa de ante galoneada de oro con cinturón del que pende un cuchillo de caza, pañuelo de batista al cuello y calzón y polainas negros. Con la derecha sostiene los blancos guantes de piel; con la izquierda, la larga escopeta de caza, que apoya en el suelo. El MARQUÉS DE ESQUILACHE *entra por la derecha, se acerca al giratorio, se arrodilla en las gradas y le pide la mano a besar: es el* REY CARLOS III.

EL REY ¿Tú aquí?

ESQUILACHE A los pies de vuestra majestad.

EL REY (*Le ayuda a levantarse.*) ¿Ocurre algo en Madrid?

ESQUILACHE Ha corrido la primera sangre, señor. A esta hora, son ya muchos los incidentes.

EL REY (*Sonríe.*) Viva el rey, muera el mal gobierno, ¿no? La fórmula es conocida. Pero yo no te quiero como víctima, Leopoldo. Mis ministros hacen lo que yo mando. Aclamarme mientras se les ataca me ofende: es suponer que soy tonto y no sé elegirlos. Pero tú y yo sabemos que no carezco de cierta inteligencia... (*Ríe y le da un golpecito en el hombro.*)

ESQUILACHE Vuestra majestad me abruma con sus bondades.

EL REY (*Apoya la escopeta contra la pared.*) La medida es justa: debes, pues, lograr que se cumpla. Pero sin violencias, ¿eh? Con toda la dulzura posible.

ESQUILACHE Sí, majestad .

EL REY Los españoles son como niños... Se quejan cuando se les lava la basura. Pero nosotros les adecentaremos aunque protesten un poco. Y, si podemos, les enseñaremos también un poco de lógica y un poco de piedad, cosas ambas de las que se encuentran bastante escasos. Quizá preferirían un tirano; pero nosotros hemos venido a reformar, no a tiranizar. (*Lo mira fijamente.*) Naturalmente, esa resistencia no es espontánea. La mueven quienes se resisten a todo cambio. Y también, ambiciones aisladas. ¿Me equivoco?

ROQUE   Right, let's go!
MARÍA   Don't hit him!
3RD EMBOZADO   God save the king!... Death to Esquilache!
ROQUE   (*Punches him.*) Go on, move!
3RD EMBOZADO   Death to Esquilache!... (*They go off upstage right, while* CRISANTO *helps the wounded constable into the house. The prisoner's voice fades away gradually. The lights dim.*) Death to Esquilache! Death to Esquilache!

The revolving platform turns to reveal the corner with two doors, covered at the moment by two tapestries featuring hunting scenes. While the rest of the stage remains in total darkness, a bright white spotlight picks out a curious figure standing in front of the tapestries. It shows a tall, lean man of about fifty, with a prominent, drooping nose, a sunken, smiling mouth and melancholy eyes. He is dressed plainly, in a black tricorn without braid or feathers, a brown coat without embroidery, a suede waistcoat trimmed with gold braid, a belt with a hunting knife, a cambric scarf around his neck, and black breeches and leggings. In his right hand he is holding white kid gloves; in his left, a long hunting gun, its butt resting on the ground. The MARQUIS OF ESQUILACHE *enters from the right, approaches the platform, kneels on the steps and kisses his hand: he is* KING CARLOS III.[34]

KING   Leopoldo, I'm surprised to see you here.[35]
ESQUILACHE   Your Majesty.
KING   (*Helps him to his feet.*) Is there trouble in Madrid?
ESQUILACHE   I'm afraid the first blood has been spilt, sire. The incidents are now multiplying.
KING   (*With a smile.*) God save the king, down with bad government. Is that it? It's a well-known formula. But I don't want you to be victimized over this, Leopoldo. My ministers do as I command them. To acclaim me while attacking them offends me: it's tantamount to suggesting that I am too stupid to choose the right ministers. But I think you and I know that I'm not entirely without intelligence... (*He chuckles and pats him on the shoulder.*)
ESQUILACHE   Your Majesty is too kind.
KING   (*Leans his gun against the wall.*) The measure is a just one: so you must make sure that it's carried out effectively. But without violence, mind you. As gently as possible.
ESQUILACHE   Yes, sire.
KING   The Spanish people are like children... They complain when they have the filth washed off them. But we shall clean them up even if they do protest a little. And if we can, we shall also teach them some logic and some godliness: they are rather short of both. Perhaps they would prefer a tyrant; but we've come here to reform, not to tyrannize. (*Looks at him steadily.*) Of course, this resistance isn't completely spontaneous. It's being stirred up by those who are opposed to all change. And a few individuals pursuing their own ambitions. Or am I wrong?

ESQUILACHE   No, majestad. Sin duda, muchos nobles mueven los hilos.

EL REY   ¿Nombres?

ESQUILACHE   Confieso mi torpeza... Aún no lo he puesto en claro...

EL REY   Quizá yo sepa algo más que tú de eso... Bien. Yo volveré a Madrid el veintidós, como de costumbre. Pero tenme informado hasta entonces. (*Saca su saboneta y mira la hora.*) ¿Algo más?

ESQUILACHE   (*Titubea.*) Confieso a vuestra majestad que estoy terriblemente perplejo... Traía un ruego, muy meditado y muy firme, y ahora no sé si debo hacerlo.

EL REY   Lo estudiaremos juntos.

ESQUILACHE   Señor: hace tiempo que me atormenta la evidencia de que la reputación de un ministro debe ser intachable en bien de su propio trabajo. Pero... vuestra majestad lo sabe... Mi esposa y mis hijos...

EL REY   ¿Cuál es tu ruego?

ESQUILACHE   (*Resuelto.*) Suplico a vuestra majestad que revoque los cargos que por su real bondad gozan inmerecidamente mis hijos mayores. Y en cuanto a mi esposa..., ruego a vuestra majestad que me permita separarme de ella. Vuestra majestad puede creerme: no existe ya solución mejor.

Baja la cabeza. El REY *lo mira, desciende de las gradas y da un paseíto. Sonríe.*

EL REY   ¿Quién es doña Fernandita?

ESQUILACHE   (*Se sobresalta y va a su lado.*) ¡Reconozco la mano de la marquesa! ¡Juro a vuestra majestad que nos ha calumniado! Es una muchacha de nuestra servidumbre; una criatura limpia y pura que...

EL REY   ¿Estás seguro?

ESQUILACHE   (*Vacila.*) Señor, yo...

EL REY   ¿La quieres?

ESQUILACHE   (*Después de un momento.*) Señor, soy un anciano.

EL REY   Pero ¿la quieres? (ESQUILACHE *baja la cabeza. El* REY *sonríe y pasea.*) ¿Sabes por qué eres mi predilecto, Leopoldo? Porque eres un soñador. Los demás se llenan la boca de las grandes palabras y, en el fondo, sólo esconden mezquindad y egoísmo. Tú estás hecho al revés: te ven por fuera como el más astuto y ambicioso, y eres un soñador ingenuo, capaz de los más finos escrúpulos de conciencia.

ESQUILACHE   Perdón, señor.

EL REY   ¿Perdón? No. España necesita soñadores que sepan de números, como tú... (*Baja la voz.*) Hace tiempo que yo sueño también con una reforma moral, y no sólo con reformas externas. Más adelante, si Dios nos sigue ayudando, te necesito para esa campaña: y si quieres iniciarla tú con un ejemplo de rectitud tan atrevido, te doy desde ahora, en nombre de mi país, las gracias. (ESQUILACHE *se inclina. El* REY *saca su saboneta.*) Un minuto de retraso.

ESQUILACHE   No, your Majesty. There's no doubt that there are noblemen pulling the strings.

KING   Any names?

ESQUILACHE   I have to confess that I've been slow... I'm still not absolutely sure...

KING   I may know more about this than you... Very well. I'll return to Madrid on the twenty-second, as usual. But keep me informed until then. (*He takes out his watch and looks at the time.*) Was there anything else?

ESQUILACHE   (*Hesitates.*) I must confess to your Majesty that I'm... torn. I was planning to ask you for something, something which I've thought over very carefully, but now I'm not sure if I should.

KING   We'll look at it together.

ESQUILACHE   Sire: for some time now I've been obsessed by the need to show that a minister's reputation should be unblemished for the sake of the integrity of his work. However..., as your Majesty is aware... My wife and my sons...

KING   What is it that you're asking for?

ESQUILACHE   (*His resolve regained.*) I wish to ask your Majesty to revoke the offices which my elder sons hold by your royal favour. And as for my wife..., I beg your Majesty to allow us to separate. I can assure you, sire: there is no better solution.

He bows his head. The KING *watches him, then steps down to the stage and begins to stroll around. He is smiling.*

KING   Who is doña Fernandita?

ESQUILACHE   (*Jumps up and goes to his side.*) I can see that my wife has been busy! Your Majesty, I swear that she's spreading slander about us! Fernandita is just a girl in our service; a sweet, pure young thing who...

KING   Are you sure?

ESQUILACHE   (*Vacillating.*) Sire, I...

KING   Do you love her?

ESQUILACHE   (*After a moment's pause.*) Sire, I am an old man.

KING   But do you love her? (ESQUILACHE *looks down. The* KING *smiles and strolls on.*) Do you know why you're my favourite, Leopoldo? Because you're a dreamer, an idealist. The others mouth fine words, but underneath it all, there's only small-mindedness and egotism. You are the other way around: from the outside, people see you as the most cunning and ambitious of all, whereas you're really an ingenuous dreamer, capable of showing the purest moral scruples.

ESQUILACHE   Forgive me, sire.

KING   Forgive you? No, no. Spain needs people like you: dreamers who know how to handle numbers... (*Lowers his voice.*) For some time now I too have been dreaming of achieving moral reform, going beyond the external reforms we have been concentrating on up to now. Later, if God continues to assist us, I shall need you for that campaign; and if you wish to start it now by setting such a bold example of rectitude, then I thank you, in the name of my country. (ESQUILACHE *bows. The* KING *takes out his watch.*) One minute late. (*He*

(*Va a recoger su escopeta.*) Y el rey debe enseñar también a los españoles la virtud de la puntualidad. (*Suspira y sonríe.*) Y ahora, a fatigarme con la caza. Es una cura que le impongo a mi pobre sangre enferma... Pero en Madrid creerán que lo hago por divertirme. No te preocupes demasiado por lo que de ti digan: ya ves que es inevitable. (*Se lleva levemente la mano al corazón.*) Nuestro juez es otro. (*El* REY *va a salir por la abertura de los tapices.* ESQUILACHE *se arrodilla. El* REY *se vuelve y le envía una penetrante mirada.*) Tienes miedo, ¿verdad?

ESQUILACHE Quizá es que estoy viejo, señor.

EL REY Dios te guarde, Leopoldo.*(Sale)*

ESQUILACHE *se levanta despacio y, pensativo, se cala el tricornio: sube las gradas y sale por el mismo sitio. El foco de luz se amortigua hasta desaparecer y una claridad suave, crepuscular, vuelve a la escena. Se oye el lejano pregón del* CIEGO.

CIEGO (*Voz de.*) El Noticioso para hoy, veintidós de marzo... Con todas las ceremonias que se celebrarán en la Pascua de Nuestro Señor...

Entretanto, el giratorio se desliza y presenta el gabinete de ESQUILACHE. *El marqués, sentado a la mesa, firma con aire cansado documentos que* CAMPOS, *a su lado, recoge. El* MAYORDOMO, *en pie junto a la puerta del fondo.*

ESQUILACHE Firmar y firmar... (*Arroja la pluma.*) A veces me parece como firmar en la arena.

CAMPOS Muy cierto, excelencia.

ESQUILACHE ¡No me dé siempre la razón! ¡Discuta!... (*Se levanta y pasea. Un silencio.*) Y usted, ¿qué hace ahí como un pasmarote?

SECRETARIO y MAYORDOMO *se miran.*

MAYORDOMO Espero las órdenes de su excelencia para el viaje a San Fernando.

ESQUILACHE (*A* CAMPOS.) ¿Usía está preparado?

CAMPOS Sí, excelencia. Podemos salir cuando lo desee.

ESQUILACHE ¿Y ese montón de papeluchos?

CAMPOS Los enviaré con un ayudante antes de partir.

ESQUILACHE ¡Hum!... Me ahorraría con gusto la excursión. Pero Grimaldi la concertó hace un mes y no hay medio de convencerle. "Para descansar con los amigos y hablar italiano." Esa es la tontería que dijo. *Bene. Parleremo il toscano.* (*Se para ante* CAMPOS.) ¿Qué era lo que tenía que contar?

CAMPOS (*Baja la voz.*) Se trata de... doña Fernandita.

Un silencio. ESQUILACHE *saca el reloj. Después, al* MAYORDOMO:

goes to pick up his gun.) And another thing the king should teach the people of Spain is the virtue of punctuality. (*He sighs and smiles.*) And now, some exercise with the hunt. I do it because it's good for my weak blood... Although in Madrid they'll think that it's just for enjoyment. Don't worry too much about what they may say about you: you can't do anything about it. (*He raises his hand slightly towards his heart.*) They are not our judge. (*The* KING *prepares to leave through the opening in the tapestries.* ESQUILACHE *kneels. The* KING *turns and looks down at him penetratingly.*) You're afraid, aren't you?

ESQUILACHE   Perhaps it's just that I'm getting old, sire.

KING   God be with you, Leopoldo. (*Exit.*)

ESQUILACHE *gets up slowly, and thoughtfully puts on his hat: he climbs the steps and goes out through the same opening. The spotlight fades out and a soft, twilight glow covers the stage. The* BALLAD-SELLER's *cry can be heard in the distance.*

BALLAD-SELLER   (*Offstage.*) The Journal for today, the twenty-second of March... Details of all the Palm Sunday ceremonies...

Meanwhile, the platform revolves to reveal ESQUILACHE's *study. The marquis is at his desk, wearily signing papers which* CAMPOS, *standing next to him, collects. The* STEWARD *is standing by the door upstage.*

ESQUILACHE   There's no end to this signing of papers... (*Throws down the pen.*) Sometimes it seems as if I'm signing my name in the sand.

CAMPOS   Very true, sir.

ESQUILACHE   Don't always agree with me! Try arguing for once!... (*He gets up and paces up and down. There is silence for a while.*) And you, what are you doing standing there like an idiot?

CAMPOS *and the* STEWARD *exchange looks.*

STEWARD   I am waiting for your Excellency's instructions about the trip to San Fernando.

ESQUILACHE   (*To* CAMPOS.) Are you ready?

CAMPOS   Yes, my Lord. We can go whenever you wish.

ESQUILACHE   What about this mountain of paperwork?

CAMPOS   I shall send an aide with it before we leave.

ESQUILACHE   Hmm!... I'd be glad not to have to go on this trip. But Grimaldi arranged it a month ago and I can't talk him out of it. "So that you can relax with your friends and talk some Italian." That's what he said. *Bene. Parleremo il toscano.* (*He stops in front of* CAMPOS.) What was it you had to tell me?

CAMPOS   (*Lowering his voice.*) It's to do with... doña Fernandita.

Pause. ESQUILACHE *takes out his watch. Then he speaks to the* STEWARD.

ESQUILACHE   Saldremos a las ocho.
MAYORDOMO   (*Que se las prometía muy felices.*) Bien, excelencia.

Y sale, muy serio, después de inclinarse, cerrando.

ESQUILACHE   (*Va a sentarse a un sillón.*) Hable.
CAMPOS   Ocurrió ayer, muy cerca de aquí. (*Se aproxima.*) Yo pasaba en ese
       momento.
ESQUILACHE   (*Glacial.*) Abrevie.
CAMPOS   Doña Fernandita estaba escuchando a un corrillo de majas y chisperos
       donde... parece que se hablaba de vuecelencia.
ESQUILACHE   Donde me estaban poniendo como chupa de dómine, vamos.
CAMPOS   Algo así... Y doña Fernandita se puso a defenderlo.
ESQUILACHE   (*Se incorpora.*) Ah, ¿sí?
CAMPOS   Con tanto ardor que... tuvo que salir corriendo hasta aquí para que no la
       golpearan.
ESQUILACHE   (*Se levanta, da unos pasos y lo mira.*) ¿Por qué me ha contado eso, don
       Antonio?
CAMPOS   (*Inmutado.*) Me pareció que le agradaría saber...
ESQUILACHE   (*Con ironía.*) Siempre es grato comprobar la lealtad y la valentía de un
       servidor. Usía, claro, no llegaría a intervenir...
CAMPOS   Están los ánimos tan excitados que, en efecto..., no juzgué prudente, en el
       propio bien de vuecelencia...
ESQUILACHE   Muy comprensible. ¿Pero a ella sí la protegería?
CAMPOS   ¡Por supuesto! La vine siguiendo..., por si le ocurría algo. (*Baja la voz.*)
ESQUILACHE   Ya. (*Golpecitos en el foro.*) ¡Adelante!

Entra el MAYORDOMO.

MAYORDOMO   Su excelencia el señor marqués de la Ensenada
ESQUILACHE   ¡Al fin! (*Sale el* MAYORDOMO. ESQUILACHE *se precipita al
       foro, al tiempo que entra* ENSENADA, *sin capa ni sombrero. La puerta se
       cierra.* CAMPOS *se inclina y* ESQUILACHE *estrecha las dos manos de*
       ENSENADA *con efusión.*) ¡Qué alegría, verte! Don Antonio puede decirte que
       te he llamado varias veces; pero siempre decían que estabas fuera.
CAMPOS   Muy cierto, excelencia.
ENSENADA   He estado en mi finca de Andalucía. Ando en tratos para venderla,
       ¿sabes? Me empieza a hacer falta algún dinero.
ESQUILACHE   ¿Pero estarás informado de todo lo ocurrido?
ENSENADA   De nada concreto... En cuanto llegué me han pasado tus recados y me he
       apresurado a venir.
ESQUILACHE   ¿Será posible que no sepas nada? ¿Las reuniones? ¿Las Ordenanzas?

ESQUILACHE We'll leave at eight.
STEWARD (*Disappointed.*) Very good, my Lord.

And after bowing, he goes out looking very serious and closes the door behind him.

ESQUILACHE (*He goes and sits down in an armchair.*) Go ahead.
CAMPOS It happened yesterday, very near here. (*Moving closer.*) I just happened to be passing at that moment.
ESQUILACHE (*Icily.*) Get to the point.
CAMPOS Doña Fernandita was listening to some of the local people who... it seems were talking about your Excellency.
ESQUILACHE And tearing me to pieces, I suppose.
CAMPOS More or less... And doña Fernandita stood up for you.
ESQUILACHE (*Sits up.*) Oh, really?
CAMPOS She defended you so fervently that she ended up having to run back here to avoid being attacked.
ESQUILACHE (*Gets up, walks a few paces and looks at him.*) Why have you told me this, don Antonio?
CAMPOS (*His face falls.*) I thought that you would be pleased to know...
ESQUILACHE (*With a touch of irony.*) It is always pleasing to be reassured of the loyalty and courage of one's servants. I don't suppose that you intervened in any way...
CAMPOS People are rather stirred up at the moment, so... I didn't think it wise, for your Lordship's sake...
ESQUILACHE Very sensible. But you made sure that she came to no harm?
CAMPOS Naturally! I followed her back..., just in case anything happened to her. (*Lowering his voice.*)
ESQUILACHE Of course. (*Someone taps on the door upstage.*) Come in!

The STEWARD *comes in.*

STEWARD His Excellency the Marquis of La Ensenada
ESQUILACHE At last! (*The* STEWARD *exits.* ESQUILACHE *hurries upstage, at the same time as* ENSENADA *comes in, without his cape and hat. The door closes behind him.* CAMPOS *bows and* ESQUILACHE *shakes both of* ENSENADA's *hands effusively.*) Wonderful to see you! Don Antonio can tell you, I've called for you several times; but they kept on saying that you were out.
CAMPOS That is true, your Excellency.
ENSENADA I've been down at my estate in Andalusia. I'm negotiating to sell it, did you know? I'm beginning to run rather short of money.
ESQUILACHE But you've been kept informed of everything that's been happening?
ENSENADA Well, not in much detail... As soon as I arrived I was given your messages and I came straight here.
ESQUILACHE How can you not know anything? Have you heard about the meetings? The Regulations?

ENSENADA ¿De qué hablas?

ESQUILACHE Toma asiento. ¿Quiere dejarnos, Campos? (ENSENADA *se sienta junto a la consola*. CAMPOS *recoge la carpeta, se inclina y sale por el foro*. ESQUILACHE *se sienta junto a* ENSENADA) Ya no hay duda, Zenón. Una conspiración muy hábil y movida por manos muy poderosas.

ENSENADA ¡Diablo!

ESQUILACHE Como los madrileños no paran de chancearse a mi costa, incluso con carnavaladas callejeras que me aluden, quise creer hasta hace poco que todo se resolvería en chistes: en esos chistes con que este país lo termina todo para no arreglar nada... Pero el diecinueve mi Policía me informó de dos reuniones.

ENSENADA ¿Gente elevada?

ESQUILACHE Sí. Una en Madrid y otra... en el propio Pardo.

ENSENADA ¿Quiénes eran?

ESQUILACHE Sin identificar. O acaso me lo callan, porque aquí está empezando ya a fallar todo... De esas juntas han salido las Ordenanzas.

ENSENADA ¿Qué Ordenanzas?

Con un gruñido sarcástico, ESQUILACHE *se levanta y va a la mesa.*

ESQUILACHE (*Mientras saca un pliego de una carpeta.*) ¡Hay más cosas! Campomanes me ha escrito un billete muy cauto pero muy revelador, como todo lo que él hace... Ha sabido por confidencias privadas que los ánimos están muy alterados en Zaragoza y en algunos puntos del País Vasco... Dicen allí que en Madrid habrá motín.

ENSENADA ¿Motín? (*Se levanta.*)

ESQUILACHE (*Esgrime el papel.*) Aquí lo tienes. Atiende: (*Lee.*) "Constituciones y Ordenanzas que se establecen para un nuevo cuerpo que, en defensa del Rey y de la Patria, ha erigido el amor español para quitar y sacudir la opresión con que intentan violar estos dominios."

ENSENADA ¿Me dejas? (ESQUILACHE *le da el pliego.*)

ESQUILACHE Son quince puntos...

ENSENADA Y muy curiosos... (*Lee.*)

ESQUILACHE (*Tras él, apunta con el dedo.*) Lee aquí.

ENSENADA "Se dará dinero a la gente de mal vivir para que en estos días no cometan excesos."

ESQUILACHE Pactan con la canalla.

ENSENADA Mucho dinero van a necesitar...

ESQUILACHE ¡Corre en abundancia, *caro amico*! Mira lo que dice aquí: "Cuanto daño se haga, se pagará sin dilación alguna."

ENSENADA (*Lee.*) "Jurar ante el Santo Sacramento no descubrirse unos a otros..."

ENSENADA What are you talking about?

ESQUILACHE   You'd better sit down. Will you leave us, please, Campos? (ENSENADA *sits down next to the console table.* CAMPOS *picks up the folder, bows and exits upstage.* ESQUILACHE *sits next to* ENSENADA) There's no doubt about it any more, Zenón. A very clever conspiracy, with some very powerful hands pulling the strings.

ENSENADA My God!

ESQUILACHE The people of Madrid are constantly making fun of me, even staging lampoons in the streets attacking me. Until recently I hoped that it would go no further than harmless jokes: the kind of jokes that this country always resorts to instead of doing things properly... But on the nineteenth my police service told me about two meetings.

ENSENADA Important people?

ESQUILACHE   Oh, yes. One meeting was in Madrid and the other... in the Pardo itself.

ENSENADA Who were they?

ESQUILACHE   They haven't been identified. Or perhaps I'm just not being told. Everything's starting to fall apart here... It was those meetings that issued the Regulations.

ENSENADA What are these Regulations?

With a snort of sarcasm, ESQUILACHE *gets up and goes to the desk.*

ESQUILACHE   (*Taking a sheet of paper from a portfolio.*) And there's more! Campomanes[36] sent me a note that was very cautious but very revealing, like everything he does... He's been told confidentially that tempers are running high in Zaragoza and some parts of the Basque Country... They're saying there that there'll be an uprising in Madrid.

ENSENADA An uprising? (*He gets to his feet.*)

ESQUILACHE   (*Waving the paper at him.*) It's all here. Listen to this: (*He reads.*) "Statutes and Regulations for the formation of a new body of men, established for the defence of the King and the Nation, and charged with the patriotic task of throwing off the oppression which seeks to ravage our land."

ENSENADA May I? (ESQUILACHE *hands him the document.*)

ESQUILACHE There are fifteen items...

ENSENADA And very odd they are too... (*He reads it.*)

ESQUILACHE (*Points over his shoulder.*) Read this bit.

ENSENADA "Money shall be paid to delinquents so that they do not cause trouble on the days in question."

ESQUILACHE They've made an alliance with the riff-raff.

ENSENADA They'll need a great deal of money...

ESQUILACHE   There's plenty of that flowing around, *caro amico*! Look what it says here: "Compensation will be paid without delay for all damages."

ENSENADA   (*Reading.*) "To swear on the Blessed Sacrament not to reveal one another's identity..."

ESQUILACHE   Muy español, ¿eh? Aquí todo se jura ante el Santo Sacramento: lo mismo las empresas más nobles que las más sucias. Tendrían que aprender más respeto... Sigue leyendo.

ENSENADA   "Sólo contra dos está permitida toda violencia."

ESQUILACHE   Los dos ministros italianos. Grimaldi y yo.

Un silencio. ENSENADA *se sienta y sigue repasando el pliego.*

ENSENADA   Pero la calle está tranquila.

ESQUILACHEE   No lo creas. Ahora no sólo protestan por el bando, sino de que la Junta de Abastos haya tenido que subir el pan por la sequía.

ENSENADA   (*Pensativo.*) ¿El pan?

ESQUILACHE   *Ecco.* La palabra que mejor comprende el humilde. ¡Los que tiran de los hilos saben mucho! Este pueblo ha tenido hambre durante siglos; pero la queja por el pan me la tenía que reservar a mí, que he desterrado el hambre de España.

ENSENADA   ¿Qué dice el rey de todo ello?

ESQUILACHE   Me sigue recomendando prudencia... Todas las guarniciones están avisadas, pero con la consigna de no actuar hasta nueva orden. ¿Qué opinas tú?

Pausa.

ENSENADA   Lo que el rey. Prudencia.

ESQUILACHE   ¿Cómo? ¿Pues no me recomendabas la mano dura?

ENSENADA   Para cumplir el bando y siempre que haga falta. Pero ¿hace verdaderamente falta ahora? Esas Ordenanzas describen un levantamiento hipotético, cuya fecha es oscura. Puede quedarse en nada, como tantas otras intentonas. La invencible fuerza del Estado amedrenta mucho.

ESQUILACHE   (*Sin mirarlo.*) Me quieren matar.

ENSENADA   (*Sonríe.*) No tanto, Leopoldo.

ESQUILACHE   ¿No lo has leído?

ENSENADA   (*Se levanta.*) Es lógico que estés intranquilo, pero también en estos trances debes aprender frialdad. El consejo del rey es bueno. (*Le pone las manos en los hombros.*) Créeme: se amenaza con demasiada facilidad.

ESQUILACHE   (*Suspira.*) Puede que lleves razón. En todo caso, mañana es Domingo de Ramos... Supongo que respetarán la santidad de la Pascua. Hay, por lo menos, una semana de tregua.

Oscurece.

ENSENADA   Me alegro de dejarte algo más tranquilo.

ESQUILACHE   ¿Te vas ya?

ESQUILACHE   Very Spanish, isn't it? Here everything is sworn on the Blessed
    Sacrament: from the noblest business to the dirtiest. They ought to have more
    respect... Go on reading.
ENSENADA "Violence will only be permitted against two individuals."[37]
ESQUILACHE   The two Italian ministers. Grimaldi and me.

Silence for a while. ENSENADA *sits down and carries on reading the paper.*

ENSENADA   It's quiet enough on the streets, though.
ESQUILACHE   I wouldn't be so sure. Now it's not only the decree that they're
    protesting about, it's also the fact that the Board of Supply has had to raise the
    price of bread as a result of the drought.
ENSENADA   (*Thoughtfully.*) Bread, eh?
ESQUILACHE   *Ecco.* The word that the common people understand best. Whoever is
    pulling the strings here certainly know what they're doing! The Spanish people
    have been hungry for centuries; but they had to save their protest about bread
    for me, the man who has banished hunger from Spain.
ENSENADA   What does the king say about all of this?
ESQUILACHE   He still advises prudence... The army has been put on alert, but told
    not to do anything without further orders. What do you think?

Pause.

ENSENADA   The same as the king. Prudence.
ESQUILACHE   That's a change. Weren't you the one who was urging me to take a
    hard line?
ENSENADA   Only in the enforcement of the decree, and only when absolutely
    necessary. But is it really necessary now? These Regulations are to do with a
    purely hypothetical uprising, with no date specified. It may come to nothing,
    like so many other plots. The crushing power of the state does intimidate
    people rather effectively.
ESQUILACHE   (*Without looking at him.*) They want to kill me.
ENSENADA   (*Smiles.*) It's not that serious, Leopoldo.
ESQUILACHE   Haven't you read it?
ENSENADA   (*Getting up.*) It's quite natural that you should feel uneasy, but you
    should learn to remain cool in crises like this. The king's advice is sound.
    (*Putting his hands on his shoulders.*) Believe me: making threats is all too easy.
ESQUILACHE   (*With a sigh.*) Perhaps you're right. In any case, tomorrow is Palm
    Sunday... I assume that they'll respect the sanctity of Easter. We'll have a
    week's truce at least.

It is getting dark.

ENSENADA   I'm glad that I can leave you in a calmer state of mind.
ESQUILACHE   Going already?

ENSENADA   Tengo un montón de cosas que arreglar después del viaje. (ESQUILACHE *agita dos veces la campanilla*.) Si me entero de algo no dejaré de informarte.

ESQUILACHE   (*Le toma las manos*.) Gracias, más que nunca, por tu visita. (*Entra el* MAYORDOMO.) Acompañe al señor marqués.

MAYORDOMO   Sí, excelencia. (*Baja la voz*.) Doña Fernandita ruega ser recibida, excelencia.

ESQUILACHE   ¿Ocurre algo?

MAYORDOMO   Parece muy inquieta...

ESQUILACHE   Que pase. Dios te guarde, Zenón.

ENSENADA   El sea contigo.

Se inclinan. Sale ENSENADA, *seguido por el* MAYORDOMO. DOÑA FERNANDITA *aparece en la puerta y se inclina*.

ESQUILACHE   Cierra. (*Ella lo hace*.)

FERNANDITA   Señor...

ESQUILACHE   ¿Te ocurre algo?

FERNANDITA   ¡Señor, tenga mucho cuidado! Vengo de la calle y nunca he visto tantas cuadrillas de embozados. ¡Algo traman!

ESQUILACHE   (*Sonríe*.) Sí, algo traman...

Se acerca y le besa la mano.

FERNANDITA   ¿Qué hace?

ESQUILACHE   Perdóname. He pensado mal de ti. Pero ahora sé que me has defendido en la calle, sin miedo a la impopularidad ni al peligro.

FERNANDITA   (*Sonríe*.) Yo soy del pueblo. No me preocupa ser impopular.

ESQUILACHE   (*La conduce a un sillón y él se sienta en el otro*.) Déjame mirarte con nuevos ojos. ¡Ah! Es maravilloso. Ya no estoy solo. Ya tengo una verdadera amiga.

FERNANDITA   (*Baja la cabeza*.) Siempre la ha tenido.

ESQUILACHE   Y me pregunto el porqué. Respeto, gratitud, incluso admiración... Eso se comprende. Pero amistad... Afecto... (*Un silencio*.) Escucha, Fernandita. Si yo fuese un tonto (y todos somos alguna vez muy tontos) empezaría a sentirme halagado sin acordarme de mis años... (*Grave*.) A veces ocurre que a una niña inexperta le deslumbra la grandeza aparente de su señor. ¡No te turbes! Nadie nos escucha y podemos llegar al fondo de los corazones. Por si..., por si tú notaras que empezabas a deslumbrarte..., yo debo recordarte que soy un anciano.

ENSENADA   I have a lot of things to sort out after being away. (ESQUILACHE *rings the bell twice*.) If I find out anything I'll certainly let you know.

ESQUILACHE   (*Takes both of his hands*.) I'm more grateful than ever for your visit. (*The* STEWARD *comes in*.) Show his lordship out.

STEWARD   Yes, my Lord. (*Lowers his voice*.) Doña Fernandita would like to see you, my Lord.

ESQUILACHE   Is something wrong?

STEWARD   She seems very worried...

ESQUILACHE   Send her in. God be with you, Zenón.

ENSENADA   And with you.

They exchange a bow. ENSENADA *leaves, followed by the* STEWARD. FERNANDITA *appears in the doorway and curtsies.*

ESQUILACHE   Close the door. (*She does so*.)

FERNANDITA   My Lord...

ESQUILACHE   Is something the matter?

FERNANDITA   You must be careful, sir! I've just come in from the street, and I've never seen so many bands of men in capes. They're plotting something!

ESQUILACHE   (*Smiles*.) Oh, yes, they're certainly plotting something...

He goes to her and kisses her hand.

FERNANDITA   What are you doing?

ESQUILACHE   Forgive me. I've done you an injustice. But now I know that you stood up for me in the street, without fear of being unpopular or in danger.

FERNANDITA   (*Smiles*.) I'm one of the people. I'm not worried about being unpopular.

ESQUILACHE   (*Leads her over to one of the armchairs and sits in the other himself*.) I'm seeing you in a new light. It's marvellous! I'm not alone any more. At last I have a true friend in you.

FERNANDITA   (*Looking down*.) You always have.

ESQUILACHE   And I wonder why. Respect, gratitude, even admiration... That's understandable. But friendship... Affection... (*Pause*.) Listen, Fernandita. If I were a fool, and we can all be very foolish at times, I might begin to feel flattered and forget how old I am... (*Solemnly*.) Sometimes an inexperienced girl can find herself dazzled by the apparent grandeur of her master. Don't worry! Nobody's listening and we can open our hearts to each other. Just in case..., in case you thought you were beginning to be dazzled..., I ought to remind you that I am an old man.

FERNANDITA   (*Sin mirarlo.*) Yo empecé a pensar mucho en su merced desde un día en que visitó a la señora marquesa en su gabinete y ella lo trató con mucho despego... Vi a su merced tan abatido, tan solo, que...

ESQUILACHE   Certo. (*Le toma las manos.*) Desde hace años. (*Melancólico.*) Y ahora, surges tú... (*Se levanta para disimular su turbación y pasea. El gabinete se encuentra ahora en una suave penumbra.*) Ya oscurece... (*Levanta la cabeza.*) Juraría que oigo el pregón... Imaginaciones que me persiguen. (*Recoge de la mesa un folleto.*) Un libro de augurios. ¿Crees tú en esas cosas?

FERNANDITA   Quizá ...

ESQUILACHE   (*Abre el libro.*) Este hombre predijo la muerte del rey Luis Primero. Escucha lo que presagia este año: "Raras revoluciones que sorprenden los ánimos de muchos. Un magistrado que con sus astucias ascendió a lo alto del valimiento, se estrella desvanecido, en desprecio de aquellos que le incensaban."

FERNANDITA   (*Temblando, dice muy quedo.*) ¡No lea eso!

ESQUILACHE   (*Exaltado.*) "Prepáranse embarcaciones que tendrán venturosos pasajes. Un ministro es depuesto por no haber imitado en la justicia el significado del enigma."

Ríe. Ella se levanta, asustada.

FERNANDITA   ¡Calle, por piedad!

Rompe a llorar. ESQUILACHE *se acerca. Ella se echa en sus brazos.*

ESQUILACHE   ¿Qué nos pasa, Fernandita? ¿Qué ocurre esta noche?...

FERNANDITA   No lo sé...

ESQUILACHE   Yo sí. Yo sí lo sé. Somos como niños sumidos en la oscuridad. (*De pronto encienden en el exterior algún farol cercano y su luz ilumina a la pareja por el ventanal.* ESQUILACHE *suspira y se separa suavemente.*) Mira. La oscuridad termina. Dentro de poco lucirán todos los faroles de Madrid. La ciudad más sucia de Europa es ahora la más hermosa gracias a mí. Es imposible que no me lo agradezcan.

Un FAROLERO *aparece por la segunda derecha. Enciende el farol de la esquina, cruza, enciende el otro farol y sale por la segunda izquierda.* BERNARDO, *embozado, aparece por la primera derecha y se disimula. A poco,* RELAÑO, *embozado, surge tras él y se aposta a su lado. Poco después,* MORÓN, *embozado, aparece por la primera izquierda y se queda espiando. Más tarde los* EMBOZADOS 1º *y* 2º *entran por la segunda derecha y se disimulan en el portal. Entretanto, continúa la escena en el gabinete:* ESQUILACHE *deja el "Piscator" sobre la mesa y saca su reloj.*

FERNANDITA   (*Without looking at him.*) I started to think a lot about you ever since
    one day when you came to her ladyship's boudoir and she treated you really
    coldly... You looked so dejected, so lonely, that...
ESQUILACHE   *Certo.* (*He holds her hands.*) I have been for years. (*Sadly.*) And now
    you've come along... (*He gets up to conceal his emotion and walks up and
    down. By now the study is enveloped in a soft half-light.*) It's getting dark...
    (*He looks up.*) I could swear that I can hear that blind man's cry... But it must
    be my imagination. (*He picks up a booklet from the table.*) A book of
    predictions. Do you believe in that kind of thing?
FERNANDITA   Maybe...
ESQUILACHE   (*Opening the booklet.*) This man foretold the death of King Luis.
    Listen to what he's predicting for this year: "Extraordinary revolutions which
    take many by surprise. A man of high office, having with great guile ascended
    to the pinnacle of royal favour, comes crashing down, despised by those who
    flattered him."
FERNANDITA   (*Trembling, she speaks very softly.*) Don't read it!
ESQUILACHE   (*Getting carried away.*) "A fleet is prepared, which will enjoy good
    fortune on its voyages. A minister is deposed for failing to administer justice in
    accordance with the significance of the enigma."[38]

He laughs. She gets up, alarmed.

FERNANDITA   No more, for pity's sake!

She begins to cry. ESQUILACHE *goes towards her. She throws herself into his arms.*

ESQUILACHE   What's happening to us, Fernandita? What's going on tonight?...
FERNANDITA   I don't know...
ESQUILACHE   I do. I know what it is. We're like children lost in the dark.
    (*Suddenly, a street lamp is lit somewhere outside and shines on the couple
    through the window.* ESQUILACHE *sighs and pulls away gently.*) Look. The
    darkness is gone. Soon all the lamps in Madrid will be alight. Thanks to me,
    the grubbiest city in Europe is now the most beautiful. I can't believe that
    they're not grateful to me for that.

A LAMPLIGHTER *comes on upstage right. He lights the lamp on the corner, crosses
the stage, lights the other lamp, and goes off upstage left.* BERNARDO, *wrapped in his
cape, appears downstage right and lurks in the shadows. Soon after,* RELAÑO, *also
muffled, follows him on and stations himself at his side. A little later,* MORÓN, *also
well disguised, appears downstage left and stands watch. After a while, the* 1ST *and*
2ND EMBOZADOS *enter upstage right and conceal themselves in the doorway.
Meanwhile, the scene in the study is continuing:* ESQUILACHE *puts the "Piscator"
down on his desk and takes out his watch.*

FERNANDITA   ¡No se vaya esta noche!

ESQUILACHE   Tengo que hacerlo... Pero volveré mañana... (*Le toma una mano.*) Fernandita... (*Conmovido.*) Fernandita. (*Ella baja la cabeza. El reacciona y agita dos veces la campanilla. Entra el* MAYORDOMO.) Luces. (*El* MAYORDOMO *se inclina y sale para volver al punto con un candelabro encendido que deposita sobre la mesa.*) A don Antonio Campos, que salimos. Mi capa. Buenas noches, Fernandita...

FERNANDITA   Que el señor marqués tenga buen viaje.

Se inclina y sale por el foro, seguida del MAYORDOMO. ESQUILACHE *se queda mirando a la puerta. Luego suspira, va a la mesa, recoge el "Piscator" y lo mira un momento para dejarlo con leve gesto melancólico. Después va al ventanal, ante el que permanece inmóvil con las manos a la espalda. Entretanto, dan las ocho en un reloj lejano. A la primera campanada,* BERNARDO *da unos pasos hacia el centro, seguido de* RELAÑO. MORÓN *cruza y se les une.* BERNARDO *sisea a los embozados del portal, que se acercan sigilosos. Todos hablan quedo.*

BERNARDO   ¿Sabéis ya la consigna contra ese hereje?

EMBOZADO lº   Sí. Mañana éste y yo, a las cuatro y media, en Antón Martín. Allí se nos reunirán otros treinta para tomar el cuartel de Inválidos.

MORÓN   ¡Chist!... Para una carroza ante el palacio.

Los embozados miran hacia la segunda izquierda y permanecen en silencio. La puerta del fondo se abre y entra el MAYORDOMO *con la espada, la capa y el sombrero del marqués.* ESQUILACHE *se ciñe la espada. El* MAYORDOMO *le pone la capa y le tiende el tricornio. Entretanto:*

BERNARDO   (*A los* EMBOZADOS 1º *y* 2º.) Vosotros ya sabéis vuestra obligación. Ojo a los corchetes. (*Disimulándose, los dos* EMBOZADOS *salen por la primera derecha.*) Nosotros tres, mañana a las cinco, aquí con todos los nuestros.

ESQUILACHE *se pone el tricornio. El* MAYORDOMO *toma el candelabro y va a la puerta.* ESQUILACHE *sale por el foro seguido del* MAYORDOMO, *que cierra.*

MORÓN   ¿Y si le propináramos un aviso al hereje?

BERNARDO   ¿Qué aviso?

MORÓN *se inclina y se lo susurra a los dos.*

RELAÑO   ¡Chist! Sale alguien...

FERNANDITA Don't go out tonight!
ESQUILACHE   I have to... But I'll be back tomorrow... (*He takes her hand.*)
Fernandita... (*Genuinely affected.*) Fernandita. (*She lowers her head. He
breaks away and rings the bell twice. The* STEWARD *comes in.*) Some light.
(The STEWARD *bows and goes out, coming back at once with a lighted
candelabra that he places on the desk.*) Tell don Antonio Campos that we are
leaving. Fetch me my cape. Good night, Fernandita...
FERNANDITA   I hope your Lordship has a good journey.

She curtsies and goes out upstage, followed by the STEWARD. *ESQUILACHE stands
gazing at the door. Then he sighs, goes to the desk, picks up the "Piscator", and looks
at it for a moment before putting it down again with a sad little gesture. Then he goes to
the window and stands in front of it, motionless, with his hands behind his back.
Meanwhile, a distant clock strikes eight. At the first stroke,* BERNARDO *strides
towards the centre of the stage, followed by* RELAÑO. MORÓN *comes across to join
them.* BERNARDO *hisses to the men in the doorway, who sneak across to join the
others. They all speak quietly.*

BERNARDO You all know the plan for getting rid of that heretic?
1ST EMBOZADO   Yes. Him and me, tomorrow at half past four, at Antón Martín.
Another thirty lads'll join us there to take the Inválidos barracks.
MORÓN Shhh!... There's a carriage stopping in front of the palace.

*The men look towards upstage left and watch in silence. The door at the back of the
study opens and the* STEWARD *comes in with the marquis's sword, hat and cape.*
ESQUILACHE *puts on his sword. The* STEWARD *puts his cape on for him and holds
out his three-cornered hat. Meanwhile:*

BERNARDO   (*To the* 1ST *and* 2ND EMBOZADOS.) You two know what to do.
Watch out for the constables. (*The two ruffians go off stealthily downstage
right.*) The three of us, back here tomorrow with the rest of the lads, right?

ESQUILACHE *puts on his hat. The* STEWARD *picks up the candelabra and goes to
the door.* ESQUILACHE *goes out upstage, followed by the* STEWARD, *who closes the
door behind him.*

MORÓN What about giving the heretic a bit of a warning?
BERNARDO What sort of warning?

MORÓN *leans towards them and whispers in their ears.*

RELAÑO Shhh! Somebody's coming out...

Los tres atisban.

BERNARDO   Yo creo que es el marqués.
RELAÑO   Ya arranca la carroza.
MORÓN   ¿Lo hacemos? Así se lo encuentra cuando vuelva esta noche.
BERNARDO   Bueno. (*A RELAÑO.*) Tú, al de la vuelta.

RELAÑO *sale rápido por la segunda derecha.* BERNARDO *y* MORÓN *van al centro de la escena y recogen algo del suelo. Tras la ventana del gabinete de* ESQUILACHE, *la luz del farol se apaga. Entonces* BERNARDO *y* MORÓN *miman, uno tras el otro, el ademán de arrojar una piedra. Con secos estallidos, los faroles de escena se apagan a sus gestos. Oscuridad.*

TELÓN

Photograph of the1958 production by Gyenes.

The three men peer towards the mansion.

BERNARDO   I think it's him, the marquis.
RELAÑO   His carriage is just setting off.
MORÓN   Shall we do it, then? It'll be a nice surprise for him when he gets back
        tonight.
BERNARDO   All right. (*To* RELAÑO.) You take the one round the other side.

RELAÑO *nips off upstage right.* BERNARDO *and* MORÓN *move to centre stage and pick up something from the ground. The lamp outside the window of Esquilache's study goes out. Then* BERNARDO *and* MORÓN, *one after the other, mime the action of throwing a stone. Each throw extinguishes one of the lamps on stage with a sharp crack. The lights go out quickly.*

CURTAIN

Ángela Molina as Fernandita and Fernando Fernán-Gómez as the Marquis of Esquilache
in the film *Esquilache* (directed by Josefina Molina).

PARTE SEGUNDA

Redoble de tambores antes de alzarse el telón, que se aleja y se pierde a los pocos segundos de levantado.

Oscurece. En los hierros del balcón de DOÑA MARÍA, *la palma del Domingo de Ramos. Asomadas al balcón,* DOÑA MARÍA *y la* CLAUDIA. *En el giratorio, el gabinete de* ESQUILACHE. *Caídos en el suelo, el cuadro de Mengs, el reloj de la consola, uno de los sillones. Todos los cristales del ventanal, rotos. Las carpetas, la escribanía, todo cuanto ocupaba la mesa, desparramado asimismo por el piso. La puerta del fondo, entreabierta. Sentado a la mesa,* RELAÑO, *que ha dejado en ella su sombrero, su capa y un pistolón. Ante él un plato con comida del que se sirve y una botella de la que bebe. Sobre la consola hay más vituallas. En el fondo, con aire atemorizado,* DOÑA EMILIA, *azafata de edad mediana. Sentada en un sillón, con aire ausente y mal peinada,* FERNANDITA. *Unos momentos de silencio, hasta que cesan los tambores.*

CLAUDIA   Me gustaría bajar a la calle.
DOÑA MARÍA   Ya has oído lo que han dicho: las mujeres, en sus casas.
CLAUDIA   Pues como mañana siga el jaleo, no nos vamos a estar quietas.
DOÑA MARÍA   Eres tú muy fuguillas. Con lo ricamente que se ve todo desde aquí.
CLAUDIA   Hace una hora que no pasa nada.
DOÑA MARÍA   Pero no te quejarás del teatro que hemos tenido.
RELAÑO   ¿No hay postre?

DOÑA EMILIA *va a la consola y lleva una fuente de dulces, de los que él empieza a comer.* FERNANDITA *no se ha movido.*

DOÑA MARÍA   Está refrescando... Vamos adentro.
CLAUDIA   Espere... Todavía no han retirado a ése de la puerta del palacio.
DOÑA MARÍA   Yo no lo distingo. Mis ojos están ya viejos.
CLAUDIA   Pues está. ¿Se fijó usté en cómo salían todos? Comiendo y fumando y con cestos enteros de botellas.
DOÑA MARÍA   Estaba la casa llena de las rapiñas de ese ladrón.
CLAUDIA   (*Misteriosa.*) ¿Y se fijó usté en unos... que parecían mandar más que los otros?
DOÑA MARÍA   No...

PART TWO

Before the curtain rises, a drum roll begins, which fades away a few seconds after the curtain has come up.

It is getting dark. A palm frond for Palm Sunday is attached to the railing on DOÑA MARÍA's balcony. DOÑA MARÍA and CLAUDIA are leaning out at the balcony. The revolving platform still shows ESQUILACHE's study. The Mengs portrait, the clock from the console table and one of the armchairs have been thrown onto the floor. All of the glass in the window is smashed. The portfolios, the writing materials, everything that was on the desk, are also scattered around the room. The door at the back has been left half open. RELAÑO is seated at the desk, on which he has left his hat, his cape and a pistol. He is helping himself from a plate of food and a bottle on the desk in front of him. There is more food and drink on the console table. DOÑA EMILIA, a middle-aged maidservant, is standing at the back looking terrified. A slightly dishevelled FERNANDITA sits distractedly in one of the armchairs. A few moments of silence, until the drum roll dies away.

CLAUDIA   I want to go down into the street.

MARÍA   You heard what they said: the women have to stay at home.

CLAUDIA   Well if this riot's still going on tomorrow, we're not going to be kept out of it.

MARÍA   I don't know why you're in such a hurry. When we can see everything nicely from up here.

CLAUDIA   It's been a whole hour since anything's happened.

MARÍA   But you can't complain about the entertainment we've had so far, can you?

RELAÑO   What about some pudding?

DOÑA EMILIA goes to the console table and brings him a dish of sweets, which he begins to eat. FERNANDITA has not moved.

MARÍA   It's getting a bit chilly... Let's go inside.

CLAUDIA   Wait... They still haven't moved him from the doorway of the palace.

MARÍA   I can't see him. My eyes aren't much good any more.

CLAUDIA   Well, he's still there. Did you see, when they were all coming out? How they were eating and smoking and carrying baskets piled high with bottles?

MARÍA   The house was full of that crook's booty.

CLAUDIA   (*In a mysterious tone.*) And did you notice that some of them... looked as if they were in charge?

MARÍA   No...

CLAUDIA. Sí, señora. Iban embozados, pero se les notaban las medias finas y la camisa de encaje.
DOÑA MARÍA   Hay muchos misterios en este mundo... ¡Mujer, que me estoy helando!
CLAUDIA Espere... Ya no hace frío...
DOÑA MARÍA ¡Qué espere, ni espere! Bien me sé yo el come come que tú tienes... (*La empuja.*) Adentro, adentro.
CLAUDIA Sí, señora.

Entra, sumisa, con DOÑA MARÍA. *Se cierra el balcón.* RELAÑO *emite un satisfecho resoplido y aparta la fuente. Elige un largo y fino cigarro puro de un montón que hay sobre la mesa.*

RELAÑO   ¡Candela! (DOÑA EMILIA *sale por el foro.* RELAÑO *mira a* FERNANDITA *y ríe.*) Vamos, niña... No hay que tomarlo tan a pecho...

Ella se estremece y no contesta. El se encoge de hombros y se arrellana en el sillón, con el cigarro en la boca. No tarda en poner los pies sobre la mesa: tiene sueño y se adormila a los pocos instantes, cayéndosele el cigarro de la boca. Entretanto, aparece por la primera derecha ESQUILACHE, *embozado en su capa, y tras él* CAMPOS, *visiblemente atemorizado. Se mueven y hablan con sigilo.*

CAMPOS ¡Es una temeridad, excelencia!...
ESQUILACHE ¡Chist!
CAMPOS ¡Aquí sólo puede encontrar ya lo peor!

ESQUILACHE *da unos pasos.* CAMPOS *lo retiene.*

ESQUILACHE ¿Qué hace?
CAMPOS ¡Vuélvase! ¡Es por su bien!
ESQUILACHE (*Lo mira de arriba a abajo.*) Vaya a la carroza.
CAMPOS Pero...
ESQUILACHE ¡Vuélvase a la carroza!

CAMPOS *se santigua y sale por donde entró.* ESQUILACHE *mira a todos lados; luego hacia su palacio. Entretanto,* DOÑA EMILIA *vuelve con una pajuela encendida y se acerca a* RELAÑO. *Al ver que está dormido apaga la pajuela y se aproxima a* FERNANDITA, *poniéndole una mano en el hombro.*

DOÑA EMILIA Váyase con su madrina, doña Fernandita.
FERNANDITA No. (DOÑA EMILIA *suspira y va a salir.*) ¿Qué hacen los otros?
DOÑA EMILIA (*Por* RELAÑO.) Lo que éste.

CLAUDIA   Oh, they were. They were wrapped up in capes like the others, but you could see that they had expensive stockings and lace shirts on.

MARÍA   Ah well, the world is full of mysteries... Come on, I'm freezing!

CLAUDIA   Wait a moment... It's not cold yet.

MARÍA   To hell with waiting! I know what you're like... (*Giving her a push.*) Come on, inside.

CLAUDIA   All right.

Submissively, she goes in with DOÑA MARÍA. *The balcony closes.* RELAÑO *makes a satisfied noise and pushes the dish away. He selects a long, thin cigar from a pile on the desk.*

RELAÑO   Bring me a light! (DOÑA EMILIA *goes out upstage.* RELAÑO *looks at* FERNANDITA *and laughs.*) Come on, girl... No need to take it so hard...

She shudders and does not answer. He shrugs his shoulders and settles down into the armchair, with the cigar in his mouth. It is not long before he has his feet up on the desk: he is feeling sleepy, and soon dozes off. The cigar drops out of his mouth. Meanwhile, ESQUILACHE *appears downstage right, muffled in his cape, followed by* CAMPOS, *who is noticeably scared. They move and speak furtively.*[39]

CAMPOS   This is very rash, sir!

ESQUILACHE   Shhh!

CAMPOS   There's nothing you can do here now!

ESQUILACHE *walks forward a few steps.* CAMPOS *holds him back.*

ESQUILACHE   What are you doing?

CAMPOS   Go back! For your own good!

ESQUILACHE   (*Looking him up and down.*) Go to the carriage.

CAMPOS   But...

ESQUILACHE   Go back to the carriage!

CAMPOS *crosses himself and goes off by the way he came on.* ESQUILACHE *looks all around; then towards his mansion. Meanwhile,* DOÑA EMILIA *returns with a lighted taper and goes towards* RELAÑO. *When she sees that he is asleep, she puts out the taper, goes over to* FERNANDITA *and puts her hand on her shoulder.*

EMILIA   You should go to your godmother's place, doña Fernandita.

FERNANDITA   No, I won't. (DOÑA EMILIA *sighs and goes towards the exit.*) What are the rest of them doing?

EMILIA   (*With a gesture towards* RELAÑO.) The same as him.

FERNANDITA   ¿Sigue Julián en el portal?
DOÑA EMILIA   Claro que sí. (*Suspira*).
FERNANDITA   (*Se levanta.*) Ayúdeme a retirarlo de allí, doña Emilia.

Tiene un vahído. DOÑA EMILIA *acude a sostenerla.*

DOÑA EMILIA   ¿Está loca?
FERNANDITA   (*Se sobrepone.*) Ayúdeme.

Sale por el fondo, seguida de DOÑA EMILIA, *que mueve la cabeza con pesar.* ESQUILACHE *se decide y da unos pasos para cruzar. De pronto, se detiene... Se oye el tap-tap de un garrote. Por la segunda izquierda entra el* CIEGO, *que cruza. Muy cerca de* ESQUILACHE, *se detiene, pues nota su presencia. Este lo mira fijamente. El* CIEGO *reanuda su marcha, gana la esquina, tantea la pared con el garrote y sale por la primera derecha bajo la aprensiva mirada de* ESQUILACHE. *Entretanto, el giratorio se desliza y presenta el ángulo de las dos puertas. Ante ellas, derribado en el suelo, el cadáver ensangrentado de un mozo. Cuando* ESQUILACHE *se vuelve está frente a su casa. Mira al caído con tristeza. Siente que la puerta se abre y se disimula en el ángulo de la derecha. Por la puerta de ese lado salen* FERNANDITA *y* DOÑA EMILIA. FERNANDITA *va a la cabeza del muerto y trata de levantarlo por los sobacos.* DOÑA EMILIA *se dirige a los pies.* ESQUILACHE *avanza, con un dedo en los labios.* FERNANDITA *da un suspiro de susto y se echa a llorar.* DOÑA EMILIA *se vuelve y lo reconoce.*

DOÑA EMILIA   ¡No entre, señor! ¡Todavía hay hombres en la casa!
ESQUILACHE   (*Por el muerto.*) ¿Quién es?
DOÑA EMILᵀA   Julián, el mozo de mulas.
ESQUILACHE   ¿Vive?
DOÑA EMILIA   Hizo resistencia y lo han matado. Al portero lo han llevado malherido al hospital. Ahora ya pasó todo, pero aún hay peligro... ¡Qué horror, señor! ¡Eran miles! Toda la calle llena. La mayor parte del servicio se ha ido, pero aún quedamos unos cuantos.
ESQUILACHE   ¿Y mi mujer?
DOÑA EMILIA   Se fue después del almuerzo a Las Delicias... No sabemos más.

Se oyen "vivas" y "mueras" lejanos.

ESQUILACHE   (*Por el muerto.*) ¿Qué iban a hacer?
DOÑA EMILIA   Llevarlo adentro.
ESQUILACHE   De nada le servirá ya.
DOÑA EMILIA   Se empeñó ella, señor... Dígale que se vaya de aquí. Nosotras podemos quedarnos todavía, pero ella no podría resistirlo.

FERNANDITA   Is Julián still in the doorway?
EMILIA   Of course. (*She sighs.*)
FERNANDITA   (*Getting up.*) Help me to get him away from there, doña Emilia.

She almost faints. DOÑA EMILIA *rushes back to support her.*

EMILIA   Are you mad?
FERNANDITA   (*Pulling herself together.*) Help me.

She goes out upstage, followed by DOÑA EMILIA *shaking her head ruefully.* ESQUILACHE *makes up his mind and starts to cross the stage. Suddenly, he stops... We hear the tap-tap-tap of a stick on the ground. The blind* BALLAD-SELLER *enters upstage left and goes across the stage. Passing very close to* ESQUILACHE, *he pauses, aware of his presence.* ESQUILACHE *stares at him. He walks on, reaches the corner, feels his way along the wall with his stick, and goes off downstage right, watched apprehensively by* ESQUILACHE. *In the meantime, the revolving platform has turned to reveal the angle between the two doors. There, dumped on the ground, lies the bloody corpse of a young man. When* ESQUILACHE *turns round, he is facing his house. He looks sadly at the body on the ground. He hears the door opening and hides around the corner to the right.* FERNANDITA *and* DOÑA EMILIA *come out of the right-hand door.* FERNANDITA *goes around to the dead youth's head and tries to lift him under his arms.* DOÑA EMILIA *goes to his feet.* ESQUILACHE *comes forward, with his finger on his lips.* FERNANDITA *makes a startled noise and bursts into tears.* DOÑA EMILIA *turns and recognizes him.*

EMILIA   Don't go in there, my Lord! There are still men in the house!
ESQUILACHE   (*Looking down at the body.*) Who is it?
EMILIA   Julián, the stable boy.
ESQUILACHE   Is he still alive?
EMILIA   He tried to resist them and they killed him. The doorman has been wounded and taken to hospital. It's all over now, but there's still danger... Oh, sir, it was awful! There were thousands of them! The whole street full of them. Most of the staff have gone, but some of us are still here.
ESQUILACHE   What about my wife?
EMILIA   She went to Las Delicias[40] after luncheon... We don't know any more than that.

Cheers and booing can be heard in the distance.

ESQUILACHE   (*Gesturing towards the body.*) What were you planning to do?
EMILIA   Take him inside.
ESQUILACHE   It won't do him any good now.
EMILIA   She insisted, my Lord... Tell her to get away from here. We can stay, but she couldn't take any more of this.

ESQUILACHE   Ven conmigo, Fernandita.

FERNANDITA *se echa en sus brazos sollozando. Gritos lejanos.*

DOÑA EMILIA   ¡Dense prisa! *(Va a entrar.)* ¡Y que Dios les proteja!

Se mete y cierra. FERNANDITA *está mirando al caído con inmenso terror. El la insta a caminar, suavemente.*

FERNANDITA   ¿Por qué ha venido, señor?
ESQUILACHE   *(Dulce.)* Por ti...

El giratorio se desliza y presenta de nuevo el gabinete de ESQUILACHE, *donde* RELAÑO *duerme.* ESQUILACHE *y* FERNANDITA *dan unos pasos y se detienen al oír gritos cercanos: "¡Viva el rey!", "¡Muera Esquilache!", que son coreados. Intentan huir por la izquierda pero no les da tiempo: por la segunda derecha aparecen* MORÓN *y los* TRES EMBOZADOS, *ahora sin capa. Vienen armados: pistolas al cinto, un trabuco, algún fusil de la infantería.* FERNANDITA *se apretuja contra* ESQUILACHE.

MORÓN   ¡Alto! *(Se acerca a la pareja seguido de los otros mientras dice:)* ¿A dónde va todavía con tres candiles? ¡Deme acá el sombrero! (ESQUILACHE *se lo tiende y él lo despunta brutalmente, devolviéndoselo.)* ¡Así! ¡Como los buenos españoles! Y ahora, grite usía con nosotros: ¡Viva el rey! (ESQUILACHE *permanece callado. El balcón se abre y salen* DOÑA MARÍA *y la* CLAUDIA) ¡Vamos, grite!
ESQUILACHE   *(Con un ardor amargo.)* ¡Viva!...
MORÓN   ¡Viva la Patria!
ESQUILACHE   ¡Viva!...
MORÓN   ¡Muera Esquilache!

ESQUILACHE *calla.*

DOÑA MARÍA   *(Haciéndose pantalla con las manos.)* Yo juraría...
CLAUDIA   ¿Qué?
DOÑA MARÍA   No es posible. ¡Veo tan mal!
MORÓN   *(Se ha ido acercando al marqués con muy mala cara.)* ¡Que grite usía muera Esquilache!
ESQUILACHE   *(Después de un momento.)* Esquilache es un anciano como yo. El morirá antes que todos vosotros, que sois jóvenes, aunque yo no grite.
MORÓN   Todo eso está muy bien. Pero ahora grite usía: ¡Muera Esquilache!
ESQUILACHE *calla.*

ESQUILACHE Come with me, Fernandita.

FERNANDITA *throws herself sobbing into his arms. More shouts in the distance.*

EMILIA Hurry! (*As she turns to leave.*) And may God protect you both!

She goes back inside and closes the door. FERNANDITA *is staring in utter terror at the body.* ESQUILACHE *leads her away gently.*

FERNANDITA Why did you come, my Lord?
ESQUILACHE (*Softly.*) For you...

The revolving platform turns back to ESQUILACHE's *study, where* RELAÑO *is fast asleep.* ESQUILACHE *and* FERNANDITA *take a few steps and stop when they hear, quite close now, a chorus of shouts of "God save the King!" and "Death to Esquilache!". They make an attempt to flee stage left, but it is too late:* MORÓN *and his three comrades (now without their capes) appear upstage right. They are armed: pistols in their belts, a blunderbuss, one or two infantry rifles.* FERNANDITA *clings to* ESQUILACHE.

MORÓN Halt! (*Followed by the others, he goes towards the couple, saying:*) And where do you think you're going with your hat still pinned up like that, eh? Give it here! (ESQUILACHE *holds it out to him and he rips open the corners before giving it back.*) That's how it's meant to be! The way proper Spaniards wear it! Now you can join in with us: God save the King! (ESQUILACHE *remains silent. The balcony opens up and* DOÑA MARÍA *and* CLAUDIA *appear.*) Go on, shout!
ESQUILACHE (*Fervently, yet bitterly.*) God save the King!
MORÓN God bless Spain!
ESQUILACHE God bless Spain!
MORÓN Death to Esquilache!

ESQUILACHE *says nothing.*

MARÍA (*Straining her eyes.*) You know, I could swear that...
CLAUDIA What?
MARÍA No, it can't be. My eyesight's getting so bad!
MORÓN (*Moving menacingly closer to the marquis.*) I want you to shout death to Esquilache!
ESQUILACHE (*After a moment's pause.*) Esquilache's an old man, like me. You're all young, and he'll die before you do, even if I don't shout it.
MORÓN That's all very well. But now say it: death to Esquilache!

ESQUILACHE *refuses.*

DOÑA MARÍA   ¿No es ésa doña Fernandita?
CLAUDIA. Creo que sí...

DOÑA MARÍA *se pasa, nerviosa, la mano por la boca.*

MORÓN (*Furioso.*) ¿Conque no grita?
EMBOZADO 3º Déjalo ya. Es un viejo y estás asustando a la niña.
MORÓN ¡No quiere gritar!
EMBOZADO 3º ¡Y qué! No vas a apiolar a todo el que no quiera. Sólo contra dos
     está permitido: ya lo sabes.
MORÓN ¡Me parece que ya han caído más de dos! (*Amenazador.*) ¡Y en cuanto a ti!...
EMBOZADO 3º (*Se crece y lo achica.*) ¡Es un viejo! (*A* ESQUILACHE.) Vaya usía
     en paz.

ESQUILACHE y FERNANDITA *cruzan y salen por la primera derecha, bajo la
intrigada mirada de las mujeres.*

DOÑA MARÍA   Oiga, mocito: ese caballero se parece muchísimo al marqués de
     Esquilache.
MORÓN (*Ríe.*) No me haga reír, abuela. Aquí iba a venir.
EMBOZADO 1º Como si fuera tonto.

Todos ríen.

DOÑA MARÍA Pues yo le he visto muchas veces... y diría que es él.
EMBOZADO 2º ¿A pie y por la calle? No son tan valientes los italianinis.
CLAUDIA Pues la niña era de su servidumbre.

Un silencio. Se miran.

MORÓN ¿Tendrá razón la vieja? (*Corre al lateral.*) Ya no se les ve.
EMBOZADO 1º Fantasías de mujeres.
EMBOZADO 2º ¡Mira por ese lado, que es caza más segura!
MORÓN (*Se vuelve.*) ¿Eh? (*Ve a quienes llegan.*) Mira... Dios nos los envía.
EMBOZADO 2º Estos son los que recortaban capas en el barrio.

El EMBOZADO 1º *se frota las manos con alegría.*

EMBOZADO 3º   Los mismos. Pero no olviden las Ordenanzas, ¿eh? Nada de
     violencias.

MARÍA   Isn't that doña Fernandita?
CLAUDIA   I think it is...

DOÑA MARÍA *wipes her hand nervously across her mouth.*

MORÓN   *(Furiously.)* So you're not going to do it, eh?
3RD EMBOZADO   Oh, leave him alone. He's just an old man, and you're frightening
    the girl.
MORÓN   But he's not doing what he's told!
3RD EMBOZADO   So what! You're not going to do in everyone who doesn't play
    along, are you?   There are only two people we're allowed to use violence
    against: you know that.
MORÓN   I reckon more than that have gone down already!   *(Threateningly.)* And as
    for you...!
3RD EMBOZADO   *(Drawing himself up to his full height, he forces him to back
    down.)* He's just an old man!   *(To* ESQUILACHE.*)* Go in peace.

ESQUILACHE *and* FERNANDITA *cross the stage and go off downstage right, under
the intrigued gaze of the two women on the balcony.*

MARÍA   Hey, young man: that gentleman looks a lot like the Marquis of Esquilache.
MORÓN   *(With a derisive laugh.)* Don't make me laugh, old woman.   As if he'd come
    round here now.
1ST EMBOZADO   He's not daft, you know.

They all laugh.

MARÍA   Well, I've seen him plenty of times... and I'd say it was him.
2ND EMBOZADO   On foot, out in the street?   Those Italians haven't got the guts.
CLAUDIA   Well, the girl was one of his servants.

Silence. They exchange looks.

MORÓN   The old woman might be right after all.   *(He dashes over to the side of the
    stage.)* No sign of them now.
1ST EMBOZADO   Just women's fantasies, I reckon.
2ND EMBOZADO   Look over there! There's an easier catch on its way!
MORÓN   *(Turning around.)* Eh?   *(He sees who is approaching.)* How about that...
    Divine intervention, I'd say.
2ND EMBOZADO   Those are the fellows who were in charge of the cape-trimming
    around here.

The 1ST EMBOZADO *rubs his hands gleefully.*

3RD EMBOZADO   You're right, it's them.   But don't forget the Regulations, eh?   No
    violence.

MORÓN ¿Y lo dices tú, que te apalearon?
EMBOZADO 3º (*Orgulloso.*) ¡Por eso mismo!
EMBOZADO 1º ¡Se van!
MORÓN (*Se vuelve.*) ¡Eh, no se vuelvan, que no les trae cuenta! ¡Aquí!... Eso es.

Aparecen, inmutados, CRISANTO *y* ROQUE. *Los* EMBOZADOS *los rodean.*

CRISANTO Cuide lo que hace, mozo...

Echa mano a la espada. Los EMBOZADOS *elevan sus armas.*

MORÓN Cálmese usía. Aquí todos somos españoles y sólo sobran los extranjeros...
EMBOZADO 2º Y lo extranjero.
MORÓN Eso. Conque traigan sus mercedes los sombreros. (ROQUE *se apresura a entregar el suyo.*) Así me gusta. (*Lo despunta y se lo devuelve.*)
EMBOZADO 3º (*A* CRISANTO.) ¡Traiga acá! (*Le quita el tricornio y se lo despunta. Las mujeres ríen.*)
MORÓN Y ahora, a gritar: ¡Viva el rey!
CRISANTO ¡Viva!
ROQUE (*Con ardor.*) ¡Viva!
MORÓN ¡Muera Esquilache!
ROQUE ¡Muera!

CRISANTO *calla.*

MORÓN Otro gallo que no canta... (*Al* EMBOZADO 3º.) ¿También vas a decir que porque es viejo?
ROQUE ¡Es que le ha pillado de sorpresa! (*Codazo a* CRISANTO.) ¡Grita, Crisanto! Sus mercedes pueden creernos: también nosotros odiamos a ese extranjero, a ese hereje. (*Y grita estentóreo:*) ¡Muera Esquilache!
EMBOZADO 3º (*Ríe.*) ¡Bravo! ¡Este lo hace muy bien por los dos!

Carcajadas.

MORÓN (*Los empuja.*) Vayan con Dios.
EMBOZADO 1º (*Tirando de la capa de* ROQUE.) ¡Y prueben a estirarse esas capitas, que son muy cortas!
EMBOZADO 3º ¡Al sastre! ¡Al sastre!

CRISANTO *y* ROQUE *salen, entre la burla general, por la primera derecha.*

MORÓN ¡Y ahora, a la cárcel de la Villa!

MORÓN   You're the one they beat up, and you still say that?
3RD EMBOZADO   (*Proudly.*) That's why I said it!
1ST EMBOZADO   They're getting away!
MORÓN   (*Turning around.*) Hey, I wouldn't head that way if I was you! Over here!...
That's right.

CRISANTO *and* ROQUE *appear, looking uneasy. The ruffians surround them.*

CRISANTO   Just watch what you're doing, laddie...

He puts his hand on his sword. The men raise their weapons.

MORÓN   No need to get excited. We're all good Spaniards here, and it's only
foreigners who don't belong...
2ND EMBOZADO   And foreign habits.
MORÓN   Right. So let's have your hats, gentlemen. (ROQUE *wastes no time in
handing his over.*) That's the way. (*He cuts loose the points and gives it back to
him.*)
3RD EMBOZADO   (*To* CRISANTO.) Give it here! (*He tears off his tricorn and cuts
the stitches. The women laugh.*)
MORÓN   And now, let's hear you shout: God save the King!
CRISANTO   God save the King!
ROQUE   (*Enthusiastically.*) God save the King!
MORÓN   Death to Esquilache!
ROQUE   Death to Esquilache!

CRISANTO *remains silent.*

MORÓN   Well, well, another cock who won't crow... (*To the* 3RD EMBOZADO.)
You're not going to say that he's an old man too, are you?
ROQUE   It's just that you took him by surprise! (*Nudges* CRISANTO.) Shout it out,
Crisanto! Honestly, lads, we hate him too, that foreigner, that heretic. (*And he
bellows impressively:*) Death to Esquilache!
3RD EMBOZADO   (*Chuckling.*) Nice one! I reckon he does it well enough for the two
of them!

Guffaws.

MORÓN   (*Giving them a push.*) Go on then, on your way.
1ST EMBOZADO   (*Tugging at* ROQUE's *cape.*) And you'd better try to make your
capes a bit longer. They look a bit short!
3RD EMBOZADO   To the tailor's! To the tailor's!

Amidst all this scoffing, CRISANTO *and* ROQUE *go off downstage right.*

MORÓN   And now, to the city jail!

CLAUDIA   (*Sobresaltada.*) ¿A la cárcel de la Villa?

MORÓN   Estamos citados allí más de doscientos para libertar a los presos. A las de la Galera las hemos soltado hace una hora.

CLAUDIA   ¡Mujeres por las calles, doña María!   ¡Y ahora sueltan a mi Pedro! ¡Aguárdenme, que bajo! (*Se mete.*)

DOÑA MARÍA   (*Tras ella.*) ¡Estás loca! ¿No comprendes que...? (*Se mete.*)

EMBOZADO 2º   ¿La esperamos?

MORÓN   Más bulto hará.

EMBOZADO 2º   Ya estarán allí otras en espera de sus hombres.

MORÓN   De lo que yo me alegro de veras, ¿eh? Porque es lo que yo digo: la calle sin mozas no resulta divertida.

Sale desalada del portal la CLAUDIA. DOÑA MARÍA *se asoma al balcón.*

EMBOZADO 1º   Aquí la tenemos.

EMBOZADO 2º   ¡Olé las mozas con redaños!

CLAUDIA   ¡Vamos allá!

Van a ponerse en marcha.

DOÑA MARÍA   ¿Adónde vas, arrastrada? ¡Conmigo estás mejor, olvídale! (*La* CLAUDIA *da unos pasos con los* EMBOZADOS.) ¡Claudia!

CLAUDIA   (*Airada.*) ¿Qué quiere?

DOÑA MARÍA   Te puede costar caro cuando él se entere de todo... ¡Piénsalo!

CLAUDIA   (*Vomita las palabras.*) ¡Vieja sucia!... ¡Que me pegue si quiere! ¡Mil veces lo prefiero a seguir con usté! ¡Ahí se queda y que el diablo se lo aumente! (*Escupe con asco. Ofendida,* DOÑA MARÍA *se mete y cierra el balcón de golpe.*) ¡Vamos!

Entre rumores de "Ha estado buena la moza", "Entera"... etc., salen todos por la segunda izquierda. Breve pausa. BERNARDO *aparece por la primera derecha, mira hacia el fondo y sale por la segunda derecha rápidamente.*

BERNARDO (*Voz de.*) ¡Relaño! (RELAÑO *se despabila con trabajo.*) ¡Relaño! ¿Sigue usté ahí?

RELAÑO *se levanta y va al ventanal.*

RELAÑO   ¿Qué hay?

BERNARDO (*Voz de.*) El hereje no habrá vuelto, claro.

RELAÑO   ¡Qué va!

BERNARDO (*Voz de.*) ¿No había por ahí un retrato suyo?

CLAUDIA (*Taken aback.*) The city jail?

MORÓN A couple of hundred of us are going to meet up there to let out the prisoners. We let the women out of the Galera an hour ago.[41]

CLAUDIA The women are in the streets, doña María! And now they'll be getting Pedro out! Hey, wait for me! I'm coming down! (*She dashes inside.*)

MARÍA (*Going after her.*) You must be crazy! Can't you see that...? (*She disappears.*)

2ND EMBOZADO Shall we wait for her?

MORÓN She'll only get in the way.

2ND EMBOZADO There'll be other women there waiting for their men.

MORÓN And a good thing too, I'd say. After all, the streets are no fun without girls, are they?

CLAUDIA *charges out of the doorway.* DOÑA MARÍA *leans out at the balcony.*

1ST EMBOZADO Here she comes.

2ND EMBOZADO That's the spirit, love!

CLAUDIA Let's go!

They prepare to go.

MARÍA Where are you off to, you hussy? You're better off with me, forget about him! (CLAUDIA *sets off with the men.*) Claudia!

CLAUDIA (*Angrily.*) What do you want?

MARÍA You'll be in trouble when he finds out what's been going on... Think about it!

CLAUDIA (*Spits out the words.*) You dirty old bitch!... He can give me a beating if he likes! I don't care: it'll be a thousand times better than staying with you! To hell with you! (*She spits on the ground in disgust. In great indignation,* DOÑA MARÍA *goes back inside and slams the balcony shut.*) Let's go!

Amidst muttered remarks such as "She did all right there" and "Really stood up for herself", they troop off upstage left. A short pause. BERNARDO *appears downstage right, glances towards the back and goes off rapidly upstage right.*

BERNARDO (*Offstage.*) Relaño! (RELAÑO *arouses himself with difficulty.*) Relaño! Are you still there?

RELAÑO *gets up and goes over to the window.*

RELAÑO What's up?

BERNARDO (*Off.*) The heretic didn't come back, did he?

RELAÑO Did he hell!

BERNARDO (*Off.*) Wasn't there a portrait of him in there somewhere?

RELAÑO   (*Vistazo a la habitación.*) Aquí está todavía...
BERNARDO   (*Voz de.*) Pues tráigalo corriendo a la plaza Mayor.

Reaparece, rápido.

RELAÑO   ¿A la plaza Mayor? ¿Para qué?
BERNARDO   ¡Allí lo verá!

Y sale apresuradamente por donde entró. RELAÑO *va a la mesa, se pone la capa y el sombrero y se guarda el pistolón, mientras bebe su último vaso de vino. Luego recoge del suelo el retrato y lo mira con un gruñido de sorna. Cargado con él, sale por el foro. A poco, reaparece por la segunda izquierda llevando el retrato del marqués y cruza para salir corriendo por la primera derecha. Entretanto, el giratorio se desliza y presenta el gabinete del Palacio Real, solitario. Oscurece en el primer término, al tiempo que se hace la luz en el gabinete. La puerta del fondo se abre y entra* ESQUILACHE, *seguido de* FERNANDITA, *que permanece a respetuosa distancia.* ESQUILACHE *considera fríamente la habitación y se despoja de la capa, que deja, con el sombrero despuntado que no llegó a ponerse, sobre una silla. Luego llega al centro de la sala y se queda pensativo. Entra* CAMPOS.

ESQUILACHE   (*Sin moverse.*) ¿A dónde da ese balcón?
CAMPOS   A la plaza de la Armería, excelencia.
ESQUILACHE   ¿Y esa puerta?

CAMPOS *cruza hacia la derecha y la abre.*

CAMPOS   A otro gabinete. Al fondo, una alcoba.

Cierra. Un silencio.

ESQUILACHE   Hay que avisar esta misma noche al Consejo de Guerra para que se reúna aquí a las siete de la mañana. Y al de Hacienda, para las nueve. Todos los secretarios de ambos despachos deberán venir igualmente: tenemos que organizar aquí el trabajo. Hable con el aposentador de Palacio para que nos destinen habitaciones al efecto.
CAMPOS   Sí, excelencia.
ESQUILACHE   Hay que llamar también a todos mis ayudantes. Cumpla inmediatamente mis órdenes.
CAMPOS   Sí, excelencia.

Cruza para salir. Un ademán del marqués lo detiene. ESQUILACHE *se vuelve lentamente y mira a* FERNANDITA, *que baja sus ojos.*

RELAÑO (*A quick glance around the room.*) It's still here.
BERNARDO (*Off.*) Bring it round to the Plaza Mayor, then. Quick as you can.

He appears on stage again, moving swiftly.

RELAÑO The Plaza Mayor? What for?
BERNARDO You'll see when you get there!

And he dashes off where he first came on. RELAÑO *goes to the desk, puts on his cape and hat and sticks his pistol in his belt, while gulping down his last glass of wine. Then he picks up the portrait from the floor and looks at it with a scornful grunt. He carries it out through the door at the back. He soon reappears upstage left carrying the marquis's portrait, crosses the stage and scurries off downstage right. Meanwhile, the platform revolves to show the study in the Royal Palace, which is empty. The lights go down on the foreground as they come up on the study. The door at the back opens and* ESQUILACHE *comes in, followed at a respectful distance by* FERNANDITA. ESQUILACHE *looks over the room coolly and takes off his cape, which he leaves on a chair together with the unstitched hat that he had not put back on. Then he walks to the middle of the room and stands there thoughtfully. Enter* CAMPOS.

ESQUILACHE (*Without moving.*) What does this balcony look out onto?
CAMPOS The Plaza de la Armería, your Excellency.
ESQUILACHE And where does that door lead to?

CAMPOS *goes to the right and opens it.*

CAMPOS Another study. Beyond that, there's a bedchamber.

He closes the door. Silence.

ESQUILACHE Notify the members of the Council of War tonight that there will be a meeting here at seven o'clock in the morning. And the Treasury Council, at nine. All the secretaries from both departments should also come: we shall have to run things from here. Ask his Majesty's chamberlain to provide us with some suitable rooms.
CAMPOS Yes, my Lord.
ESQUILACHE And summon all of my aides. At once.
CAMPOS Yes, my Lord.

He goes across towards the exit. A gesture from the marquis stops him. ESQUILACHE *turns slowly and looks at* FERNANDITA, *who bows her head.*

ESQUILACHE   Pero antes, don Antonio..., presente a doña Fernandita al sumiller de
cocinas. No quiero nada con el servicio de la casa: ella debe encargarse de
atenderme en todo.
CAMPOS   Una precaución muy oportuna, excelencia.

ESQUILACHE *lo mira, asombrado. Al fin comprende y sonríe con ironía.*

ESQUILACHE   Usía piensa siempre en todo. Aquí también tengo enemigos, en efecto.
Que dispongan una habitación para ella en los altos del Palacio.
CAMPOS   Bien, excelencia.

La puerta del fondo se abre y entra un LACAYO *de librea.*

LACAYO   ¡Su majestad el rey!

Entra CARLOS III, *destocado. Los tres se arrodillan. El* REY *mira con recatada
curiosidad a* FERNANDITA *y a* CAMPOS, *y los despide con un ademán. Ellos se
levantan, hacen la reverencia y salen con el* LACAYO. *La puerta se cierra. El* REY
llega junto a ESQUILACHE *y lo alza, reteniéndolo un momento por los brazos.*

EL REY   ¿Sano y salvo?
ESQUILACHE   Gracias a Dios, señor.
EL REY   ¿Tus familiares?
ESQUILACHE   Nada sé de ellos, señor. Mis hijos... supongo que llegarán a Madrid de
un momento a otro. Mis hijas, en las Salesas.
EL REY   ¿Doña Pastora?
ESQUILACHE   Fue a Las Delicias después del almuerzo. No sé más.
EL REY   De eso me ocuparé yo. No te inquietes. (*Se sienta en una de las sillas del
primer término.*) Bien. Ya tenemos aquí el anunciado motín. Ha sido
providencial que estuvieses fuera. Han saqueado tu casa pero sin llevarse nada
de valor. Parece que había quienes vigilaban eso. Han desistido de quemarla
porque pertenece al marqués de Murillo. Después han ido a la de Grimaldi,
pero allí se han limitado a apedrear los cristales... Y luego, a la de otra persona,
a vitorearla.
ESQUILACHE   No sé nada, señor...
EL REY   (*Sonríe.*) Ya, ya lo veo. Pero no te preocupes. Yo he trabajado en tu
ausencia. (*Grave.*) Siéntate. Noto que sufres ese dolor tuyo y que lo disimulas
por respeto.
ESQUILACHE   (*Agotado.*) Con vuestra venia, señor.

Se sienta en la otra silla.

ESQUILACHE   But first, don Antonio..., introduce doña Fernandita to the head chef. I
     don't want to be served by palace staff: she must take charge of everything.
CAMPOS   A very wise precaution, sir.

ESQUILACHE *gives him a look of astonishment. Finally he understands and smiles
ironically.*

ESQUILACHE   You always think of everything. It's true, I have enemies here too.
     Arrange for her to have a room in the palace servants' quarters.
CAMPOS   Very well, my Lord.

The door at the back of the stage opens and a liveried FOOTMAN *enters.*

FOOTMAN   His Majesty the King!

CARLOS III *comes in, bare-headed. All three of them kneel. The* KING *scrutinizes*
FERNANDITA *and* CAMPOS *discreetly, and gestures to them to leave. They get up,*
bow and go out with the FOOTMAN. *The door closes. The* KING *goes to*
ESQUILACHE *and helps him to his feet, holding him by the arms for a moment.*

KING   Safe and sound?
ESQUILACHE   Yes, sire, thanks to God.
KING   And your family?
ESQUILACHE   I don't know how they are, sire. My sons... I suppose they will be
     arriving in Madrid at any moment. My daughters are in the Salesian Convent.[42]
KING   Doña Pastora?
ESQUILACHE   She went to Las Delicias after luncheon. I don't know any more.
KING   I shall find out. There's no need for you to worry. (*He sits on a chair
     downstage.*) Well. Here it is, the revolt that we were warned about. It was
     fortunate that you were away. They have sacked your house, but without taking
     anything valuable. It seems that they were being kept in check by someone.
     They refrained from burning the place because it belongs to the Marquis of
     Murillo.[43] Next, they went to Grimaldi's house, but did no more than throw
     stones at the windows... And then, they went to another person's house, where
     they cheered.
ESQUILACHE   I know nothing, your Majesty...
KING   (*With a smile.*) Yes, I can see that. But don't worry. I've been busy in your
     absence. (*Becoming serious.*) Sit down. I can see that your pain is troubling
     you and you're concealing it out of respect.
ESQUILACHE   (*Exhausted.*) With your permission, sire.

He sits on the other chair.

EL REY   Han estado aquí también, con sus consabidos "vivas" y "mueras". Querían verme... Suplicarme. Pero yo me he negado a verlos: no quiero entrar en ese juego sin tenerte a mi lado. ¿Qué opinas tú?

ESQUILACHE   No sé qué decir, señor.

EL REY   Lo diré yo por ti. Hasta ahora hemos sido prudentes. Pero hay una noticia que... nos obligaría a reconsiderar el asunto.

ESQUILACHE   ¿Cuál, señor?

EL REY   Disturbios en Zaragoza.

ESQUILACHE   ¡Gran Dios!

EL REY   Debemos estudiar fríamente si, ante una oposición tan flagrante a la autoridad real, no habrá que emplear, y de inmediato, la mano dura.

ESQUILACHE   He citado aquí para mañana al Consejo de Guerra.

EL REY   Luego eres partidario de aplastar sin contemplaciones la revuelta. (*Un silencio.*) ¿No es así?

ESQUILACHE   Perdón, señor... En este momento no sabría responder nada.

EL REY   Estás enfermo... Mañana lo decidiremos todo. Entretanto, nos mantendremos muy unidos. Pero con mucha reserva...

ESQUILACHE   ¿Es que he perdido la confianza de vuestra majestad?

EL REY   (*Suspira.*) La reserva es necesaria porque... tampoco en Palacio podemos confiar. (*Baja la voz.*) Ni siquiera, lo sabes, en mi augusta madre... (*Mira al suelo.*) Hoy he comprendido lo solos que estamos. Somos nosotros los conspiradores contra una mayoría... (*Calla un momento. Se levanta.* ESQUILACHE *trata de hacerlo también y él lo detiene.*) Permanece sentado. Lo necesitas.

ESQUILACHE   (*Se levanta.*) No, no, majestad. Ya ha pasado.

EL REY   Te designaré inmediatamente un mayordomo. Echaré mano de quien pueda, porque mis mejores gentileshombres están ya muy ocupados... Me ha costado bastante poner hoy un poco de orden aquí. Bien. No desesperemos. (*Saca su saboneta y la mira.*) Tengo mucho que hacer. Te dejo.

ESQUILACHE   Puedo ayudaros, señor...

EL REY   No. Tú descansa y tranquilízate. A mí todavía me aclaman... Es contra ti contra quien van, pero aquí no van a poder hacerte nada. (*Se encamina al foro.*)

ESQUILACHE   Señor... (*El* REY *se vuelve.*) Señor...

Se le quiebra la voz de gratitud y va a besarle la mano, muy conmovido.

EL REY   (*Le pone la mano en el hombro.*) Descansa. (ESQUILACHE *se precipita a abrirle la puerta. Antes de salir, el* REY *repara en el sombrero de* ESQUILACHE *y lo levanta.*) ¿Cómo? ¿También te lo han despuntado?

ESQUILACHE   (*Baja los ojos.*) Bajé un momento de la carroza, señor.

EL REY   (*Afectuoso.*) Loco...

KING   They've been here too, with the usual shouts of "God save so-and-so" and "Death to whatsisname". They wanted to see me... To petition me. But I refused to see them: I'm not prepared to become involved in that game without having you at my side. What do you think?

ESQUILACHE   I don't know what to say, sire.

KING   Well, I shall say it for you. Until now, we have acted with caution. But there has been a development that may... oblige us to reconsider our approach.

ESQUILACHE   What is that, sire?

KING   Rioting in Zaragoza.[44]

ESQUILACHE   Good God!

KING   We shall have to consider, calmly, whether such a flagrant challenge to royal authority demands a firm response, and a swift one.

ESQUILACHE   I've called a meeting of the Council of War here tomorrow.

KING   So you're in favour of crushing the revolt without compromise. (*Silence.*) Aren't you?

ESQUILACHE   Forgive me, your Majesty... I really do not know how to reply at the moment.

KING   You're not well... We'll decide everything tomorrow. In the meantime, you and I must be completely united on this, although I cannot allow that to be known.

ESQUILACHE   Have I lost your Majesty's confidence, then?

KING   (*With a sigh.*) We must be careful because... because even in the Palace not everyone can be trusted. (*Lowering his voice.*) Not even my mother, as you know...[45] (*Looks down.*) It has become clear to me today how isolated we are. It is we who are the conspirators against a majority... (*He says nothing for a moment. He gets up.* ESQUILACHE *tries to follow suit, and the* KING *stops him.*) Don't get up. You need to rest.

ESQUILACHE   (*Getting up.*) No, no, sire. It's gone now.

KING   I shall assign you a chamberlain at once. I'll have to use whoever is available, as my best gentlemen are already very busy... I've had to work hard to restore some order around here today. Fine. Let's not lose hope. (*Takes out his watch and looks at the time.*) I have a great deal to do. I'll leave you now.

ESQUILACHE   I can help you, sire...

KING   No. You need rest and quiet. They are still supporting me... It's you they're after, but they can't do anything to you here. (*He heads upstage.*)

ESQUILACHE   Your Majesty... (*The* KING *turns.*) Your Majesty...

He breaks into a sob of gratitude, and goes to kiss the KING's *hand, deeply moved.*

KING   (*Putting his hand on* ESQUILACHE's *shoulder.*) Get some rest. (ESQUILACHE *hurries ahead to open the door for him. Before going out, the* KING *notices* ESQUILACHE's *hat and picks it up.*) So they took a knife to yours too, did they?

ESQUILACHE   (*Looking down.*) I got out of my carriage for a moment, sire.

KING   (*Affectionately.*) You're a mad fool...

Sale, y ESQUILACHE *se arrodilla. Se levanta y se queda perplejo. Mira a todos lados y siente el peso de su soledad. Con la respiración entrecortada, va al foro y tira de la campanilla. Una pausa. Tira otra, y otra vez, mirando a la puerta más y más nervioso. Golpecitos en la puerta.*

ESQUILACHE   ¡Sí! ¡Sí, adelante! (*Entra* FERNANDITA.) ¿No hay nadie en mi antecámara?

FERNANDITA   Nadie, señor.

ESQUILACHE   (*Con angustia.*) ¿Ni siquiera un criado?

FERNANDITA   Yo sola, señor. (ESQUILACHE *va a la mesita y se sienta, sombrío, en una de las sillas.*) ¿Quiere que le prepare algo?

ESQUILACHE   No, gracias. Nada por esta noche. (*La mira.*) Pero tú sí debes reparar tus fuerzas...

FERNANDITA   No se preocupe su merced... Ya tomaré algo.

ESQUILACHE *se levanta, nervioso, y va al balcón.*

ESQUILACHE   Ya es de noche... Y muy oscura... Madrid no brilla como otras veces. (*Se vuelve. Ella no se ha movido: está ensimismada, con una expresión dolorosa en su rostro. El se acerca.*) Soy un egoísta... Sólo pienso en mí y tú estás destrozada. (*Ella lo mira, temerosa, pero no ve en su cara nada especial, y baja los ojos. El la obliga a sentarse en el sillón que hay ante la mesa.*) Le querías, ¿verdad?

FERNANDITA   (*Con un grito de alimaña asustada que desconcierta a* ESQUILACHE.) ¿A quién?

ESQUILACHE   (*Recostándose sobre la mesa.*) A... ese mozo que ha caído por defender mi casa... A Julián...

FERNANDITA   (*Casi no se la oye.*) No...

Y deniega, en silencio, varias veces.

ESQUILACHE   *Allora*... La mala impresión, ¿*è vero*?... Pero tú eres muy entera... *Molto brava*... ¿Le querías? (FERNANDITA *estalla en sollozos y deniega otra vez.*) ¡Criatura! ¿Qué te ocurre? (*Golpecitos en la puerta.* ESQUILACHE *se incorpora y dice con otra voz:*) Cálmate ahora. (*Ella procura calmarse, se seca con los dedos alguna lágrima. Nuevos golpecitos. Ella se levanta y corre a refugiarse en el aposento de la derecha.*) ¡Adelante! (*Entra el* DUQUE DE VILLASANTA. ESQUILACHE *retrocede instintivamente.*) ¿Qué desea?

VILLASANTA   Todo lo que a usía se le ofrezca... He sido designado por su majestad para ponerme a las órdenes de usía en funciones de mayordomo mientras permanezca en Palacio.

*As he goes out, ESQUILACHE kneels. He gets to his feet and stands for a moment in
confusion. He looks all around, painfully aware of his isolation. Breathing with some
difficulty, he goes upstage and rings the bell. A pause. He pulls the cord again, and
again, and looks increasingly anxiously towards the door. Someone knocks gently.*

ESQUILACHE   Yes! Yes, come in! (*Enter* FERNANDITA.) Is there no-one in the
   antechamber?
FERNANDITA   No-one, sir.
ESQUILACHE   (*In anguish.*) Not even a servant?
FERNANDITA   Only me, my Lord. (ESQUILACHE *goes over to the small table and
   sits down on one of the chairs.*) Would you like me to make you anything?
ESQUILACHE   No thank you. Nothing for tonight. (*Looks at her with concern.*) But
   you do need something to get your strength back...
FERNANDITA   There's no need for your Lordship to worry about me... I'll have
   something soon.

ESQUILACHE *gets up nervously and goes towards the balcony.*

ESQUILACHE   It's night already... Very dark... Madrid isn't as lit up as it has been
   recently. (*He turns towards her. She has not moved: she is sunk in her own
   thoughts, an expression of pain on her face. He goes to her.*) How selfish I
   am... All I can think about is myself, while you are devastated. (*She looks up
   at him warily, but finding his face inexpressive, she lowers her eyes again. He
   makes her sit down in the armchair in front of the desk.*) You loved him, didn't
   you?
FERNANDITA   (*Shrieks like a startled animal, which alarms ESQUILACHE.*) Loved
   who?
ESQUILACHE   (*Leaning on the desk.*) That boy... the one who was killed defending
   my house... Julián...
FERNANDITA   (*Almost inaudible.*) No...

And she shakes her head several times in silence.

ESQUILACHE   *Allora*... It's had a bad effect on you, hasn't it? *E vero?*... But you're
   taking it well... *Molto brava*... Did you love him? (FERNANDITA *sobs and
   shakes her head again.*) Come, come, my girl, what's the matter? (*Someone
   taps on the door.* ESQUILACHE *straightens up and says in a very different
   tone of voice:*) Pull yourself together. Now. (*She tries to calm down, wiping
   away a few tears with her fingers. More taps on the door. She gets up and runs
   into the room on the right to hide.*) Enter! (*The* DUKE OF VILLASANTA
   comes in. ESQUILACHE *recoils instinctively.*) What do you want?
VILLASANTA   To serve your Excellency in whatever way you wish... I have been
   assigned by his Majesty to act as your chamberlain while you are at the Palace.

ESQUILACHE (*Con asombro y disgusto.*) ¿Usía?

VILLASANTA Era el único gentilhombre que quedaba libre. Deploro lo que pueda tener de humillante la elección para usía... Y me permito hacerle notar que la humillación es mutua.

ESQUILACHE Está bien. Dígnese retirarse.

VILLASANTA (*Con un leve tono de reto.*) Estoy a las órdenes de usía para cuanto necesite, incluso si es información. Información veraz, por supuesto. ¿Desea saber las últimas novedades?

ESQUILACHE (*Acepta el reto.*) ¿Por qué no? Dígalas.

VILLASANTA El pueblo ha destrozado los cinco mil faroles que usía mandó instalar. En la plaza Mayor han encendido una gran hoguera... donde sólo queman cuadros y otras cosas, claro.

ESQUILACHE   Le felicito, duque... Los madrileños vuelven por sus fueros: impunidad, insania y basura. Ahora puede retirarse.

Reverencia del duque, correspondida por el marqués, que se queda mirando a la puerta cuando VILLASANTA *sale. La luz baja, hasta desaparecer casi totalmente. Poco antes,* DOÑA MARÍA *se asoma a su balcón con un perol de desperdicios y otea a una y otra parte.*

DOÑA MARÍA ¡Agua va!

Tira el contenido del perol a la calle y cierra. "Mueras" y "vivas" lejanos animan la noche y van aumentando de intensidad conforme vuelve, lentamente, la luz diurna. Con la misma lentitud pasa de la segunda derecha a la segunda izquierda, como si fuese él quien trajese el nuevo día, el CIEGO. *La luz vuelve también al gabinete, donde* ESQUILACHE, *sin espada y sentado ahora a la mesa, escribe.* CAMPOS, *de pie, al lado de la mesa.* FERNANDITA, *de pie, junto al balcón. En la mesita, un servicio de chocolate. Se oye la airada voz de* ESQUILACHE *antes de que la luz vuelva del todo.*

ESQUILACHE ¡Ya sé que gritan "muera Esquilache"!

CAMPOS También dan "vivas", excelencia.

ESQUILACHE ¿Y ésas son todas las noticias que me trae?

CAMPOS Hago lo que puedo, excelencia.

ESQUILACHE Lo que puede, ¿eh?... (*Termina de escribir y arroja la pluma.*) ¿Por qué no ha habido manera de reunir esta mañana al Consejo de Guerra? ¿Por qué han venido sólo dos consejeros de Hacienda?

CAMPOS No puedo asegurar que a todos les llegara el aviso, excelencia.

ESQUILACHE ¡Ah! ¿No puede asegurar...?

CAMPOS Excelencia, yo...

ESQUILACHE (*Se levanta.*) ¡No me interrumpa! Usía no cumplió mis órdenes. Si no puede asegurar que llegaron los recados es que no se ha cerciorado de si fueron

ESQUILACHE   *(Surprised and displeased.)* You?

VILLASANTA   I was the only gentleman at Court not occupied. May I say that I regret the humiliation that this must cause you... And I would have you know that I feel no less humiliated myself.

ESQUILACHE   Very well. You may go.

VILLASANTA   *(As if laying down a challenge.)* I am at your Excellency's disposal, with instructions to supply you with whatever you need, including information. Accurate information, naturally. Would you like to hear the latest news?

ESQUILACHE   *(Accepting the challenge.)* Why not? Tell me, then.

VILLASANTA   The people have destroyed the five thousand street lights that you had installed. In the Plaza Mayor they've lit a large bonfire... but of course they're only burning pictures and a few other things in it.

ESQUILACHE   Congratulations, your Grace... The people of Madrid are back to their old ways: anarchy, insanity and filth. Now I would like you to leave me.

The duke bows, the marquis bows in reply, and stands staring at the door as VILLASANTA *goes out. The lights fade, until the stage is almost completely dark. Just before it gets dark,* DOÑA MARÍA *leans out at her balcony with a pan full of leftovers and checks that the coast is clear.*

MARÍA   Gardyloo![46]

She tips the contents of the pan into the street and closes the balcony. The night is enlivened by distant shouts and cheers, which intensify as daylight slowly returns. Just as slowly, the blind BALLAD-SELLER *moves across the stage from upstage right to upstage left, as if it were he who was bringing in the new day. The light also comes up on the study, where* ESQUILACHE, *without his sword, is sitting at the desk writing.* CAMPOS *is standing next to the desk.* FERNANDITA, *near the balcony. On the side table is a tray with hot chocolate. Before the room is completely lit, we hear* ESQUILACHE *speaking angrily.*

ESQUILACHE   You don't need to tell me that they're shouting "Death to Esquilache"!

CAMPOS   There are also people cheering, my Lord.

ESQUILACHE   And is that all the news you have for me?

CAMPOS   I am doing what I can, sir.

ESQUILACHE   Doing what you can, are you?... *(He finishes writing and flings down the pen.)* Then why couldn't we have a meeting of the Council of War this morning? Why have only two members of the Treasury Council come?

CAMPOS   I cannot guarantee that the notice will have reached all of them.

ESQUILACHE   Ah! So you can't guarantee...?

CAMPOS   My Lord, I...

ESQUILACHE   *(Gets up.)* Don't interrupt me! You failed to carry out my orders. The reason why you can't guarantee that the messages arrived is that you didn't

cumplidos, lo cual es otra falta. Pero ¿para qué cerciorarse? Era tan difícil ayer encontrar en mi antecámara oficiales que obedeciesen... *Allora*, la falta empezó ayer: no me lo niegue. Justificó el encargo con unas pocas llamadas y hoy no me puede asegurar que los demás fuesen avisados. *¡E chiaro!* ¡Qué va a poder asegurar!

Va a la mesita para servirse una jícara. FERNANDITA *se adelanta y se la lleva.*

CAMPOS   Excelencia...

ESQUILACHE   ¡Don Antonio! Soy un ministro de su majestad. Le advierto lealmente que su falta de celo es, por lo menos, prematura. Esos revoltosos que piden mi muerte en la calle van a saber todavía quién es Esquilache. Dentro de unos minutos se reunirá el Consejo Real y allí haré aprobar medidas decisivas. ¡Acabo de redactarlas! ¡Aprenderán a andar derechos por la fuerza y si hay que barrerlos a cañonazos, es preferible no vacilar! Y los servidores que cumplan mal con su deber, también tendrán que sentir. ¿O es que usía cree que he caído en desgracia? (*Bebe de su taza.*)

CAMPOS   Aseguro a vuecelencia que en ningún momento he pensado...

ESQUILACHE   ¡Míreme a los ojos! ¡Ah!... ¡Le cuesta trabajo!... (*Su voz cambia: se hace más reflexiva.*) Le cuesta trabajo. (*Golpecitos en la puerta.*) ¡Adelante!

Entra VILLASANTA.

VILLASANTA   Debo informar a usía de que la explanada de Palacio se ha llenado de paisanos armados. Quieren entrar aquí (*Señala al balcón.*), en la plaza de armas, pero la infantería valona ha acordonado el Arco de la Armería y lo impide.

ESQUILACHE   ¿Se sabe qué quieren?

VILLASANTA   Ver al rey.

ESQUILACHE   Gracias. Téngame al corriente de cuanto suceda. (VILLASANTA *se inclina y sale, cerrando.*) ¡Y usía también, don Antonio! Ya se ve que sobran noticias. Salga y muévase.

Le interrumpen dos tiros lejanos. FERNANDITA *gime y corre al balcón.* ESQUILACHE *deja la taza y va tras ella.*

FERNANDITA   No se ve nada...

ESQUILACHE   (*Se vuelve.*) ¿Qué espera? Ya ve que las novedades se suceden.

CAMPOS   Ahora mismo, excelencia. Pero antes... permítame vuecelencia hacerle notar respetuosamente una cosa. (ESQUILACHE *se acerca, intrigado.*) No es la

bother to make sure that they would: another failure. But then, why should you bother to check? Yesterday it was so difficult to find any staff here who would do what they were told... *Allora*, your failure began yesterday: don't try to deny it. You made one or two calls just to show that you were doing something, and now you can't be sure that the others were notified. *E chiaro!* You can't be sure of anything, can you?

He goes towards the table to serve himself a cup of chocolate. FERNANDITA *gets there first and brings it to him.*

CAMPOS Your Excellency...

ESQUILACHE Don Antonio! I am still a minister of the Crown. As a friend, I would advise you that your lack of zeal is, at the very least, premature. I intend to show those rebels calling for my head out there just who they are dealing with. In a few minutes there will be a meeting of the Royal Council, at which I'll push through some decisive measures. I've just been drawing them up! I'll make that rabble stay in line, and if we have to blast them out of our way, it's best not to waste any time! And any of my staff who fall short in their duties will regret it soon enough, too. Or did you think that I've fallen out of favour already? (*He takes a sip of chocolate.*)

CAMPOS I can assure you, my Lord, that not for one moment have I thought...

ESQUILACHE Look me in the eye! Ah!... You find that difficult, don't you?... (*The tone of his voice changes, becoming more thoughtful.*) You find it difficult to look me in the eye. (*Someone knocks lightly on the door.*) Come in!

VILLASANTA *comes in.*

VILLASANTA My Lord, I must inform you that the esplanade outside the palace is full of armed civilians. They are trying to force their way into the courtyard (*Pointing towards the balcony.*), but the Walloon guards have cordoned off the arch to stop them.

ESQUILACHE Do we know what they want?

VILLASANTA To see the king.

ESQUILACHE Thank you. Keep me informed of everything that happens. (VILLASANTA *bows and leaves, closing the door behind him.*) And that goes for you too, don Antonio! It's obvious that there's a lot going on out there. Get to work.

He is interrupted by two shots in the distance. FERNANDITA *moans and rushes towards the balcony.* ESQUILACHE *puts down his cup and follows her.*

FERNANDITA I can't see anything...

ESQUILACHE (*Turning towards his secretary.*) What are you waiting for? You can see that events are moving quickly, can't you?

CAMPOS At once, sir. But first... I hope that your Lordship will allow me respectfully to draw something to your attention. (ESQUILACHE *moves*

primera vez que vuecelencia censura con dureza mis supuestos errores...
delante de criados.

ESQUILACHE *eleva las cejas, irritado.*

FERNANDITA Si el señor marqués me permite retirarme...
ESQUILACHE (*Se calma súbitamente e interrumpe con un gesto a* FERNANDITA.)
¿Y qué más?
CAMPOS Soy un hidalgo español. No me gusta que se falte a mi dignidad de ese
modo.
ESQUILACHE (*Muy tranquilo.*) Y claro: es su hidalguía la que le obliga a hacerme esa
observación, ¿no?
CAMPOS Con todo respeto.
ESQUILACHE (*Llega a su lado.*) ¿Y por qué su hidalguía no le obligó a hablar la
primera vez que ocurrió? (*Un silencio.*) O la segunda. (*Un silencio.* CAMPOS
baja los ojos. ESQUILACHE *sonríe con amargura.*) ¡O la tercera!... ¿Por qué
ha esperado a hoy precisamente para decírmelo?... (CAMPOS *baja la cabeza.*)
Salga, don Antonio. Y procure estar cerca cuando le llame. (CAMPOS *sale y
cierra.*) ¡Mascalzone! (*Vuelve a la mesita para beber otro sorbo. Se sienta,
melancólico.*) Me pregunto si tengo derecho a hacerte compartir todas estas
amarguras...
FERNANDITA (*Suspira.*) El rey lo llamará en seguida... Ya lo verá. Y en el Consejo
Real lo arreglará todo...
ESQUILACHE No... He escrito durante toda la mañana... Pero a ti no puedo mentirte.
Lo hacía para no pensar en la terrible evidencia de que todos... me abandonan.
FERNANDITA Tome algo más, señor... Ha comido muy poco este mediodía...
ESQUILACHE (*Deniega.*) Ahora no podría. (*Otro tiro. Se miran, sobresaltados.*)
¿Qué va a ocurrir, Fernandita? ¿Qué nos va a ocurrir a los dos? (*Golpecitos en
la puerta.* ESQUILACHE *se levanta.*) ¡Adelante! (*Entra* VILLASANTA.)
¿Qué sucede ahora?
VILLASANTA (*Cierra la puerta.*) Muchas cosas, marqués. (*Cruza hacia el balcón.*)
En primer lugar, debo obtener su palabra de que no se asomará a este balcón.
ESQUILACHE ¿Por qué?
VILLASANTA Podría ser peligroso. (ESQUILACHE *va a abrir el balcón.*) ¡Marqués,
no debe abrirlo! ¡Hay orden de que nadie se asome a esta fachada! En este
momento su majestad ocupa el balcón central con su confesor y varios
gentileshombres.
ESQUILACHE ¿El rey? ¿Qué hace?
VILLASANTA Contesta a una delegación.
ESQUILACHE ¿A una delegación? (*Sube al poyete y trata de atisbar tras los
cristales.* VILLASANTA *pone rápidamente su mano sobre la falleba.*) ¡No
voy a abrir, duque!

towards him, intrigued.) This is not the first time that your Lordship has severely reprimanded me for supposed errors... in the presence of servants.

ESQUILACHE *raises his eyebrows in irritation.*

FERNANDITA   If your Lordship will give me leave to withdraw...
ESQUILACHE   (*Calms down suddenly and stops* FERNANDITA *with a gesture.*) Anything else?
CAMPOS   I am a gentleman and a Spaniard. I am displeased by such a lack of respect for my dignity.
ESQUILACHE   (*Very calmly.*) And naturally, it's your status as a gentleman that prompts you to point this out to me, is it?
CAMPOS   With the greatest respect.
ESQUILACHE   (*At his side.*) And why didn't your gentlemanly dignity make you speak up the first time this happened? (*Silence.*) Or the second? (*Silence.* CAMPOS *looks down.* ESQUILACHE *smiles bitterly.*) Or the third!... Why did you wait until today, precisely today, before saying something?... (CAMPOS *lowers his head.*) Get out of here, don Antonio. And make sure that you're nearby when I call you. (CAMPOS *goes out, closing the door behind him.*) *Mascalzone!* (*He goes back to the table to drink another sip of chocolate. He sits down, gloomily.*) I'm not sure that I have the right to make you share all these tribulations.
FERNANDITA   (*Sighs.*) The king'll call for you soon... You'll see. And in the Royal Council you'll sort it all out...
ESQUILACHE   No... I've been writing all morning... But I can't lie to you. I've been trying not to think about what's becoming painfully obvious: the fact that they are all abandoning me.
FERNANDITA   You ought to have something else to eat, my Lord... You've hardly had anything today...
ESQUILACHE   (*Shaking his head.*) No, I couldn't eat anything now. (*Another shot. They exchange a look of alarm.*) What's going to happen, Fernandita? What's going to happen to us? (*A knock on the door.* ESQUILACHE *gets up.*) Come in! (*Enter* VILLASANTA.) What's happening now?
VILLASANTA   (*Closing the door.*) A great deal, my Lord. (*He moves over towards the balcony.*) First, I must ask you to give me your word that you will not go out onto this balcony.
ESQUILACHE   Why not?
VILLASANTA   It could be dangerous. (ESQUILACHE *goes to open it.*) My Lord, you must not open it! The order has been given that no-one should be seen along the whole of this side of the palace! At this very moment his Majesty is on the central balcony with his confessor and some of his gentlemen-in-waiting.
ESQUILACHE   The king? Why, what is he doing?
VILLASANTA   He is responding to a delegation.
ESQUILACHE   A delegation? (*He gets up onto the step and tries to look out.* VILLASANTA *quickly puts his hand on the handle.*) I'm not going to open it!

VILLASANTA   ¿Ni siquiera cuando me retire?

ESQUILACHE   ¿Tan necesario es?

VILLASANTA   Si no me da su palabra, me veré obligado a poner aquí dos soldados de la guardia.

ESQUILACHE   ¡Qué!

VILLASANTA   ¿Tengo o no tengo su palabra?

ESQUILACHE   (*Baja iracundo del poyete y pasea.*) ¡La tiene! Y ahora, explíquese. (FERNANDITA *sube al poyete y trata de ver algo, muy nerviosa.*) ¿Qué delegación es ésa?

VILLASANTA   Gente del pueblo. Se les ha dejado entrar desarmados. Era la única forma de lograr una tregua.

ESQUILACHE   ¿Una tregua?

VILLASANTA   Las cosas empeoran, marqués. Ahí fuera un valón ha matado a una mujer y a él lo han arrastrado. En la plaza Mayor se acaba de librar un encuentro sangriento entre el pueblo y el piquete de valones que estaba de guardia allí. Los amotinados los han apedreado con las piedras apiladas para la nueva pavimentación... (ESQUILACHE *se muerde los labios.*) Luego se han cruzado tiros. El pueblo ha logrado dispersarlos y ha cogido a tres o cuatro... que también han muerto bárbaramente.

ESQUILACHE   ¡Inaudito!

VILLASANTA   No olvide que el pueblo odia a los valones desde que cargaron contra la multitud en los esponsales del príncipe de Asturias. Hubo varios muertos...

ESQUILACHE   Fue un accidente deplorable.

VILLASANTA   Los valones que acaban de morir también son... accidentes deplorables.

ESQUILACHE   ¿Qué pide esa delegación?

VILLASANTA   Lo ignoro. Para mayor garantía del rey, venía con ellos un fraile de San Gil que ha subido a entregarle las peticiones. (ESQUILACHE *va al foro y tira nerviosamente del cordón de la campanilla.*) ¿Puedo saber a quién llama usía?

ESQUILACHE   A mi secretario.

VILLASANTA   No está en la antecámara.

ESQUILACHE   Que se le busque.

VILLASANTA   Me temo que no esté en Palacio...

ESQUILACHE   ¿Qué sabe usía?

VILLASANTA   Juzgo por lo que dijo cuando salió de aquí.

ESQUILACHE   Ah, ¿sí?... ¿Qué dijo?

VILLASANTA   No sé si debo repetirlo.

ESQUILACHE   (*Ruge.*) ¿Usía es o no es mi mayordomo?

VILLASANTA   Dijo que... ya había soportado bastante los malos modales de un extranjero advenedizo y que sabía muy bien a quién tenía que ofrecer ahora sus servicios.

VILLASANTA   Not even when I leave?
ESQUILACHE   Why is it so important?
VILLASANTA   If you do not give me your word, I shall be obliged to post two guards
   here.
ESQUILACHE   What?!
VILLASANTA   Do I or do I not have your word?
ESQUILACHE   (*In a rage, he steps down and begins to walk around.*) You do! And
   now, you can explain yourself. (FERNANDITA, *looking very anxious, gets up
   onto the step and attempts to see something.*) What is this delegation you were
   talking about?
VILLASANTA   Oh, just some of the rabble. They've been let through without their
   weapons. It was the only way of winning a truce.
ESQUILACHE   A truce?
VILLASANTA   Things are getting worse, my Lord. One of the Walloons has killed a
   woman and his body has been dragged around the city. There has just been a
   bloody encounter in the Plaza Mayor between the crowd and the squad of
   Walloons that was on guard there. The rioters stoned them with the cobbles
   that were piled up for the new paving... (ESQUILACHE *bites his lip.*) Then
   there was some shooting. The crowd managed to split them up and got hold of
   three or four of them... and killed them brutally.
ESQUILACHE   This is incredible!
VILLASANTA   Don't forget that the people hate the Walloons, ever since the time
   when they fired on the crowd at the Prince of Asturias's wedding. Several
   people were killed...[47]
ESQUILACHE   It was a regrettable accident.
VILLASANTA   Just as these deaths of a few Walloons are... regrettable accidents, I
   suppose.
ESQUILACHE   What does the delegation want?
VILLASANTA   I don't know. To reassure the king, they came with a friar from San
   Gil, who has come up to hand over the petitions. (ESQUILACHE *goes upstage
   and jerks the bell pull.*) May I ask for whom you are ringing?
ESQUILACHE   My secretary.
VILLASANTA   He's not in the antechamber.
ESQUILACHE   Then I'll send for him.
VILLASANTA   I'm afraid he's not in the palace at all...
ESQUILACHE   How should you know?
VILLASANTA   I'm simply judging by what he said as he left here.
ESQUILACHE   Oh, yes?... And what did he say?
VILLASANTA   I'm not sure that I should repeat it.
ESQUILACHE   (*With a roar.*) Are you my aide or aren't you?
VILLASANTA   He said... that he had put up for long enough with the rudeness of a
   certain foreign upstart, and that he knew very well to whom he could offer his
   services now.

Un silencio. ESQUILACHE *se apoya en la mesa.*

FERNANDITA   Parece que se oyen vivas...

VILLASANTA *sube al poyete y mira.*

VILLASANTA   Los delegados salen de la plaza.
ESQUILACHE   Una pregunta, duque. ¿Me equivoco si supongo que en este momento hay soldados en mi antecámara?
VILLASANTA   (*Baja los ojos.*) Han sido puestos para velar por la seguridad de usía.
ESQUILACHE   (*Sonríe con amargura.*) ¡De modo que estoy prisionero!
VILLASANTA   Custodiado solamente, marqués.

Baja del poyete y se acerca a la puerta.

ESQUILACHE   (*Se interpone y le aferra por un brazo.*) ¿Está seguro de no excederse en sus atribuciones?
VILLASANTA   (*Se suelta.*) ¡No me toque!
ESQUILACHE   ¡No ha respondido a mi pregunta!
VILLASANTA   ¡Sólo cumplo órdenes!
ESQUILACHE   (*No se fía.*) Ya. Así que no soy un prisionero. De modo que si ahora quiero salir de aquí para ver al rey...
VILLASANTA   No comprende la situación, marqués. Es el rey quien ruega al marqués de Esquilache que aguarde aquí su visita.
ESQUILACHE   (*Rojo.*) ¡Eso es mentira!
VILLASANTA   (*Palidece.*) Ese insulto no quedaría impune en otra ocasión. (ESQUILACHE, *muy alterado, va hacia la puerta y empuña el pomo.*) ¡No le dejarán salir, Esquilache! (ESQUILACHE *lo mira con un principio de temor en los ojos.*) ¡Es el rey quien lo ordena y no yo, marqués! ¡Lo juro por mi honor!

ESQUILACHE *retrocede, sintiendo que el temor le crece, sin dejar de mirarlo.*

ESQUILACHE   (*Jadea.*) Allora... Le ordeno que vea al rey en mi nombre... y le diga... que solicito respetuosamente la inmediata reunión del Consejo Real.
VILLASANTA   (*Baja la cabeza.*) Es un ruego tardío, marqués.
ESQUILACHE   ¿Tardío?
VILLASANTA   El rey se reunió con el Consejo Real hace media hora.
ESQUILACHE   (*Trastornado.*) ¿Sin mí?
VILLASANTA   Lo ha interrumpido sólo para salir al balcón.
ESQUILACHE   (*En voz queda.*) Sin mí... (*Avanza para sentarse pesadamente junto a la mesita.*) ¿Por qué no me lo dijo hace media hora, duque?

A pause. ESQUILACHE *leans against the desk.*

FERNANDITA   I think I can hear some cheering...

VILLASANTA *steps up and looks out.*

VILLASANTA   The delegates are leaving the courtyard.
ESQUILACHE   I'd like to ask you one thing, your Grace. Would I be wrong to
     suppose that there are soldiers in my antechamber right now?
VILLASANTA   (*Looks down.*) They have been posted there for your securitv
ESQUILACHE   (*Smiles ruefully.*) So I'm a prisoner, then!
VILLASANTA   Your Excellency is merely being guarded.

He steps down and goes towards the door.

ESQUILACHE   (*Intercepting him and grabbing his arm.*) Are you sure that you're not
     exceeding your powers?
VILLASANTA   (*Breaks free.*) Do not touch me!
ESQUILACHE   You haven't answered my question!
VILLASANTA   I'm only obeying orders!
ESQUILACHE   (*Not convinced.*) Fine. You said that I'm not a prisoner. So if I want
     to leave here now to go and see the king...
VILLASANTA   I'm afraid you don't understand the situation. It's the king himself who
     wishes the Marquis of Esquilache to wait for him here.
ESQUILACHE   (*Reddening.*) That's a lie!
VILLASANTA   (*He stiffens.*) At any other time, that insult would not go unchallenged.
     (ESQUILACHE, *extremely agitated, marches to the door and grasps the
     handle.*) They won't let you leave, Esquilache! (ESQUILACHE *looks at him
     with fear welling up in his eyes.*) The king's orders, not mine! I swear it on my
     honour!

ESQUILACHE *retreats, feeling the fear growing inside him, without taking his eyes off*
VILLASANTA.

ESQUILACHE   (*Panting.*) Allora... I order you to go and see the king in my name...
     and tell him... that I respectfully request an immediate meeting of the Royal
     Council.
VILLASANTA   (*Lowers his head.*) Your request is too late, my Lord.
ESQUILACHE   Too late?
VILLASANTA   The king held a meeting with the Royal Council half an hour ago.
ESQUILACHE   (*Confused.*) What, without me?
VILLASANTA   His Majesty came directly from the meeting and out onto the balcony.
ESQUILACHE   (*Very quietly.*) Without me... (*He moves forward and slumps down
     onto a chair next to the side table.*) Why didn't you tell me this half an hour
     ago?

Se vuelve para mirarlo al ver que no contesta.

VILLASANTA   No soy tan cruel como usía cree.

ESQUILACHE.   Cuando el enemigo ha caído ya. ¿No era eso lo que pensaba añadir? *Ecco.* Yo ya era un caído, aunque me obstinase en engañarme. Los demás ven nuestro destino antes que nosotros. (VILLASANTA *se inclina en silencio y sale, cerrando.*) Si es uno de los jefes de la conspiración, me tiene entre sus garras. Si no ha mentido, el rey me ha abandonado. Ya no sé qué pensar. (*Mira a* FERNANDITA.) No debí traerte. Hay agonías que un hombre debe pasar solo.

FERNANDITA   (*Sin mirarlo.*) Hay agonías tan terribles que nunca se debieran pasar en soledad. Cuando se sufren, es mejor tener a nuestro lado al más pobre, al más desvalido de los seres, con tal de que tenga un poco de piedad.

Lo ha dicho pensando en sí misma; pero ESQUILACHE *se siente bruscamente quebrado por sus palabras y estalla en un sollozo. Para disimular sus lágrimas, para luchar contra ese destructor sentimiento de autocompasión que le atenaza, se levanta y va hacia la derecha, tragando, jadeando, intentando en vano retener el llanto.* FERNANDITA *corre a su lado.* ESQUILACHE *habla de espaldas, rehuyendo los tímidos contactos que ella, en su angustia, osa, se vuelve a uno y otro lado para que ella no vea sus mejillas mojadas. El diálogo se hace entrecortado, confuso: dos grandes desgracias se buscan a ciegas a su través.*

ESQUILACHE   Una vida perdida...
FERNANDITA   Perdóneme... No debí decir nada...
ESQUILACHE   Prisionero del rey...
FERNANDITA   Aún no se ha perdido todo...
ESQUILACHE   Del rey...
FERNANDITA   Confíe...
ESQUILACHE   Creí que era mi amigo y me sacrifica...
FERNANDITA   Es necesario confiar...
ESQUILACHE   Pero sobre todo, me engaña...
FERNANDITA   Aunque el dolor nos desgarre las entrañas...
ESQUILACHE   Todo es ingratitud...
FERNANDITA   Señor...
ESQUILACHE   Ya sólo tengo al lado a ese pobre ser humano, al más desvalido de todos, al único que aún sabe apiadarse... A ti... Tú... Tú...
FFRNANDITA   (*En voz baja.*) ¡Dios mío!
ESQUILACHE   (*Se vuelve de improviso y escucha, aferrándole una muñeca.*) Calla. ¿No oyes?

Los dos miran hacia el balcón.

As the duke does not answer at once, he turns to look at him.

VILLASANTA I'm not as cruel as you think I am.
ESQUILACHE When your enemy is already down. Isn't that what you were thinking
of adding? *Ecco.* I had already fallen, even though I was insisting on deceiving
myself. Others see our destiny before we do. (VILLASANTA *bows in silence
and goes out, closing the door behind him.*) If he's one of the leaders of the plot,
he has me in his grasp. If he's telling the truth, the king has abandoned me. I
don't know what to think any more. *(He looks at* FERNANDITA.) I shouldn't
have brought you here. There are agonies that a man should suffer alone.
FERNANDITA *(Without looking at him.)* There are some agonies so terrible that they
should never be suffered alone. When we go through them, it's best to have at
our side someone utterly poor and helpless, as long as that person has some
compassion.

*She has been referring to herself; but her words have a powerful effect on
ESQUILACHE, who lets out a heartfelt sob. In an attempt to conceal his tears and
fight off the dangerous temptation to wallow in self-pity, he stands up and walks over to
the right, swallowing hard, panting, struggling in vain to control his weeping.
FERNANDITA runs to his side. ESQUILACHE talks with his back to her, shrinking
from the tentative contacts that she, in her anguish, dares to make; he keeps turning
away so that she should not see his wet cheeks. The dialogue becomes staccato,
confused: two victims of terrible wrongs groping towards each other in the dark.*

ESQUILACHE My whole life wasted...
FERNANDITA Forgive me... I shouldn't have said anything.
ESQUILACHE A prisoner of the king...
FERNANDITA Everything's not lost yet...
ESQUILACHE Of the king...
FERNANDITA Trust him...
ESQUILACHE I thought he was my friend and he's sacrificing me...
FERNANDITA We must have faith in someone...
ESQUILACHE But worst of all, he's deceiving me...
FERNANDITA Even if the pain is tearing us apart...
ESQUILACHE Ingratitude... there's nothing but ingratitude.
FERNANDITA My Lord...
ESQUILACHE The only one who's standing by me now is the poorest, the most
helpless of all, the only one who can still take pity on me... You are all I've got
left... You... You...
FERNANDITA *(Quietly.)* God help us!
ESQUILACHE *(Turns round suddenly and listens, grasping her wrist.)* Quiet. Can
you hear something?

They both look towards the balcony.

FERNANDITA   Parecen gritos.
ESQUILACHE   Aclamaciones. Dan vivas a alguien.
FERNANDITA   Y además... Ese fragor...
ESQUILACHE   Es como el sonido del mar.

FERNANDITA *corre al balcón, mira y se vuelve.*

FERNANDITA   El pueblo está llenando la plaza... Ha debido de romper el cordón de
          soldados.
ESQUILACHE   Los delegados les habrán transmitido las promesas del rey... y no les
          habrán parecido suficientes.
FFRNANDITA   (*Vuelve a mirar.*) Se acercan... (ESQUILACHE *llega al balcón para
          mirar también.* FERNANDITA *se pone a observar algo, de repente, con
          enorme sorpresa.*) ¡Pero...! (*Se vuelve descompuesta, con la mano en los labios
          y ahoga un gemido. Trastornada, histérica, dice:*) El... Es él... Es él... El...
ESQUILACHE   ¿Quién?
FERNANDITA   Ese... El que va delante... El...

ESQUILACHE *mira. Ella solloza y se refugia en sus brazos.*

ESQUILACHE   Pero ¿quién es él?
FERNANDITA   (*Presa de una tremenda crisis.*) ¡Mató a Julián! ¡Lo mató delante de
          mí por defenderme!...

A ESQUILACHE *le agranda los ojos una súbita sorpresa.*

ESQUILACHE   ¿Por defenderte? (*La baja a viva fuerza del poyete mientras ella sigue
          musitando, con ojos extraviados: "El... El...*") ¿Por defenderte de quién?
FERNANDITA   ¡De él!
ESQUILACHE   ¿Lo conoces?
FERNANDITA   ¡Sí!...
ESQUILACHE   (*Horrorizado, la aprieta contra sí.*) Fernandita...
FERNANDITA   ¡No puedo más!...

Se desprende y corre hacia la derecha, pero él la retiene por una muñeca.

ESQUILACHE   ¡Fernandita!

Ella se detiene, con los ojos bajos, turbadísima.

FERNANDITA   No puedo más...
ESQUILACHE   (*Suelta su mano.*) ¿Quién es?

FERNANDITA   It sounds like shouting.
ESQUILACHE   Cheering, I'd say. They're cheering someone.
FERNANDITA   And there's a roaring noise too...
ESQUILACHE   It's like the sound of the sea.

FERNANDITA *rushes to the balcony, peers out, and then turns towards him.*

FERNANDITA   The crowd's pouring into the courtyard... They must have broken
      through the cordon of soldiers.
ESQUILACHE   Their delegates must have announced the king's promises to them...
      and they're not satisfied.
FERNANDITA   (*Looking out again.*) They're coming this way... (ESQUILACHE *goes
      to the balcony to have a look for himself. FERNANDITA suddenly notices
      something that takes her by surprise.*) But it can't be...! (*She turns away,
      obviously upset, with her hand over her mouth, stifling a moan. Shocked,
      hysterical, she says:*) Him... It's him... It's him... Him...
ESQUILACHE   Who?
FERNANDITA   That one... The one at the front... It's him...

ESQUILACHE *takes a look. She sobs and takes refuge in his arms.*

ESQUILACHE   But who is he?
FERNANDITA   (*In great suffering.*) He was the one who killed Julián! He killed him
      right in front of me because he was defending me!

ESQUILACHE'*s eyes suddenly widen in surprise.*

ESQUILACHE   Julián was defending you? (*He drags her down from the step, while
      she continues, wild-eyed, to mutter: "Him... Him...".*) Defending you from
      whom?
FERNANDITA   From him!
ESQUILACHE   Do you know him?
FERNANDITA   Yes!
ESQUILACHE   (*Horrified, he holds her tightly in his arms.*) Fernandita...
FERNANDITA   I can't take any more!

She breaks away from him and runs towards the right, but he holds onto her wrist.

ESQUILACHE   Fernandita!

She stops, her head hanging in shame and anguish.

FERNANDITA   I can't take any more...
ESQUILACHE   (*Lets go of her hand.*) Who is he?

FERNANDITA   (*Muy bajo.*) Bernardo. Un calesero.

ESQUILACHE   ¿Te perseguía?

FERNANDITA   Sí.

ESQUILACHE   (*Muerde la palabra en un rapto de desesperación.*) ¡Fernandita! (*La atrae hacia sí y la abraza con fuerza.*)

FERNANDITA   ¡Se encerró conmigo! ¡Yo gritaba, pero toda la casa era un puro grito!... A Julián lo arrastraron después a la puerta... Querían llevarlo por las calles, pero allí lo dejaron, y yo... Yo... (*Llora desconsoladamente.*)

ESQUILACHE   ¡Y no poder vengarte! (*Crispa una de sus manos.*) En esta mano estaba el Poder de España y ahora está vacía... ¡Dios mío, dame el Poder de nuevo!

FERNANDITA   (*Se desprende y retrocede.*) ¡No soy digna de piedad! ¡Yo también soy despreciable, porque sé que al final... no he resistido!

ESQUILACHE   ¿Que no has resistido?... ¿Le querías? (*Ella asiente levísimamente.*) ¡Le querías!...

FERNANDITA   He tratado de olvidarlo, de aborrecerlo. El representa toda la torpeza y toda la brutalidad que odio. ¡Es como el que mató a mi padre! ¡Y yo he querido salir de esa noche, de ese horror... y no puedo! ¡Yo he querido curarme con un poco de luz, con un poco de piedad! ¡Huir hacia su merced y hacia todo lo que su merced representaba! ¡Huir de ese infierno de mi infancia aterrorizada y asqueada por el asesinato! ¡Y no puedo!... (*Estalla en sollozos.*)

ESQUILACHE   (*Musita.*) ¡Dios mío!

FERNANDITA   Intenté olvidarle con Julián. Pero no era posible... Y al fin... me pareció que un sentimiento nuevo y más grande me llenaba las entrañas... Una ternura nueva, limpia..., hacia un anciano bondadoso, triste, solitario... Y esa ternura no ha cesado... Pero ¿qué puede contra este demonio que me habita? (ESQUILACHE *suspira.*) Y ahora está ahí, abajo. Es el enemigo de los dos. ¡Viene por los dos!... ¡Y nos vencerá!

ESQUILACHE   (*Se acerca.*) Escucha, hija mía...

FERNANDITA   ¡No me toque! (*Retrocede.*) ¡No me diga nada! Todo está perdido y yo... ¡no puedo más! (*Se vuelve y llega, rápida, a la puerta de la derecha, que abre.*) ¡No puedo más! (*Sale.*)

ESQUILACHE   (*Tras ella.*) ¡Fernandita!

Se detiene ante la puerta en el mismo instante en que la del fondo se abre sin ruido. El REY CARLOS III entra y cierra. ESQUILACHE oye algo y se vuelve. Vuelve a mirar al aposento de la derecha y cierra la puerta. Después se arrodilla. El REY avanza.

EL REY   Levanta, Leopoldo. Tenemos poco tiempo. (ESQUILACHE *se levanta. El REY llega a la mesita: observa el servicio del chocolate y luego levanta sus ojos para mirar a la puerta de la derecha. ESQUILACHE no lo pierde de*

FERNANDITA   (*Very quietly.*) Bernardo. A cab driver.

ESQUILACHE   Was he after you?

FERNANDITA   Yes.

ESQUILACHE   (*He blurts out her name in despair.*) Fernandita! (*He pulls her towards him and embraces her forcefully.*)

FERNANDITA   He shut me in with him! I was screaming, but the whole house was full of shouting!... They dragged Julián down to the front door afterwards... They were going to carry him through the streets, but they just left him there in the end, and I... I... (*She weeps inconsolably.*)

ESQUILACHE   And to think that I can't avenge you! (*He clenches his fist.*) I had all the power of Spain in this hand, and now it's empty... Oh, God, give me back the power!

FERNANDITA   (*Pulling free and backing away.*) I don't deserve your pity! You ought to despise me too, because I know that in the end... I didn't really resist!

ESQUILACHE   You didn't resist?... Did you love him, then? (*She nods almost imperceptibly.*) You loved him!...

FERNANDITA   I've tried to forget him, to loathe him. I see in him all the crudeness and brutality that I hate. He's just the same as the man who murdered my father! And I've tried to get away from all that darkness, all that horror... and I can't! I wanted to make myself better by finding a little light and a little human kindness. To escape towards you and everything you stood for! To get away from the hell of that childhood, terrorized and brutalized by murder! And I can't! (*She breaks into uncontrollable sobbing.*)

ESQUILACHE   (*Mutters to himself.*) My God!

FERNANDITA   I tried to forget him by being with Julián. But it was impossible... And then... I found a new, greater feeling growing inside me... A new, clean kind of tenderness..., towards a kind-hearted, sad, lonely old man... And that tenderness hasn't gone away... But what chance does it have against this demon that's taken me over? (ESQUILACHE *sighs.*) And he's down there right now. He's your enemy as well as mine. He's coming to get us both!... And he will get us!

ESQUILACHE   (*Moving towards her.*) Now listen, my child...

FERNANDITA   Don't touch me! (*Backing away.*) Don't say anything to me! Everything's gone wrong and I... I can't take any more! (*She rushes out.*)

ESQUILACHE   (*Going after her.*) Fernandita!

He stops just as he gets to the door, at the very moment when the door at the back of the stage opens silently. KING CARLOS III *comes in and closes the door.* ESQUILACHE *hears something and turns around. He casts another glance into the room off to the right and shuts the door. Then he kneels down. The* KING *walks downstage.*

KING   Get up, Leopoldo. We haven't got much time. (ESQUILACHE *gets to his feet. The* KING *pauses by the side table: he notices the tray with the chocolate, and looks up towards the door at stage right.* ESQUILACHE *watches him*

vista.) Bien... Te supongo al corriente de todo. Desde aquí habrás visto y habrás oído.

ESQUILACHE Muy poco, señor. Vuestra majestad prohibió, al parecer, que me asomara.

EL REY Corrías peligro. ¿No has oído las peticiones?

ESQUILACHE Sólo un rumor sordo, señor.

EL REY ¿Ni siquiera las aclamaciones?

ESQUILACHE Pero las supongo. El pueblo aclama siempre a su rey.

EL REY (*Enigmático.*) No sólo a mí.

ESQUILACHE Nada he oído, señor. Pero sé lo bastante. Sé, por ejemplo, que vuestra majestad ha reunido al Consejo Real...

EL REY Acaba de terminar y por eso vengo.

ESQUILACHE (*Inclina la cabeza.*) Aguardo vuestra decisión, señor.

EL REY ¿Mi decisión? (*Una pausa.*) No, Leopoldo. Yo vengo a que decidas tú.

ESQUILACHE (*No cree lo que oye.*) ¿Yo?

EL REY Comprendo... Has llegado a creer que te abandonaba. Pero ¿cuándo he abandonado yo a mis amigos? No podía citarte a un Consejo donde el principal asunto eras tú y en un momento en que todo el aire de Palacio está envenenado contra ti... Pero nada se ha acordado y nada acordaré sin ti.

ESQUILACHE *se precipita a besar su mano.*

ESQUILACHE He llegado a creerme prisionero de vuestra majestad.

El REY *elude, suave, el comentario y va a sentarse junto a la mesita.*

EL REY (*Le indica la otra silla.*) Así estaremos más cómodos. (ESQUILACHE *se sienta.*) Y ahora, escucha. Arcos, Gazola y Priego recomiendan restablecer con toda dureza la autoridad real. Sarriá, Oñate y Revillagigedo abogan por acceder a las peticiones de los amotinados, aunque alguno de ellos reconoce la necesidad de castigar después a los inductores. El pueblo espera abajo la decisión definitiva. ¿Qué dices tú?

ESQUILACHE (*Se levanta, con una nueva luz en los ojos.*) ¿Vuestra majestad me confiere toda mi autoridad?

EL REY Nunca la has perdido.

ESQUILACHE, *nervioso, va a la mesa del fondo y recoge el papel donde escribió, volviendo con él.*

ESQUILACHE Señor: he redactado una exposición de medidas urgentes que...

EL REY (*Le interrumpe con un ademán.*) Un momento. (*Le señala una silla y* ESQUILACHE *vuelve a sentarse.*) Antes de que pronuncies una palabra,

carefully.) Well then... I imagine you know what has been happening. You must have seen and heard it all from here.

ESQUILACHE   Very little, sire. I was told that your Majesty had forbidden me to go out onto the balcony.

KING   It would have been dangerous for you. Didn't you hear the demands?

ESQUILACHE   Only a vague noise.

KING   Not even the cheering?

ESQUILACHE   I assumed that's what it was. The people always cheer for their king.

KING   (*Enigmatically*.) It's not only for me, though.

ESQUILACHE   I've heard nothing, sire. But I know enough. I know, for example, that your Majesty has held a meeting of the Royal Council...

KING   Yes, it has just finished; that's why I'm here.

ESQUILACHE   (*Bowing his head*.) I await your decision, your Majesty.

KING   My decision? (*Pause*.) No, Leopoldo. I've come to hear your decision.

ESQUILACHE   (*Cannot believe what he hears*.) Mine?

KING   I can understand your surprise... You've begun to think that I was deserting you. But when have I ever deserted my friends? I couldn't call you to a meeting at which you were the main subject of debate, at a time when the whole court has turned against you... But nothing has been decided, and I shall decide nothing without you.

ESQUILACHE *rushes to kiss his hand.*

ESQUILACHE   I'd begun to think that I was your Majesty's prisoner.

The KING *gently brushes aside the remark and goes to sit down by the side table.*

KING   (*Pointing towards the other chair*.) Let's make ourselves more comfortable. (ESQUILACHE *sits down*.) And now, listen. Arcos, Gazola and Priego recommend that we re-establish royal authority by force. Sarriá, Oñate and Revillagigedo are in favour of giving way to the demands of the rioters, although at least one of them recognizes the need to punish the ringleaders later. The people are waiting below for the final decision. What do you say?[48]

ESQUILACHE   (*Stands up, his eyes shining again*.) Your Majesty gives me full authority?

KING   You have never lost it.

ESQUILACHE, *looking agitated, goes to the desk upstage, picks up the piece of paper on which he had been writing, and returns with it in his hand.*

ESQUILACHE   Sire: I've drawn up a set of urgent measures that...

KING   (*Interrupts him with a gesture*.) Just a moment. (*He points towards the chair and* ESQUILACHE *sits down*.) Before you say anything, I think you should get

conviene que conozcas la situación en todo su alcance. En uno de los platillos de la balanza estás tú... Bueno, y otras pocas cosas: la supresión de la Junta de Abastos, la salida de la Corte de la infantería valona, que el pueblo vista según su costumbre...

ESQUILACHE ¿Y Grimaldi?

EL REY De ése ya no hablan. En el fondo, va contra ti todo. Piden...

ESQUILACHE No me lo diga vuestra majestad. Presumo lo peor: un proceso, con jueces elegidos entre mis enemigos, del que pueda salir, incluso... la prisión.

EL REY (*Lo mira curiosamente.*) Bien. Pongamos que es lo peor.

ESQUILACHE ¿Y en el otro platillo de la balanza?

EL REY (*Baja la voz y se inclina hacia él.*) Se han recibido más noticias. No sólo Zaragoza y las Vascongadas, sino Valencia, Murcia, Cartagena, Valladolid, Salamanca, están alborotadas. (ESQUILACHE *mira el papel que conserva en las manos.*) En el otro platillo de la balanza está la subversión contra todo lo que hemos traído, la terca ceguera de un país infinitamente menos adelantado que sus gobernantes... La necesidad, tal vez, de defender todo eso a sangre y fuego antes de que lo destruyan... Pero con el riesgo, con la seguridad casi, que nos traen esas noticias, de una guerra fratricida.

Un silencio.

ESQUILACHE ¿Puedo preguntar a vuestra majestad de qué lado se inclina en su ánimo la balanza?

EL REY (*Se levanta, y* ESQUILACHE *también.*) Por primera vez estoy perplejo... (*Pasea.*) Los dos caminos son igualmente malos. Por eso he decidido confiar en tu inteligencia y en tu corazón. (*Se para y lo mira.*) Tú decides.

ESQUILACHE Así, pues, he llegado al momento supremo de mi vida. Debo elegir, y elegir bien... De un lado, la fuerza. O sea, mi continuidad personal, por lo pronto... (*Se enardece.*) La ocasión de devolver golpe por golpe, de atrapar y fusilar a los traidores, de vengar atropellos repugnantes..., de imponer, sí, de imponer lo bueno a quienes no quieren lo bueno... Y de seguir moldeando a esta bella España, y de dar un poco de luz y de alegría... (*Mira a la puerta de la derecha.*) a algunos corazones angustiados que la merecen... La vida, de nuevo. Con sus luchas, sus riesgos, su calor... (*Grave.*) Y también, el fuego. El infierno en la Tierra, y ahora por mi mano. Cincuenta muertos en Madrid no son nada. Caerán a miles por las llanuras... Una mujer forzada es un gran dolor, pero la guerra lo multiplica... España entera, roja de sangre. Esa misma plaza, dentro de unos minutos, barrida por la fusilería... La política. Y ahora, desnuda, en su más crudo aspecto. El Poder, pero cueste lo que cueste... (*Suspira.*) Sí. Sería una hermosa embriaguez. Mandar de nuevo... Restituir, todavía, la sonrisa a un rostro amado...

a clear picture of the situation. You are on one side of the scales... Together with a few other things: the abolition of the Board of Supply, the withdrawal of the Walloon Guard from Madrid, allowing the people to dress according to custom...[49]

ESQUILACHE   What about Grimaldi?

KING   They're no longer talking about him. Essentially, the whole thing is directed against you. They're demanding...

ESQUILACHE   Please don't tell me, sire. I'm assuming the worst: a trial, with judges chosen from amongst my enemies, which could even result in... prison.

KING   (*Stares at him curiously.*) Very well. Let's assume the worst.

ESQUILACHE   And on the other side of the scales?

KING   (*Lowers his voice and leans towards him.*) More news has come in. It's not only Zaragoza and the Basque Country where there are disturbances, but also in Valencia, Murcia, Cartagena, Valladolid and Salamanca. (ESQUILACHE *glances at the paper he is still holding.*) On the other side of the scales is the undermining of everything we've brought with us, the pigheaded blindness of a country infinitely less advanced than its rulers... The necessity, if it comes to that, of defending it all by fire and sword before they destroy it... But at the risk (and judging by the news we've received, it's almost a certainty) of a fratricidal war.

A moment of silence.

ESQUILACHE   And will your Majesty allow me to ask which way the balance tips in your mind?

KING   (*Gets up;* ESQUILACHE *does likewise.*) For the first time ever, I'm at a loss... (*Pacing up and down.*) Both options are equally unattractive. That is why I've decided to trust in your intelligence and your heart. (*Stops and looks at the other man.*) You decide.

ESQUILACHE   So it seems that I've reached the supreme moment of my life. I must choose, and choose well... On one side, force. Which would mean, for one thing, my political survival... (*Becoming ardent.*) The chance to hit back blow for blow, to capture and shoot the traitors, to avenge hateful outrages..., to impose, yes, impose, the good on those who don't want it... And to continue shaping this beautiful land of Spain, and to bring a little light and a little joy... (*Looks towards the door at the right.*) to some suffering souls who deserve it... To live life again. With its struggles, its risks, its warmth... (*Sombrely.*) And the fire, too. Hell on earth, and now at my hands. Fifty dead in Madrid is nothing. Thousands will fall across the country... One woman raped is a terrible thing, but it's multiplied in war... The whole of Spain, bathed in blood. The courtyard out there, a few minutes from now, swept clear by gunfire... Politics. And now, naked, at its crudest. Power, at any price... (*Sighs.*) Yes. It would be a marvellous thrill. To be in command again... To bring back, even now, the smile to the face of a loved one...

Calla.

EL REY   (*Que ha dirigido una grave mirada a la puerta de la derecha.*) ¿Y bien?
ESQUILACHE   Vuestra majestad debe aceptar todas las peticiones de los rebeldes para
   evitar la guerra.

Rompe el papel que tomó y deja los trozos sobre la mesita.

EL REY   (*Conmovido.*) Ven aquí. (ESQUILACHE *se acerca y el* REY *lo abraza con
   los ojos húmedos. Luego se desprende y va hacia el foro. Se detiene.*) No
   habrá prisión para ti. Ni proceso. No piden tanto.
ESQUILACHE   ¿Qué piden?
EL REY   Tu destierro, con toda tu familia. (ESQUILACHE *baja la cabeza. El* REY *se
   acerca y le habla en tono confidencial.*) Esta noche saldré con la familia real
   para Aranjuez. No volveré hasta que este pueblo díscolo no me dé completas
   muestras de su pacificación. Tú me acompañarás... Mañana haré ir allí a tu
   mujer y a tus hijos.
ESQUILACHE   ¿Dónde se encuentra mi mujer?
El REY   (*Suspira.*) Estaba en la Legación de Holanda. (ESQUILACHE *baja la
   cabeza.*) He mandado que se traslade a las Salesas y que aguarde allí mis
   órdenes. Ya no te separarás de ella... Ahora sería inútil.
ESQUILACHE   (*Que asiente, amargo.*) Así que todo se ha perdido...
EL REY   Acaso. Pero yo no dejaré por eso de seguir probando a que comprendan...
   (*Le pone una mano en el hombro.*) ¿Hemos soñado, Leopoldo?   ¿Hay un
   pueblo ahí abajo?
ESQUILACHE   Hemos hecho lo que debíamos.
EL REY   (*Se aparta unos pasos.*) No volverás a Madrid. Saldrás de Aranjuez para
   Cartagena y allí embarcarás para tu patria. Irás bien guardado.
ESQUILACHE   Como un preso...
EL REY   Para que nada te suceda.
ESQUILACHE   Sé muy bien que mi calvario no ha terminado. Será un viaje de
   insultos y de infamia.

Un silencio.

EL REY   Olvidaba una cosa. (*Saca de la manga de su casaca un pliego sellado.*)
   Muchas veces me has rogado a favor de Ensenada Le he llamado a Palacio, y
   he dado orden de que lo conduzcan aquí en cuanto llegue. Dale esto en mi
   nombre: será tu último acto de Gobierno.
ESQUILACHE   Gracias también en su nombre, señor.

He falls silent.

KING   *(After glancing towards the door at the right.)* Well?
ESQUILACHE   Your Majesty should concede all of the rebels' demands in order to avoid war.

He tears up the paper he was holding, and drops the pieces onto the table.

KING   *(Moved.)* Come here. (ESQUILACHE *goes to him and the* KING *hugs him with tears in his eyes. Then he lets go and walks upstage. He pauses.)* There'll be no prison for you. Nor a trial. They're not demanding as much as that.
ESQUILACHE   What do they want?
KING   They want you banished, along with your whole family. (ESQUILACHE *bows his head. The* KING *moves closer to him and speaks in a confidential tone.)* I'll be going to Aranjuez tonight with the royal family. I shan't come back to Madrid until these unruly people convince me that they've quietened down. You'll come with me... Tomorrow I'll have your wife and children brought there too.
ESQUILACHE   Where is my wife now?
KING   *(With a sigh.)* She was at the Dutch Legation. (ESQUILACHE *lowers his head.)* I've given instructions that she should be moved to the Salesian convent and wait there for my orders. There'll be no separation for you two now... There would be no point.
ESQUILACHE   *(Nods bitterly.)* So I've lost everything...
KING   Perhaps. But that won't stop me trying to make them understand... *(Puts one hand on* ESQUILACHE's *shoulder.)* Have we just been dreaming, Leopoldo? Is there a real people down there?
ESQUILACHE   We did what we had to do.
KING   *(Moving away a few steps.)* You won't come back to Madrid. You'll go directly from Aranjuez to Cartagena, and sail from there back to your own country. You'll be well guarded all the way.
ESQUILACHE   Like a prisoner...
KING   So that nothing happens to you.
ESQUILACHE   I know very well that my Calvary hasn't ended yet. I'll be followed by insults and slander everywhere I go.

Silence.

KING   There's something else that I almost forgot. *(He takes a sealed document from the sleeve of his coat.)* You've often pleaded with me in favour of Ensenada. I've summoned him to the Palace, and given orders that he be brought here as soon as he arrives. Give him this in my name: it will be your last act of government.
ESQUILACHE   I thank you in his name as well as in mine, sire.

Toma el pliego. El REY *va, rápido, al foro. Con la mano en el pomo de la puerta se vuelve.*

EL REY   Me duele sacrificarte.
ESQUILACHE   La decisión ha sido mía, señor.   Y más dolorosa de lo que vuestra majestad supone.
EL REY   Lo comprendo.
ESQUILACHE   No se trata del Poder, señor.
EL REY   Sé muy bien que no se trata del Poder... *(Baja los ojos.)* Si... puedo hacer algo por esa criatura..., *(Tímido movimiento de cabeza hacia la otra puerta.)* pídemelo.
ESQUILACHE   *(Se le quiebra la voz, cae de rodillas.)* ¡Gracias, señor! *(El* REY *sale.*

ESQUILACHE *se incorpora, mira al pliego y lo deja sobre la mesa, al tiempo que dice con melancolía:)* "Prepáranse embarcaciones que tendrán venturosos pasajes... *(Marcha hacia la puerta de la derecha.)* Un ministro es depuesto por no haber imitado en la justicia el significado del enigma." *(Golpecitos en el foro.* ESQUILACHE *suspira y reacciona.)* ¡Adelante!

Entra VILLASANTA.

VILLASANTA   El señor marqués de la Ensenada
ESQUILACHE   Que pase.

VILLASANTA *vacila.*

VILLASANTA   Creo que debo informar a usía de una particularidad... extraña.
ESQUILACHE   ¿Y es?
VILLASANTA   El secretario de usía acompaña al señor marqués de la Ensenada

ESQUILACHE *alza las cejas, sorprendido; después baja, sombrío, la cabeza.*

ESQUILACHE   Que entre el señor marqués. (VILLASANTA *se inclina y va a salir. La voz de* ESQUILACHE *lo detiene en la puerta.)* Un momento... *(Mira hacia el balcón.)* Todos han callado... *(Sube al poyete y mira.)* Es que el rey sale al balcón. *(Una pausa. Aclamaciones entusiastas al rey en el exterior.)* Le aclaman... *(Se vuelve con una amarga sonrisa hacia* VILLASANTA.) Les acaba de decir que seré desterrado. (VILLASANTA *desvía la mirada.)* Pero no importa. Ahora sé que he vencido. (VILLASANTA *lo mira, sorprendido. El sonríe.)* Usía no comprende, claro. Usía no me comprenderá nunca. *(Se repiten las aclamaciones.* ESQUILACHE *vuelve a mirar a la plaza.)* Todo ha terminado... Empiezan a replegarse hacia la salida. *(Desciende lentamente del poyete. Un silencio. Suspira, melancólico.)* Haga pasar al señor marqués.

He takes the document. The KING *walks rapidly upstage. With his hand on the doorknob, he turns.*

KING It hurts me to have to sacrifice you.
ESQUILACHE The decision has been my own, sire. And more painful than your Majesty supposes.
KING I understand.
ESQUILACHE It's not a question of power, sire.
KING I know that it's not a question of power... (*Looking down.*) If... if there's anything I can do for that poor girl..., (*He makes a slight gesture with his head towards the door at the right.*) just ask me.
ESQUILACHE (*His voice cracking, he falls to his knees.*) Thank you, your Majesty! (*The* KING *leaves.* ESQUILACHE *gets up, glances at the folded document and leaves it on the desk, while muttering gloomily:*) "A fleet is prepared, which will enjoy good fortune on its voyage... (*He goes towards the door at the right.*) A minister is deposed for failing to administer justice in accordance with the significance of the enigma." (*Someone taps on the door at the back of the stage.* ESQUILACHE *sighs before calling out.*) Come in!

Enter VILLASANTA.

VILLASANTA The Lord Marquis of La Ensenada.
ESQUILACHE Show him in.

VILLASANTA *hesitates.*

VILLASANTA I think I should inform your Excellency of a... curious detail.
ESQUILACHE And what is it?
VILLASANTA Your secretary is with the Marquis of La Ensenada.

ESQUILACHE *raises his eyebrows in surprise; then he bows his head glumly.*

ESQUILACHE Show his lordship in. (VILLASANTA *bows and heads for the door.* ESQUILACHE's *voice stops him as he reaches the door.*) Just a moment... (*Looks towards the balcony.*) They've all gone quiet... (*Gets up on the step and looks out.*) It's because the king is coming out onto the balcony. (*A pause. Enthusiastic cheers outside for the king.*) They are cheering him... (*He turns with a wry smile towards* VILLASANTA.) He has just told them that I am to be banished. (VILLASANTA *looks away.*) But it doesn't matter. Now I know that I have won. (VILLASANTA *looks at him in astonishment. He smiles.*) Of course, you don't understand. You will never understand me. (*The cheers are heard again.* ESQUILACHE *takes another look out*) It's all over now...[50] They're moving back towards the arch. (*He steps down slowly. There is a moment of silence. He sighs sadly.*) Show his lordship in.

VILLASANTA *se inclina y sale. Entra* ENSENADA, *con capa y el sombrero en la mano. Una banda azul le cruza el pecho; dos placas adornan su casaca. La puerta se cierra.* ENSENADA *va al encuentro de* ESQUILACHE *y le estrecha las manos.*

ENSENADA   Siento verdaderamente lo ocurrido.

ESQUILACHE   (*Sonríe.*) Poco importa, si te llaman a ti.

ENSENADA   Tal vez no me creas. Quizá supongas que me alegro de...

ESQUILACHE   ¿Por qué no iba a creerte?

ENSENADA   Lo que me sorprende es que me hayan conducido a tu presencia.

ESQUILACHE   Su majestad lo ha dispuesto así y me felicito por ello. (*Va a la mesa y toma el pliego.*) Toma. No sé si vienes a sustituirme o a algún otro puesto. Sea lo que sea, me alegro de haberlo conseguido al fin. (ENSENADA *toma el pliego.*) Nuestro amo y señor tarda en madurar las cosas: pero ya ves cómo no se equivoca. (*Grave.*) No te equivoques tú en adelante.

ENSENADA   Lo procuraré.

ESQUILACHE   (*Desvía la mirada.*) Lo digo por... mi secretario, a quien acabas de admitir. Es un falso.

ENSENADA   Como la mayoría. (*Deja el sombrero sobre la mesa.*) ¿Me permites?

ENSENADA *rompe el sello y lee la orden. No puede evitar un sobresalto. Enrojece y mira a* ESQUILACHE *con rencor.*

ENSENADA   Sencillamente perfecto. Sobre todo, ahora que me quedé sin dinero para poder pagar a toda esa canalla.

ESQUILACHE   ¿Cómo?

ENSENADA   (*Fuera de sí.*) La jugada es tuya, ¿verdad? ¡Me admiras!

ESQUILACHE   ¿Qué jugada?

ENSENADA   ¡Vamos, italiano! Basta de fingimientos. Sabes de sobra que el rey me destierra a Medina del Campo.

ESQUILACHE   (*Después de un momento.*) ¿Que te destierra...? (*Le arrebata el papel y lee.*) No dice por qué.

ENSENADA *le quita el papel y se aparta.*

ENSENADA   (*Desdeñoso.*) Sabes muy bien por qué.

ESQUILACHE   (*Que no deja de mirarlo fijamente.*) No, no lo sabía... Pero estoy empezando a comprenderlo... (*En tanto se abalanza al cordón de la campanilla y tira:*) Y me parece tan increíble, que...

ENSENADA *se guarda la orden en el bolsillo y lo mira, suspicaz.*

ENSENADA   ¿De verdad no sabías?...

VILLASANTA *bows and goes out. Enter* ENSENADA, *with his cape and hat in his hand. He wears a blue sash across his chest, and two decorations on his coat. The door closes behind him.* ENSENADA *goes forward to greet* ESQUILACHE *and shake his hands.*

ENSENADA   I'm truly sorry about what has happened.

ESQUILACHE   (*Smiling.*) It's not important, as long as you are being called back.

ENSENADA   Perhaps you don't believe me. Perhaps you think that I'm pleased that...

ESQUILACHE   Why shouldn't I believe you?

ENSENADA   What surprises me is that they've brought me to you.

ESQUILACHE   His Majesty ordered it himself, and I'm glad. (*Goes to the desk and picks up the document.*) Here. I don't know if you're here to replace me or for some other post. In any case, I'm delighted to have done something for you at last. (ENSENADA *takes the document.*) Our lord and master takes his time in bringing things to fruition, but as you can see, he doesn't get them wrong. (*Gravely.*) I hope you won't go wrong from now on.

ENSENADA   I shall try not to.

ESQUILACHE   (*Looking away.*) I say that because of my secretary, whom you've just taken on. He's disloyal.

ENSENADA   Like most of them. (*He puts his hat down on the desk.*) May I?

ENSENADA *breaks the seal and reads the orders. He cannot conceal his surprise. He reddens and glares resentfully at* ESQUILACHE.

ENSENADA   Perfect. Simply perfect. Especially now that I've been left without a penny after paying off that rabble.

ESQUILACHE   What?

ENSENADA   (*Beside himself with rage.*) This is your doing, isn't it? Only you could have pulled a trick like this!

ESQUILACHE   What trick? What do you mean?

ENSENADA   Come on, you sly Italian schemer! Don't try to pretend any more. You know damned well that the king is banishing me to Medina del Campo.[51]

ESQUILACHE   (*After a moment.*) He's banishing you...? (*He grabs the paper out of his hand and reads it.*) He doesn't say why.

ENSENADA *takes back the document and moves away.*

ENSENADA   (*Scornfully.*) You know very well why.

ESQUILACHE   (*Staring at him intensely.*) No, I didn't know... But I'm beginning to see it now... (*As he lurches towards the bell-pull and tugs it, he says:*) And it seems so unbelievable, that...

ENSENADA *puts the order in his pocket and eyes* ESQUILACHE *suspiciously.*

ENSENADA   You really didn't know?...

Entra VILLASANTA.

ESQUILACHE   Duque: después de asaltar mi casa, las turbas fueron a la de otra persona para vitorearla. ¿Puede decirme qué persona?

VILLASANTA   (*Sonríe con malicia.*) El señor marqués de la Ensenada

ESQUILACHE   Hoy han aclamado también a alguien ante estos balcones. ¿Era a la misma persona?

VILLASANTA   A la misma.

ESQUILACHE   Gracias.

VILLASANTA *sale y cierra.*

ENSENADA   (*Sin mirarlo.*) Te equivocas si crees que he sido el único en mover todo esto.

ESQUILACHE   Basta con que hayas sido uno de ellos. (*Se acerca.*) Pero ¿cómo es posible que tú, uno de los hombres más grandes que hoy tiene España, hayas podido pactar con nuestros enemigos? Y sobre todo: ¿qué te he hecho yo, di?

ENSENADA   (*Amargo.*) ¿Y lo preguntas?

ESQUILACHE   ¡Yo era tu amigo!

ENSENADA   (*Irónico.*) Sí... Un amigo que me suplanta en el Gobierno del país y en el favor real, valiendo mucho menos que yo. Porque tú vales menos que yo, Leopoldo. ¡Yo empecé todo esto! Y tú te has limitado a continuarlo..., trabajando incansablemente, sí; pero con bastante mediocridad. Tú, un extranjero, le quitas el puesto al marqués de la Ensenada ¡Era ridículo!... E intolerable.

ESQUILACHE   Pero era el rey quien...

ENSENADA   ¡Vamos, Esquilache! No pretendas hacerme creer que intercediste por mí. Nadie se busca competidores peligrosos y tú no ibas a ser el primero. Para ti era más cómodo aceptar mis consejos manteniéndome en la sombra, y eso es lo que hiciste.

Va hacia el balcón, entristecido.

ESQUILACHE   (*Se recuesta en la mesa.*) ¡Reconozco el estilo del rey! El hombre por cuya causa me destierran, tiene que sufrir la humillación de ser desterrado por mi mano. Para mí, una reparación completa. Pero no es sólo eso: él nos enfrenta para ofrecernos una silenciosa y formidable lección.

ENSENADA   (*Se vuelve.*) ¿Qué lección?

ESQUILACHE   Nos enfrenta para compararnos. Yo me comparo contigo y comprendo.

ENSENADA   ¿El qué?

Enter VILLASANTA.

ESQUILACHE   Tell me, Villasanta: after the crowds had stormed my house, they went
   on to cheer outside another person's house. Whose was it?
VILLASANTA   (*With a malicious smirk.*) The Marquis of La Ensenada's.
ESQUILACHE   And today they have been acclaiming someone outside these
   balconies. Was it the same person?
VILLASANTA   It was.
ESQUILACHE   Thank you.

VILLASANTA *goes out and closes the door.*

ENSENADA   (*Without looking at him.*) You're mistaken if you think I've set this whole
   thing up on my own.
ESQUILACHE   It's bad enough that you've been one of them. (*Moves towards him.*)
   You're one of the greatest men Spain has at the moment. How can you have
   conspired with our enemies? And above all, what have I done to you? Tell me.
ENSENADA   (*Bitterly.*) You're asking me that?
ESQUILACHE   I was your friend!
ENSENADA   (*With irony.*) Oh, yes... A friend who is worth much less than I am, yet
   takes my place in the government of the country and the king's favour. Yes,
   you are worth less than I am, Leopoldo. I started all this! And all you've done
   is to continue it..., working tirelessly, yes; but in a mediocre sort of way. You, a
   foreigner, taking the Marquis of La Ensenada's job from him. It was
   ridiculous!... And intolerable.
ESQUILACHE   But it was the king who...
ENSENADA   Come on, Esquilache! Don't try to make me believe that you really did
   anything for me. No-one wants dangerous rivals around, and you were not
   going to be an exception. It was more convenient for you to accept my advice
   while keeping me in the shadows, and that is exactly what you did.

ENSENADA, *saddened, walks towards the balcony.*

ESQUILACHE   (*Leaning on the desk.*) I can recognize the king's hand in this! The
   man who has brought about my exile has to suffer the humiliation of being
   exiled by me. For me, complete reparation. But it's not just that: he has
   brought us face to face in order to give us a tremendous, silent lesson.
ENSENADA   (*Turning around.*) What lesson?
ESQUILACHE   He has brought us together to compare us. I can compare myself with
   you and understand.
ENSENADA   What can you understand?

ESQUILACHE   Tienes razón. Valgo menos que tú. Y sin embargo, soy más grande
    que tú. ¡El hombre más insignificante es más grande que tú si vive para algo
    que no sea él mismo! Desde hace veinte años tú ya no crees en nada. Y estás
    perdido.
ENSENADA   ¿Y en qué podemos creer nosotros, los que trabajábamos para el pueblo?
    Ya ves que no hay pueblo. La tragedia del gobernante es descubrirlo.
ESQUILACHE   ¡Buen pretexto para la mala política! Pero ellos podrían decir lo
    contrario: que su tragedia es ver cómo al más grande político le pierde la
    ambición.
ENSENADA   ¿Quiénes van a decir eso, iluso? ¿Los que piden tu cabeza ahí fuera?

ESQUILACHE *lo mira largamente. Después va a la derecha y abre la puerta.*

ESQUILACHE   Fernandita...   (ENSENADA *se yergue, desconcertado.*
    FERNANDITA *entra, mira a los dos y se inclina ante* ENSENADA) No le
    saludes... No merece tanto.
ENSENADA   ¿Quién es esa mujer?
ESQUILACHE   (*Mientras la conduce a la mesita.*) Nadie importante: una muchacha de
    mi servicio. Una insignificante mujer... del pueblo. (ENSENADA *va a la
    mesa. Recoge su sombrero y se encamina a la puerta.* ESQUILACHE *ruge:*)
    ¡Quieto! (*Corre a su lado, le arrebata el sombrero y lo tira sobre la mesa.*)
    ¡Me sobran fuerzas para retenerte! (*Lo empuja lenta, pero enérgicamente,
    hacia el sillón que hay ante la mesa.*) Siéntate.
ENSENADA   ¿Delante de una criada?
ESQUILACHE   Una criada que puede juzgarnos a los dos. ¡No temas! Lo hará en
    silencio. Desde ayer no habla mucho. (*Le obliga a sentarse.*)
FERNANDITA   (*Suplicante.*) ¡Señor!
ESQUILACHE   Siéntate también, Fernandita... Lo que voy a decir, tú debes oírlo.
    (FERNANDITA *se sienta a la izquierda.* A ENSENADA) Mírala... Hasta ayer
    mismo estaba con nuestra obra. Nos admiraba. Quizá desde hoy no comprenda
    ya nada, cuando sepa que tú, que el gran Ensenada sublevó a Madrid contra
    Esquilache. (FERNANDITA *levanta la cabeza, desconcertada.*) ¿Lo ves? No
    le cabe en la cabeza. Pensará: Si entre ellos riñen, ¿en qué se puede creer ya?
    No advierte que puede creer en lo más grande, en lo que yo creo: en ella misma.
ENSENADA   ¡Esto es intolerable!
ESQUILACHE   ¿Intolerable? ¿Qué podría ella decirte a ti? Ella, que sufrió el asalto de
    mi casa, que ha visto a tus asesinos matar a un pobre mozo que la quería, que...
FERNANDITA   (*Asustada.*) ¡Señor!

ESQUILACHE You're right. I'm worth less than you. And yet I'm greater than you. The most insignificant man is greater than you if he lives for something other than himself! You haven't believed in anything for twenty years. And you're lost.

ENSENADA And what can we believe in, those of us who used to work for the people? You can see now that there's no such thing as the people. The tragedy of the politician is realizing that.

ESQUILACHE A good excuse for bad government! But the people could say the opposite. They see how even the greatest politician is ruined by ambition. That is their tragedy.

ESQUILACHE Who's going to say that, you fool? The mob outside calling for your head?

ESQUILACHE *stares at him for some time. Then he goes to the right and opens the door.*

ESQUILACHE Fernandita... (ENSENADA *stiffens, puzzled.* FERNANDITA *comes in, looks at both men and curtsies to* ENSENADA.) You needn't do that... He doesn't deserve it.

ENSENADA Who is this woman?

ESQUILACHE (*Leading her towards the side table.*) No-one important: one of my serving women. An insignificant woman... of the people. (ENSENADA *goes to the desk. He picks up his hat and heads for the door.* ESQUILACHE *roars at him:*) Stay where you are! (*He strides after him, tears his hat out of his hand and flings it onto the table.*) I've more than enough strength to stop you! (*Pushes him slowly, but forcefully, towards the armchair by the desk.*) Sit down.

ENSENADA In front of a servant?

ESQUILACHE A servant who's good enough to judge us both. Don't worry! She'll do it in silence. She hasn't been speaking much since yesterday. (*He makes him sit down.*)

FERNANDITA (*Pleading.*) Sir!

ESQUILACHE You sit down too, Fernandita... You ought to hear what I'm going to say. (FERNANDITA *sits at the left.* ESQUILACHE *speaks to* ENSENADA.) Look at her... Until yesterday, she supported our work. She admired us. Perhaps from now on she won't be able to understand anything, once she knows that you, the great Ensenada, stirred up Madrid's revolt against Esquilache. (FERNANDITA *looks up in bewilderment.*) You see? She can't take it in. She'll be thinking: if they fight amongst themselves, what is there left to believe in? She doesn't see that she can believe in the greatest thing of all, what I believe in: herself.

ENSENADA This is intolerable!

ESQUILACHE Intolerable, is it? She could tell you about what's intolerable. She had to suffer the attack on my house, she had to watch your assassins murder a poor young man who loved her, she...

FERNANDITA (*Alarmed.*) Sir!

ESQUILACHE   (*Exaltado.*) ¡Sabe mucho de tus primeras víctimas! ¡Ha tenido que
    soportar el horror de...!
FERNANDITA   (*Se levanta.*) ¡Señor, por caridad, calle!

ENSENADA *empieza a incorporarse también, mirándola, impresionado a su pesar.*

ESQUILACHE   (*Después de un momento.*) ... El horror de ver cómo... a otra azafata...,
    a una entrañable amiga suya, la forzaban. (*Un silencio.* FERNANDITA *llora.*
    ENSENADA, *de pie, la mira muy turbado: ha comprendido.* ESQUILACHE
    se acerca a ENSENADA) ¿Te desagrada tu obra?... (ENSENADA *desvía la
    vista.*) Pero eso no es nada al lado de lo que iba a ser: tú has conspirado
    fríamente para encender el infierno en toda España.   Por fortuna, yo lo he
    apagado.

FERNANDITA *lo mira, sorprendida, y atiende con emoción a sus palabras.*

ENSENADA   ¿Tú?
ESQUILACHE   (*Se enardece.*) ¡No eres tú quien me destierra, Ensenada sino yo
    mismo! ¡Una sola palabra mía y el infierno de la guerra habría ardido! Pero yo
    no he dicho esa palabra.   Al teniente general, al ministro de la Guerra
    Esquilache, no le gusta la guerra, ni la crueldad... Abomina del infierno en la
    Tierra...   Y decide no aumentar el sufrimiento (*Mira a* FERNANDITA.) de esa
    pobre carne triste, ultrajada..., de los de abajo, que todo lo soportan.
ENSENADA   (*Hosco.*) Déjame salir.
ESQUILACHE   ¡Puedes hacerlo! (*Se acerca a* FERNANDITA *y le rodea los hombros
    con su brazo.*) Nosotros dos, que valemos menos que tú, te condenamos.   El
    pueblo te condena.
ENSENADA   ¿El pueblo?
ESQUILACHE   Nací plebeyo, Ensenada.. Fui y soy como ella.   Tú dices: nunca
    comprenderán.   Nosotros decimos: todavía no comprenden.
ENSENADA   ¡Deliras! ¡Sueñas!
ESQUILACHE   Tal vez. Pero ahora sé una cosa: que ningún gobernante puede dejar de
    corromperse si no sueña ese sueño. (*Con un repentino cansancio que le abate,*
    ENSENADA *toma su sombrero y se encamina, cabizbajo, al foro.*
    ESQUILACHE *recita, lento, unas curiosas palabras:*) "Un personaje bien visto
    de la plebe no se rehúsa de entrar en un negocio por el bien del público; pero le
    cuesta entrar en el significado del enigma." (ENSENADA *se vuelve desde la
    puerta, asombrado.* ESQUILACHE *le dedica una inquietante sonrisa.*) Son
    palabras del Piscator de Villarroel. Te estaban destinadas. Pídele a Campos
    que te lo adquiera, antes de que también te deje solo.
ENSENADA   ¿Estás loco?

ESQUILACHE   (*Impassioned.*) She knows a lot about your first victims! She has had
    to go through the horror of...!
FERNANDITA   (*Jumping to her feet.*) Please don't, sir, for pity's sake!

ENSENADA *also begins to stand up, watching her, moved despite himself.*

ESQUILACHE   (*After pausing for a moment.*) ... The horror of seeing... another
    maidservant..., a dear friend of hers, raped. (*Silence. FERNANDITA weeps.
    ENSENADA, on his feet now and very troubled, watches her: he has
    understood. ESQUILACHE moves towards him.*) Aren't you pleased with your
    work?... (ENSENADA *looks away.*) But that's nothing in comparison with
    what would have happened: you've plotted cold-bloodedly to set off an inferno
    throughout Spain. Luckily, I've been able to put it out.

FERNANDITA *looks at him in surprise, and listens anxiously to what he says.*

ENSENADA   You?
ESQUILACHE   It's not you who is sending me into exile, Ensenada! I'm banishing
    myself! One word from me and the inferno of war would have raged! But I
    didn't utter that word. Esquilache the lieutenant-general, the Minister of War,
    doesn't like war, nor cruelty... He has a horror of hell on earth... And he has
    decided not to increase the torment (*Glances at* FERNANDITA.) of the poor,
    abused flesh... of the people down below, the people at the bottom of the heap,
    who take the brunt of everything.
ENSENADA   (*Sullenly.*) Let me leave.
ESQUILACHE   You can go! (*He goes to* FERNANDITA *and puts his arm around her
    shoulders.*) We two, who are worth so much less than you, condemn you. The
    people condemn you.
ENSENADA   The people?
ESQUILACHE   I was born into a humble family, Ensenada. I was and am the same as
    her. You say: they will never understand. We say: they don't yet understand.
ENSENADA   You're deluding yourself! Dreaming!
ESQUILACHE   Perhaps. But now I know one thing for sure: no ruler can avoid being
    corrupted if he doesn't dream that dream. (*Weighed down by a sudden
    weariness,* ENSENADA *picks up his hat and walks, with his head hanging,
    upstage. ESQUILACHE slowly recites some curious lines:*) "A personage well
    regarded by the common people does not hold back from a certain affair for the
    public good; but he has great difficulty in penetrating the significance of the
    enigma." (ENSENADA *turns back from the door in astonishment.
    ESQUILACHE gives him an unnerving smile.*) Some lines from Villarroel's
    Piscator. They were meant for you. Ask Campos to get hold of it for you,
    before he deserts you too.
ENSENADA   Are you mad?

178 PARTE SEGUNDA

ESQUILACHE ¡Envidia también mi locura, Ensenada! ¡Y vete! Ella te ha juzgado ya. (ENSENADA *dirige una triste mirada a* FERNANDITA, *que le vuelve la espalda. Sintiéndose repentinamente viejo, sale. Una pausa.*) Ese ciego insignificante llevaba el destino en sus manos. Nada sabemos. Tan ciegos como él, todos... (*Se acerca y le toma las manos a* FERNANDITA.) ¡Ayúdame tú a ver!

FERNANDITA Yo también estoy ciega.

ESQUILACHE Tú puedes juzgarnos a todos, y ahora debes juzgarme a mí.

FERNANDITA ¿Yo, señor?

ESQUILACHE Mírame. No sufriré la muerte de los héroes: no la merezco. Me quejaré desde Italia, pediré nuevos puestos, lo sé... Soy pequeño. Pero ahora es el momento de la verdad. Acaba de salir de aquí un egoísta a quien la ambición ha perdido, pero dentro queda otro... Esquilache.

FERNANDITA ¡No es verdad!

ESQUILACHE Lo fue... He sido abnegado en mi vejez porque mi juventud fue ambiciosa... Intrigué, adulé durante años... Mi castigo es justo y lo debo pagar. No se puede intentar la reforma de un país cuando no se ha sabido conducir el hogar propio. Nada se puede construir sobre fango, si no es fango. ¡Condéname, Fernandita!

FERNANDITA Yo no puedo condenar.

ESQUILACHE Pues perdóname entonces, si puedes, en tu nombre y en el de todos.

FERNANDITA Si yo tuviera que decir a su merced algo en nombre de todos, no sería una palabra de perdón, sino de gratitud.

ESQUILACHE ¿Por lo que he hecho? Es muy poco...

FERNANDITA Pero ha evitado una inmensidad de dolor. (*Se echa a llorar.*)

ESQUILACHE ¡Fernandita!

FERNANDITA ¡Lléveme consigo, tenga piedad!...

ESQUILACHE No puedo llevarte. Vuelvo a Italia a terminar mi vida con mi esposa y mis hijos. Tu presencia entre nosotros ya no sería posible.

FERNANDITA ¡Me perderé aquí si no me ayuda! ¡Dijo que me ayudaría! ¡No me abandone!... (*Se echa en sus brazos.*)

ESQUILACHE Si pudiera... Pero yo he hecho mi mayor sacrificio hoy: sabía que, al dejar España, te perdería... Y tú sabes que yo... Tú sabes, Fernandita, que este anciano ridículo... te... quiere... (*Un silencio. Habla muy quedo.*) Y sufre al verte perdida en una pasion ciega... por un malvado.

FERNANDITA ¡Perdón!...

ESQUILACHE ¿Por qué? Es la cruel ceguera de la vida. Pero tú puedes abrir los ojos.

FERNANDITA ¡No sabré!...

ESQUILACHE ¡Sí! ¡Tú has visto ya!

FERNANDITA ¡No podré!...

ESQUILACHE ¡Tienes que intentarlo!

FERNANDITA (*Desesperada.*) ¡No!

ESQUILACHE   You can envy my madness too, Ensenada! And now get out of here! She has judged you now. (ENSENADA *looks sadly at* FERNANDITA, *who turns her back. Feeling suddenly old, he goes out. A pause.*) That insignificant blind man had our destiny in his hands. We know nothing. As blind as he is, all of us... (*He goes to* FERNANDITA *and takes her hands.*) Help me to see!

FERNANDITA   I'm blind as well.

ESQUILACHE   You can judge all of us, and now you must judge me.

FERNANDITA   Me, my Lord, judge you?

ESQUILACHE   Look at me. I'm not going to die a hero's death: I don't deserve that. I'll send complaints from Italy, I'll ask for new posts, I know...[52] I'm a weak, small man. But this is the moment of truth. One egotist ruined by ambition has just left this room, but there's another still here... Esquilache.

FERNANDITA   That's not true!

ESQUILACHE   It used to be... I've been self-denying in my old age because I was ambitious when I was young... For years I schemed, I flattered... My punishment is just, and I must submit myself to it. You can't attempt to reform a country when you haven't been able to put your own house in order.. Nothing but mud can be built on mud. Condemn me, Fernandita!

FERNANDITA   I can't.

ESQUILACHE   Then forgive me, if you can, in your name and in everyone else's.

FERNANDITA   If I was to say something to you on behalf of everyone, it would be a word of gratitude, not forgiveness.

ESQUILACHE   For what I've achieved? It's very little...

FERNANDITA   But you've prevented massive suffering. (*She bursts into tears.*)

ESQUILACHE   Fernandita!

FERNANDITA   Take me with you, have pity on me!...

ESQUILACHE   I can't take you. I'm going back to Italy to spend the rest of my days with my wife and children. It wouldn't be possible to have you with us now.

FERNANDITA   I won't stand a chance here if you don't help me! You said you'd help me! Don't leave me!... (*Throws herself into his arms.*)

ESQUILACHE   If only I could... But I've already made my greatest sacrifice today: I knew that leaving Spain would mean losing you... And you know that I... You know, Fernandita, that this ridiculous old man... loves you... (*A moment of silence. Then he speaks very quietly.*) And suffers seeing you caught up in a passion for an evil man.

FERNANDITA   Forgive me!...

ESQUILACHE   Why? It's just the cruel blindness that's part of life. But you can open your eyes.

FERNANDITA   I won't know how!...

ESQUILACHE   You will! You've already begun to see!

FERNANDITA   I can't.

ESQUILACHE   You have to try!

FERNANDITA   (*In despair.*) No!...

ESQUILACHE   ¿De verdad no quieres que prendan a ese hombre?

FERNANDITA   ¡No!...

ESQUILACHE   (*La toma de los brazos.*) ¡Dime qué puedo hacer por ti! ¿Quieres entrar al servicio del rey?

Un silencio. FERNANDITA *se separa y niega.*

FERNANDITA   (*Sombría.*) Volveré con mi madrina.

ESQUILACHE   ¿Con tu madrina... o con él? (*Un silencio, entrecortado por el llanto de ella.*) Te queda la lucha peor. Ese hombre no será detenido: tú debes vencer con tu propia libertad. (*Le aferra los brazos.*) ¡Creo en ti, Fernandita! El pueblo no es el infierno que has visto: ¡el pueblo eres tú! Está en ti, como lo estaba en el pobre Julián, o como en aquel embozado de ayer, capaz de tener piedad por un anciano y una niña... ¡Está, agazapado, en vuestros corazones! Tal vez pasen siglos antes de que comprenda... Tal vez nunca cambie su triste oscuridad por la luz... ¡Pero de vosotros depende! ¿Seréis capaces? ¿Serás tú capaz?

FERNANDITA   (*Llorosa.*) Que el Cielo le colme de bendiciones...

Se encamina, lenta, hacia el foro.

ESQUILACHE   Te vas?... Sí, *è chiaro.* Debemos separarnos ya. Y él está ahí fuera... (*La mira con melancólica fijeza.*) Dispuesto a atraparte para siempre. (*Se acerca y le toma las manos.*) Dios te guarde, Fernandita. Y gracias por haberme hecho sentir, aunque sea tardíamente, ¡y con tanta tristeza!..., el sabor de la felicidad.

Con los ojos llenos de pena, FERNANDITA *le besa la mano, desesperadamente. Después sale, rápida. La puerta se cierra.* ESQUILACHE *va al foro, va a abrir: lo piensa mejor y baja la mano. Entretanto,* DOÑA MARÍA *y la* CLAUDIA *salen al balcón.* DOÑA MARÍA *se muestra contenta; la* CLAUDIA, *triste.* ESQUILACHE *suspira y va hacia el balcón, por cuyos cristales mira al exterior con indecible melancolía. Por la primera izquierda entra presuroso* BERNARDO, *lleno de alegría.*

BERNARDO   ¡Doña María! ¡Va a salir un rosario de Santo Tomás en acción de gracias al rey con todas las palmas del domingo! ¡Desate la suya y échemela!

DOÑA MARÍA   (*Mientras desata.*) Pero ¿es verdad que han echado al hereje?

CIEGO   (*Voz de, muy lejana.*) ¡El Gran Piscator de Salamanca, con el pronóstico confirmado de la caída de Esquilache!...

BERNARDO   ¿Lo oye? ¡Sus mercedes pueden venir también!

La CLAUDIA *se echa a llorar y se mete dentro.*

ESQUILACHE Do you really not want him arrested?
FERNANDITA No!...
ESQUILACHE (*Holds her by the arms.*) Tell me what I can do for you! Do you want
to be in the king's service?

Silence. FERNANDITA *pulls herself away and shakes her head.*

FERNANDITA (*Gravely.*) I'll go back to live with my godmother.
ESQUILACHE With your godmother... or with him? (*A moment of silence,
punctuated by her weeping.*) Your hardest struggle is still ahead of you. He
won't be arrested: the only way you can win through is by your own free will.
(*He squeezes her arms.*) I believe in you, Fernandita! That inferno you've seen
is not the people: you are the people! The true spirit of the people is in you, as
it was in poor Julián, or in that man yesterday who took pity on an old man and
a girl... It's there, hidden in your hearts! Maybe it'll be centuries before the
people understand... They may never make it out of their grim darkness into the
light... But it depends on you and on others who are like you! Is it possible?
Will you make it possible?
FERNANDITA (*Tearfully.*) God bless you...

She walks slowly towards the back of the stage.

ESQUILACHE Are you going?... Yes, *è chiaro.* We should part now. And he's out
there... (*Gazing at her sadly.*) Ready to trap you for ever. (*He goes to her and
takes her hands.*) May God protect you, Fernandita. And thank you for having
made me experience, however late in life, and with so much sadness..., a taste
of happiness.

Her eyes full of sorrow, FERNANDITA *kisses his hand despairingly. Then she leaves
quickly. The door closes.* ESQUILACHE *goes to the back of the stage, begins to open
the door: he decides not to, and drops his hand. In the meantime,* DOÑA MARÍA *and
CLAUDIA *have appeared on their balcony.* DOÑA MARÍA *looks pleased;
CLAUDIA, however, looks gloomy.* ESQUILACHE *sighs, goes to the balcony, and
stands looking out with ineffable melancholy. A joyful* BERNARDO *dashes on
downstage left.*

BERNARDO Doña María! They're going to offer prayers of thanksgiving to the king,
with all the palms from Sunday! Untie yours and toss it down here!
MARÍA (*As she unties it.*) Is it true, then? Have they thrown the heretic out?
BALLAD-SELLER (*Off, in the distance.*) The Great Piscator of Salamanca, with the
confirmed prediction of the fall of Esquilache!
BERNARDO Did you hear that? You two can come along as well!

CLAUDIA *bursts into tears and goes inside.*

DOÑA MARÍA   Bueno, ésta no vendrá.

BERNARDO   ¿Qué le pasa ?

DOÑA MARÍA   (*Suspira.*) Que han matado a su Pedro en la plaza Mayor... (*Le hace pantalla a los ojos.*) Calla. ¿Quién viene por ahí?

BERNARDO *se vuelve, y ve entrar a* FERNANDITA *por la segunda izquierda. Ella va a cruzar, pero lo ve y se detiene, trémula. Él se acerca, lento.* DOÑA MARÍA *interrumpe su faena y atiende.*

BERNARDO   Si me buscabas, aquí me tienes. Te dije que serías mía y ahora te digo: ven conmigo. (*En la fisonomía de* FERNANDITA *se dibuja una tremenda lucha. El la toma de un brazo con brusca familiaridad.*) ¡No lo pienses! ¡Soy yo quien te lo manda! (FERNANDITA *se desprende bruscamente y retrocede, turbadísima, denegando mientras lo mira con ojos empavorecidos.*) ¿Que no?

Ella baja la cabeza y da unos pasos. BERNARDO, *chasqueado, da un paso tras ella.* FERNANDITA *se vuelve y le envía una dolorosa mirada, en la que se evidencia una definitiva ruptura.*

FERNANDITA   Adiós, Bernardo.

Sigue su camino. DOÑA MARÍA *se encoge de hombros con un gesto de perplejidad.*

BERNARDO   (*Que se ha quedado mudo de despecho, escupe la palabra:*) ¡Ramera!...

El "Concierto de Primavera" de Vivaldi comienza al punto, mientras FERNANDITA *sale y el telón va cayendo. Tal vez parece crearse una recatada armonía entre sus alegres notas y la melancólica figura de* ESQUILACHE, *que no se ha movido.*

TELÓN

MARÍA Well, she won't be coming.

BERNARDO What's the matter with her?

MARÍA (*With a sigh.*) They killed her Pedro in the Plaza Mayor... (*She shades her eyes with her hand.*) Hang on. Who's this coming along?

BERNARDO *turns around, and sees* FERNANDITA *coming on upstage left. She is heading across the stage, but notices him and stops, trembling. He moves slowly towards her.* MARÍA *stops what she is doing and watches carefully.*

BERNARDO If you were looking for me, here I am. I said you'd be mine, and now I'm telling you to come with me. (FERNANDITA's *face reveals a tremendous struggle. He grabs her arm with rough familiarity.*) Don't even think about it! You'll do what you're told! (FERNANDITA *wrenches herself free and backs away, very agitated, shaking her head as she stares at him in terror.*) You will, you know!

She lowers her head and walks on a few steps. BERNARDO, *disappointed, sets off after her.* FERNANDITA *turns and gives him a sorrowful look, a look that signals a definitive separation.*

FERNANDITA Goodbye, Bernardo.

She walks on. DOÑA MARÍA *shrugs her shoulders in bewilderment.*

BERNARDO (*Who has been shocked into silence, manages to spit out the word:*) Slut!...

Vivaldi's "Spring Concerto" starts playing immediately, while FERNANDITA *goes off and the curtain falls. Perhaps some kind of harmony can be sensed between the sunny tone of the music and the melancholy figure of* ESQUILACHE, *who has not moved.*

CURTAIN

Esquilache, Ensenada and Fernandita. Photograph of the 1958 production by Gyenes.

NOTES TO THE PLAY

1   The adjective *majo* is defined in the Real Academia's *Diccionario de la lengua española* as describing "a person, typically lower-class, of easygoing and flamboyant appearance, manner and dress". In the context of 18th- and 19th-century Spain (especially Madrid), the *majo* and *maja* tend to be thought of as typifying the spirit of the common people: colourful, roguish, street-wise characters whose exuberant customs and style of dress come to be imitated by the aristocracy. The *sainetes* (short comic plays) of Ramón de la Cruz (1731-94) and the paintings and engravings of Francisco de Goya (1746-1828) reflect this reality, and help to build up the mythic status of the *majo* and *maja* as representatives of earthy Spanish vitality in contrast with the effete French-dominated culture of the Bourbon court.

2   Bernardo is a *majo* who makes a living by driving a *calesa* (from the French *calèche*; calash or caleche in English): a light two-wheeled carriage with a folding hood.

3   Morón, Bernardo and their accomplices all appear wrapped up in long capes, with broad-brimmed hats drooping over their faces. They are therefore referred to simply as *embozados*: men in disguise, with their faces concealed.

4   Another typical figure of 18th- and 19th-century Madrid was the *cesante*: a former civil servant, either retired on a meagre pension or dismissed (often after a change of government, but in this case, as a result of Esquilache's trimming of the administration).

5   The house on the Calle de las Infantas known as *La Casa de las Siete Chimeneas* was built in the 16th century. From around 1760, Esquilache rented the house and surrounding estate from the Count of Polentinos. The house still stands (with its seven chimneys intact) on the Plaza del Rey, now part of the headquarters of the Ministerio de Cultura. The Ministry has published an information sheet giving a brief history of the house: *Hoja informativa 1/008* (Ministerio de Cultura, Plaza del Rey 1, 28071 Madrid). For more details, see José Navarro Latorre, *La Casa de las Siete Chimeneas* (Madrid: Ayuntamiento, 1970).

6   Although the dramatic importance of the blind man in this play lies in his role as purveyor and announcer of the predictions in the Piscator almanac, such figures have traditionally made a precarious living by selling and reciting ballads and *aleluyas* (stories in rhyming couplets, illustrated with cartoons). "El Gran Piscator de Salamanca" was the name under which Diego de Torres Villarroel published a lucrative, and sometimes controversial, series of almanacs between the 1720s and 1760s, distributed through bookshops and street sellers. Torres (1693-1770) was a poet, satirist, mathematician and astrologer, best known for his autobiography: *Vida, ascendencia, nacimiento, crianza y aventuras del doctor don Diego de Torres y Villarroel.*

7   The *Diario Noticioso, Curioso, Erudito y Comercial, Público y Económico* was founded by Francisco Mariano Nipho in 1758, the first daily newspaper published in Spain.

8   Claudia is going to the church of Nuestra Señora de los Desamparados to light a candle as an offering to the Virgin Mary. *La Virgen de los Desamparados* is known to English-speaking Catholics as either "Refuge of the Homeless" or "Comforter of the Afflicted".

9   There may have been two *caleseros* who played prominent roles in the rebellion: "The most famous, Avendaño (Diego? Bernardo?), is a *calesero*, but in his name and in his reported appearance before the king as spokesman for the people, both at the Palace on the afternoon of the 24th, and bearing the message written under duress by Bishop Rojas to Aranjuez on the 25th and bringing back Roda's reply on the morning of the 27th, he seems to have become confused with another *calesero* whom some accounts call Juan the Malagueño" (José Navarro Latorre, *Hace doscientos años* (Madrid: Instituto de Estudios Madrileños, 1966), p.49) [translations of this and other Spanish sources are mine]. The Count of Fernán-

Núñez describes the man chosen by the crowd to meet the king as "un caleseruelo, con chupetín encarnado y sombrero blanco" ("a young cab-driver, in a red waistcoat and white hat")(*Vida de Carlos III* (Madrid: Fernando Fé, 1898), p.200).

10   The district of Maravillas lies to the north of the centre of Madrid. The church of Las Maravillas stands next to the Puerta de Monleón.

11   This *décima* is genuine: the text, with slight variations, is printed in Teófanes Egido, *Sátiras políticas de la España Moderna* (Madrid: Alianza, 1973), p.262. Egido also quotes several other lampoons attacking Esquilache for dishonesty, disloyalty and excessive ambition.

12   Zenón (often spelt Cenón) de Somodevilla, Marquis of La Ensenada (1702-81), had distinguished himself in diplomacy and naval administration in the reign of Felipe V; as a minister of Fernando VI (from 1746), he revitalized the navy and army, the merchant marine, state finances, agriculture, trade and industry. He was ousted by his rivals and banished to Granada in 1754, and although he had been on very good terms with Carlos III when the latter was King of Naples (Carlos had given him his title), he was freed from exile but not recalled to government when Carlos succeeded Fernando in 1759. There is a portrait of Ensenada by Jacopo Amigoni in the Prado Museum in Madrid.

13   The palace of El Pardo lies in the midst of extensive hunting grounds to the north-west of Madrid. Carlos III's court followed an expensive annual round of five royal *sitios*: El Pardo, Aranjuez, the Palacio Real in Madrid, San Ildefonso, and El Escorial. More recently, El Pardo was a favourite retreat of Francisco Franco, who shared Carlos's passion for hunting.

14   Leopoldo di Gregorio (1700-85) was born in Sicily of a humble family. His successful service as administrator of customs, then Treasury Secretary, of the Kingdom of Naples, won him Carlos's favour and several titles: Marquis of Squillace (adapted to Esquilache in Spain), of Trentino and of Valle-Santoro, and Prince of Santa Elía. He travelled to Spain with Carlos in 1759, and was the only new minister appointed by the new king on his accession: he was given the key financial ministry (*Hacienda*). He soon came to dominate the government, and took over the ministry of war in 1763.

15   Francisco Sabatini (1721-97) was a Sicilian architect and engineer who had worked for King Carlos in Naples before coming to Madrid in 1760 to complete the Palacio Real. The gardens next to the palace are named after him. Other Madrid landmarks designed by Sabatini are the Puerta de Alcalá and the Casa de la Aduana (now the Ministerio de Hacienda).

16   As a result of the signing of the Third Family Compact in February 1762, Spain joined France in the Seven Years' War against Britain and Portugal: an unpopular, costly and unsuccessful move to which Esquilache was opposed. Spanish forces occupied parts of Portugal, but Britain's naval superiority resulted in the humiliating loss of Havana and Manila. These possessions were recovered at the Treaty of Paris in February 1763, but at the cost of ceding Florida and other territories to Britain and withdrawal from Portugal.

17   Fernán-Núñez attributes this phrase to Esquilache himself. Commenting on Carlos III's enthusiasm for agriculture, the arts, industry and, "to an excessive degree", building, he adds that "because of this, the Marquis of Squilache used to tell him that his *mal de piedra* was ruining him" (vol.2, p.49).

18   There were several issues over which Carlos, while King of Naples, disagreed with his brother, Fernando VI. The most important of these were the proposal referred to here, by which a small part of Galicia was to be ceded to Portugal, and the Treaty of Madrid of 1750, by which Spain and Portugal agreed to exchange territories in Brazil and Paraguay: Ensenada opposed both of these agreements, and informed Carlos, who protested (and later annulled the Treaty of Madrid). These actions contributed to Ensenada's downfall in 1754. There is no specific evidence that Esquilache attempted to persuade the king to bring

Ensenada back into government, but he does seem to have admired Ensenada's achievements. Ferrer del Río suggests that the king distrusted Ensenada's evident desire for power, and that Esquilache's initially friendly attitude towards him quickly cooled (Antonio Ferrer del Río, *Historia del reinado de Carlos III en España*, vol.2 (Madrid, 1856), p.50).

19 Geronimo, Marquis of Grimaldi was Genoese, and had moved from the priesthood to diplomacy, serving under Felipe, Fernando and Carlos and reaching the influential position of ambassador to Versailles. When he replaced Ricardo Wall as minister of State in 1763, the government was dominated by the two Italian ministers. He survived the crisis of 1766, remaining in government until 1776, when he was appointed ambassador to Rome.

20 Esquilache had married Pastora Paternó in Barcelona before 1759. She soon became notorious for her arrogance and blatant abuse of her husband's position to acquire wealth and influence for herself and for her family.

21 These details are given by Ferrer del Río, but in a different order: the eldest was made lieutenant colonel, then field marshal; "his second son, while still an adolescent, enjoyed the income of a very well-endowed archdeaconship; his third son, hardly out of his cradle, had been appointed administrator of customs at Cádiz, with a stand-in chosen by his father until he came of age and a stipend of 3000 *duros*" (vol.2, p.7).

22 The term *petimetre*, a corruption of the French *petit maître*, was used to mock the affected imitation of French manners and fashions. The foppish *petimetre* was a stock caricature in the *sainetes* of Ramón de la Cruz.

23 The Count of Fernán-Núñez gives a graphic first-hand account of the squalor ("el estado de porquería") of Madrid in 1760, and praises the progress made in following years in the paving, lighting and cleaning-up of the capital (vol.2, pp.63-4).

24 These are the last six lines of Dante's sonnet "Tanto gentile e tanto onesta pare", from *Vita nuova* (written around 1294). The "new life" of the title refers primarily to youth. The following translation is by Barbara Reynolds:
Her beauty entering the beholder's eye
Brings sweetness to the heart, all sweets above:
None comprehends who does not know this state;
And from her lips there seems to emanate
A gentle spirit, full of tender love,
Which to the soul enraptured whispers: "Sigh!"
(Dante Alighieri, *Vita Nuova* (Harmondsworth: Penguin, 1969), p.76)

25 There is no neat equivalent in English of the noun *ilustrado*: a man of the Enlightenment. Although Carlos and his ministers were clearly influenced by rationalist, reformist ideas from other parts of Europe, particularly France, the impact of the Enlightenment in Spain in the 18th century was limited: "In spite of the Encyclopaedic influences which some of the ministers absorbed there was little ideology in their policies and no overt attack on religion. [...] As for the mass of the people, they remained Catholic in conviction and devoted to absolute monarchy" (John Lynch, *Bourbon Spain, 1700-1808* (Oxford: Basil Blackwell, 1989), pp.254-61).

26 *Redingote* is a French word, borrowed into English and Spanish, but derived in the first place from the English *riding-coat*. The *Oxford English Dictionary* defines it as "a double-breasted outer coat for men, with long plain skirts not cut away in the front", giving the year 1835 for the word's first use in English. This coat should have fuller, plainer, squarer skirts than those of the *casacas* worn by the aristocratic characters in this play, which would be cut away in the front. The greasy *casacón* worn by the blind ballad-seller might be a rougher, heavier garment, something like a greatcoat.

27   Buero reproduces here, in an abbreviated form, the original wording of the decree issued by
      Esquilache on 10 March 1766. He had been encouraged by the successful imposition of this
      measure on civil servants in January, and swept aside the doubts of the Council of Castile
      about its general application. The full text is given in Fernando Díaz-Plaja, *La historia de
      España en sus documentos: El siglo XVIII* (Madrid: Instituto de Estudios Políticos, 1955),
      p.261.

28   Ferrer del Río and Danvila both describe the tearing down of the notices, and their
      replacement with lampoons and posters declaring that there were fifty (Danvila) or three
      thousand (Ferrer) loyal Spaniards ready to defend the long cape and round hat, and that there
      were arms available for any who wished to join them (Ferrer del Río, vol.2, pp.13-14;
      Manuel Danvila y Collado, *Reinado de Carlos III*, vol.10 of *Historia general de España*, ed.
      A. Cánovas del Castillo (Madrid: El Progreso, 1891), p.312).

29   No duke of Villasanta is mentioned by historians in relation to this period. The character is
      introduced by Buero to represent the opposition of the traditional nobility to the erosion of
      their influence and privileges. The feudal stranglehold of the aristocracy and the church on
      land ownership and influence at court was gradually loosened during the 18th century in a
      variety of ways: fiscal and land reform, a shift away from the traditional Councils of state to
      bureaucratic ministries, the appointment of talented officials and ministers from humbler
      backgrounds. "Not that the Spanish nobility was a beleaguered species in the eighteenth
      century. Even reformers accepted the existing social structure and justified nobility in terms
      of its service to the state" (Lynch, p.233). The Duke of Medinaceli, mentioned earlier by the
      cesante, was one of the wealthiest grandees in Spain, who ran several large households with
      thousands of servants and hangers-on. He may have had some part in stirring up the
      rebellion against Esquilache, as he was carried to the Palace on the shoulders of the crowd
      on 23 March to take their demands to the king: a vivid demonstration of the alliance of the
      nobility with the common people against the reformist state.

30   Modern Castilian employs two different sets of pronouns for what in English has become
      simply "you": the familiar *tú* (singular) and *vosotros* (plural); and the formal *usted* and
      ustedes (used with the third-person form of a verb). *Usted* is derived from *vuestra merced*
      (contracted to *usarced*), and has displaced the form *usía* (from *vuestra señoría*) used in this
      play. A century earlier, two noblemen would have addressed each other as *vos*: this form is
      only used by Esquilache when addressing the king. As this scene makes clear, the use of
      forms of address reflected a very strict social hierarchy in this period: *tú* is used by a high-
      ranking person to someone clearly inferior (Esquilache to Fernandita, the king to
      Esquilache), or between equals (husband and wife, Esquilache and Ensenada); otherwise,
      usía shows deference (by Fernandita to Esquilache) or a polite distance (between
      Esquilache and Campos).

31   *L'Encyclopédie*: "a dictionary of universal knowledge published between 1751 and 1776 in
      35 volumes under the editorship of Diderot, with (until 1758) D'Alembert as his chief
      assistant, and with the leading intellectuals of the age, including Voltaire, Montesquieu,
      Rousseau, Buffon, and Turgot, as contributors. It attempted nothing less than the provision
      of a rational explanation for all aspects of existence, and it can be regarded as the most
      representative monument of the Enlightenment. Its attacks on superstition and incredulity
      attracted the hostility of church and state" (*The Oxford Companion to English Literature*, ed.
      Margaret Drabble (Oxford: OUP, 1985)). The *Encyclopédie* was banned by the Spanish
      Inquisition in 1759, but was known to the educated élite. "The writings of Montesquieu, in
      many ways a crucial test of enlightenment, contained too many arguments for individual
      liberty, religious toleration and constitutional monarchy to escape the attention of the

Inquisition, but in spite of its prohibition his thought still penetrated the peninsula" (Lynch, pp.256-57).

32   The Inquisition still played a formidable role as defender of traditional Catholicism, particularly through censorship, but was gradually brought under the control of the crown. Only four times in the 18th century were people burnt alive: in 1714, 1725, 1763 and 1781 (Lynch, pp.287-88).

33   *Velay* is a dialect word (from Valladolid, amongst other places), used in an emphatic way to mean something like "of course", or "well there it is and what are you going to do about it?" (María Moliner, *Diccionario de uso del español* (Madrid: Gredos, 1990)). It is therefore very close in tone and usage to the phrase "why-aye" used in the north-east of England.

34   This description of the king in hunting clothes is based on the portrait by Goya that hangs in the Prado Museum. Carlos was born in 1716, the son of the first Bourbon king of Spain, Felipe V, and the formidable Isabel Farnese. He was king of Naples (strictly speaking, of the Two Sicilies, a kingdom that included the whole of southern Italy and the island of Sicily) from 1734 until 1759, when he succeeded his brother Fernando VI as king of Spain. Historians' assessments of his personal qualities and the effectiveness of his administration are generally favourable: "Charles III excelled by contrast, a prodigy among Bourbon misfits, a marked improvement on the past and a neglected model for the future" (Lynch, p.247). He presided over reform and modernization, yet his ideas and beliefs remained traditional, his policies absolutist, and his cultural interests limited (shooting game twice a day being his main pastime). He died in 1788, leaving to his son Carlos a greatly strengthened regime, but an empire on the verge of rapid decline.

35   This dialogue between Esquilache and the king contains three lines that Buero was obliged by the government censors to change. The king's first line originally read: "¿Tú, en el Pardo?". The censors appear to have been uneasy about a possible association between Carlos and Esquilache in the past and Franco in the present. The censors were also unhappy about the passage from "Los españoles son como niños" ("the Spanish people are like children") to "a reformar, no a tiranizar" ("to reform, not to tyrannize"), but Buero insisted on keeping it in. Two other changes were accepted by the author, however (he is reported as confessing that he "had gone too far"). "Los demás se llenan la boca de las grandes palabras y, en el fondo, sólo esconden mezquindad y egoísmo" ("the others mouth fine words...") had originally been shorter and more mordant: "Los demás son políticos; o sea, malvados" ("the others are politicians, that's to say, villains"). "España necesita soñadores que sepan de números, como tú..." ("Spain needs people like you...") was originally followed by "y no ésos que llamamos políticos" ("not the kind of men we call politicians"), but this phrase was deleted. These details are given by Patricia O'Connor: 'Censorship in the contemporary Spanish theater and Antonio Buero Vallejo', in Mariano de Paco (ed.), *Estudios sobre Buero Vallejo* (Murcia: Universidad, 1984), pp.87-88. O'Connor gives a useful summary of the impact on Spanish theatre of the censorship imposed by Franco's regime, and gives other examples of Buero's skilful skirmishing with the deadening and unpredictable influence of the censors.

36   Pedro Rodríguez de Campomanes (1723-1802), was a talented lawyer and historian from a poor background, who had been appointed fiscal of the Council of Castile in 1762. He was president of the Council (effectively Minister of the Interior) from 1783 to 1791, and became Count of Campomanes in 1780.

37   These anonymous *Constituciones y Ordenanzas* (or *Estatutos*, according to some sources) were issued on 12 March 1766. The wording used by Buero is slightly different from the text given in full (together with other documents relating to the *motín*) in Laura Rodríguez Díaz, *Reforma e Ilustración en la España del siglo XVIII: Pedro Rodríguez de Campomanes*

(Madrid: Fundación Universitaria Española, 1975), pp. 307-11. Two of the items not read out by Esquilache and Ensenada have a particular bearing on the dramatic action: item 4 states that the call to action will be cries of "viva el rey" or "viva España", and that anyone not joining in these shouts will be regarded as a traitor; and item 14 rules that "women shall not be included".

38   These words (and the second part recited by Esquilache towards the end of the play) appear in the Piscator almanac entitled *La tía y la sobrina*. What Buero did not know when he used them was that this almanac was published in October 1766, with predictions for 1767. This is made clear by Guy Mercadier, who quotes this prediction in full (with the two enigmas or riddles), together with a prediction for 26 March 1766 from Torres Villarroel's almanac published in 1765, entitled *El santero de Majalahonda y el sopista perdulario*: "A powerful figure at a certain court suffers trials and tribulations, from which he could have delivered himself if he had known how to penetrate the significance of the enigma" (*Diego de Torres Villarroel, masques et miroirs* (Lille: Université de Lille III, 1976), vol.1, pp.253-54). Both of these almanacs were banned by order of Campomanes, and Torres was obliged to promise not to make any more political predictions.

39   Esquilache's return to his looted house and confrontation with some of the rioters on 23 March is invented. Ferrer del Río records that the marquis heard of the uprising as he was passing the Puerta de Alcalá on his way back from San Fernando, and immediately headed for the Royal Palace (vol.2, p.17). There are differing accounts of his wife's movements before and after the riots. According to Fernán-Núñez, she took refuge in the house of the Dutch ambassador, Monsieur Doublet, and on 24 March "was cool and daring enough to pass through the crowds, enter her house in disguise, hear Mass twice, collect her jewels, and get safely away" (vol.1, p.199). Danvila offers another version, according to which doña Pastora was rescued by the Danish ambassador; when his coach was stopped, he pretended that she was his wife, and the two of them were forced to shout "God save the king! Death to Esquilache and his whore of a wife!" (p.322).

40   The Paseo de las Delicias: an avenue running from the southern end of the Paseo del Prado to the River Manzanares.

41   The word *galera* has several meanings, the main ones being: large cart for carrying people; ship powered by sails and oars; women's prison.

42   The church and convent of Las Salesas (built 1750-58) are on the Calle Bárbara de Braganza, not far from the House of the Seven Chimneys. Part of this large complex is now the Palace of Justice.

43   Both Ferrer del Río (p.17) and Danvila (p.323) give this reason for the mob not carrying out the plan to burn down the House of the Seven Chimneys. However, according to Navarro Latorre, someone talked the crowd out of arson by arguing that it would damage the property across the street (the Calle de las Infantas) belonging to the Count of Murillo, an "honourable Spaniard" who may have been a supporter of Ensenada (pp.30-31).

44   The news of the success of the Madrid uprising spread rapidly, setting off a chain reaction of disturbances in April and May (not as early as is shown here) in Zaragoza, Cuenca, the Basque Country and dozens of other locations. The elements of political conspiracy behind the Madrid rebellion were not present in these riots. They were mostly spontaneous expressions of popular discontent over the high price of bread: classic food riots.

45   Isabel Farnese had continued to be an abrasive presence at the courts of Fernando and Carlos, and was certainly no friend of Esquilache, but she had little real power, became physically decrepit, and died in July 1766. The year before, her coach had been surrounded by a crowd protesting about food prices; she reported this to the king, who sent for Esquilache and "partly reproached him with being the cause of this disturbance" (Lord

Rochford quoted by Lynch, p.262). Perhaps because of this episode, it was rumoured that the rioters of March 1766 were assured that they had the Queen Mother's support.

46   Gardyloo: "1771 [apparently formed on *gare de l'eau*, pseudo-French for *gare l'eau*]. An old Edinburgh cry before throwing slops, etc. into the street" (*Oxford English Dictionary*). Esquilache's government discouraged the practice of throwing waste into the street with a cry of *¡Agua va!*; reviving it seems to be doña María's own contribution to the rebellion.

47   This occurred in 1764. A display of fireworks was given in the Plaza del Buen Retiro as part of the celebrations of the marriage of Prince Carlos and María Luisa of Parma. The foreign Walloon Guard used excessive force to control the crowd, killing about twenty spectators, and many people believed that it was Esquilache who had given the order to charge.

48   This dramatically crucial development, in which the king leaves the decision entirely to Esquilache, is an invention of Buero's, but is not implausible. Danvila provides several hints: "His Majesty did not allow the use of military force against the rebels, although it would have been easy enough to overcome them in a few hours, and Squillace ordered that the uprising be contained with the utmost restraint" (p.346); Carlos wrote in a letter that "poor Squillace [...] has sacrificed himself for me in these unfortunate circumstances, and I must give him full credit for having always served me well" (pp.350-51); and on arrival in Naples in May, Esquilache gave the impression that he "was satisfied with what he had done" and regarded his downfall as "a kind of triumph" (p.355).

49   Two other demands figured in the list presented to the king. While the demand that all non-Spaniards be removed from the government was not insisted upon, the reduction of the price of bread and oil was an important component of the eventual agreement.

50   This was the end of the affair as far as Esquilache was concerned, but the *motín* was far from over. The king's decision to depart for Aranjuez at two o'clock on the morning of 25 March (whether out of fear for his safety or as a means of showing his displeasure) was a mistake: the people took it as a sign that he was planning to renege on the agreement made in the palace courtyard, and continued their virtual occupation of the city. Only when a written promise that all the concessions would be carried out was brought back from Aranjuez did the crowds disperse.

51   Having Esquilache himself give Ensenada the order banishing him without explanation to Medina del Campo is another masterly invention of the playwright's. Ensenada was certainly expecting good news on 25 March: "Ensenada thought that the time had come for him to obtain a ministry, now that the dismissal of Esquilache was leaving two vacant"; he left word with palace officials that any message for him from the king should be brought to him at once; "a document did indeed come and was immediately delivered to him, but rather than his nomination as minister, it contained an order naming Medina del Campo as his place of exile" (Ferrer del Río, p.51).

52   Esquilache wrote several letters from Cartagena and Naples to Roda (Minister of Justice) in the following months, asking for an ambassadorial post and an opportunity to clear his name. He was finally appointed ambassador to Venice in 1772, a post he held until his death in 1785.

FERNÃO LOPES
THE ENGLISH IN PORTUGAL 1383–1387 (edd. D.W. Lomax & R.J. Oakley)

Federico GARCIA LORCA
GYPSY BALLADS (ed. R.G. Havard)
MARIANA PINEDA (ed. R.G.Havard)
YERMA (edd. I. R.Macpherson & J. Minett)

THE POEM OF MY CID (edd. P. Such & J. Hodgkinson)

Francisco de QUEVEDO
DREAMS AND DISCOURSES (ed. R.K.Britton)

Fernando de ROJAS
CELESTINA (ed. Dorothy Sherman Severin)

CHRISTIANS AND MOORS IN SPAIN
Vol I (711-1150) C.C. Smith
Vol II (1195-1614) C.C. Smith
Vol III ARABIC SOURCES (711-1501) (edd. Charles Melville & Ahmad Ubaydli)

TIRSO DE MOLINA
DAMNED FOR DESPAIR (ed. N.G. Round)
DON GIL OF THE GREEN BREECHES (ed. G.G. Minter)
TAMAR'S REVENGE (ed. J.E. Lyon)
THE TRICKSTER OF SEVILLE AND THE STONE GUEST (ed. G. Edwards)

Ramon Maria del VALLE- INCLAN
MR PUNCH THE CUCKOLD (edd. R. Warner & D. Keown)
LIGHTS OF BOHEMIA (ed. J. Lyon)

Roger Wright **SPANISH BALLADS**